HISTORIOGRAPHY

MYTH

LITERATURE

CONFERENCE PAPERS SERIES #21

HISTORIOGRAPHY
MYTH
LITERATURE

EDITED BY

Larraitz Ariznabarreta

CENTER FOR BASQUE STUDIES
UNIVERSITY OF NEVADA, RENO
2023

This book was published with generous financial support from the Basque Government.

Center for Basque Studies
University of Nevada, Reno
1664 North Virginia St,
Reno, Nevada 89557 usa
http://basque.unr.edu

Library of Congress Cataloging-in-Publication Data

Names: Ariznabarreta, Larraitz, editor.
Title: Historiography, myth, literature / edited by Larraitz Ariznabarreta.

Description: Reno, Nevada : Center for Basque Studies Press/University of Nevada, Reno, 2023. | Series: Conference papers series ; 21 | Includes bibliographical references and index. | Summary: "Since antiquity, poets have been tossed as untrustworthy chroniclers of history. However, the intersections of history, legend, and literature remain blurry scholarly junctions, and the study of literature continues to be central in deciphering the distant past of a nation and decoding its narratives, shared tropes, and legends. Therefore, poetry and literature seem evocative enough for both approaches to history: exploring it and inventing it. Both, apparently contradictory slants, are central to this volume"-- Provided by publisher.
Identifiers: LCCN 2023046498 (print) | LCCN 2023046499 (ebook) | ISBN 9781949805741 (paperback) | ISBN 9781949805741 (epub)
Subjects: LCSH: Literature and history. | Historiography.
Classification: LCC PN50 .H576 2023 (print) | LCC PN50 (ebook) | DDC 809/.93358--dc23/eng/20231016
LC record available at https://lccn.loc.gov/2023046498
LC ebook record available at https://lccn.loc.gov/2023046499

Printed in the United States of America

CONTENTS

INTRODUCTION

POETRY IS A WEAPON LOADED WITH FUTURE[1]

On the intersections of historiography, orality, legend, myth, and literature

Larraitz Ariznabarreta

Since antiquity, poets have been tossed as untrustworthy chroniclers of history. However, the intersections of history, legend, and literature remain blurry scholarly junctions, and the study of literature continues to be central in deciphering the distant past of a nation and decoding its narratives, shared tropes, and legends. To quote Roland Barthes: "there is not, there has never been anywhere, any people without narrative."[2] Therefore, poetry and literature seem evocative enough for both approaches to history: exploring it and inventing it. Both, apparently contradictory slants, are central to this volume.

Literature is a historically significant testimony in its own right. As the Basque literary critic Mikel Ayerbe fittingly suggests, literature remains: "an effort to gather and create testimonies of hypothetical realities." According to Ayerbe, gathering narrative evidence is the real purpose of all testimony (including literature) even when those collected signs are, in fact, fragments reconstructed from fragile memories.[3] Ayerbe's reflections most eloquently frame this volume on the intersections of history, literature, and myth:[4]

All testimonies want to leave their mark. Literature, too, has that aim. And, in fact, the main distinguishing feature of real literature is that it leaves an intangible impression on readers' memories. But memory all too often gives us away, being an effort to unite and create the hypothetical fiction we call reality. Memory is fragile and limited because it is an interpretive action, as well as being an invention that we (re) invent each time we remember things.[5]

In 2021, the backdrop of the 700th anniversary of the Basque battle of Beotibar (1321)—and the accumulation of apocryphal texts and cultural artifacts that were inspired by the historical event within the Basque cultural realm through the years—served as the perfect scholarly milieu to interrogate the relationship of history, literature, and the construction of national myths, while revisiting them from a contemporary cultural perspective. The 18th annual conference organized by the Center of Basque Studies at the University of Nevada, Reno—October 29th, 2021—attempted to plumb that intersection of historiography, orality, folklore, legend, and literature. The organizers encouraged proposals that related broadly to the topic of historiography and the construction, nature, and transmission of national narratives. The conference was inspired by the belief that, as Judith Neulander highlights, "tradition will never be static; the most stable part of tradition is that the next generation changes it to fulfil the needs of different times and the places."[6] It is worth quoting Neulander at length for the evocative nature of her reflections when it concerns this particular volume and its foremost commission.

> (. . .) Past traditions do not always speak to contemporary issues or current events, and many skilled oral productions will lose their communicative genius in written form. Therefore, the overarching impulse on the part of tradition bearers is to "improve" traditional materials by transforming them to suit contemporary times, tastes and means of transmission. This creative impulse speaks to the fact that tradition is not and has never been something static, the most stable aspect of any tradition being its ability to changing needs of different generations, different times, and different places. The impulse to keep traditions timely and relevant is characteristic of each generation of bearers. As a result, patterns of stability and change in an oral tradition give us access to the spirit and mentality of the different groups who have shaped the tradition over time and across space.[7]

With regard to Beotibar's prominent presence in this volume, the battle's treatment in literature is of particular interest in the context of Basque chronicles;[8] since, as Xabier Paia explains:

> Epic songs, poetic tales of wartime events or feats, are the oldest Basque literary creations. Epic poems are the equivalent in written literature, long narratives with the same purpose. Epic songs that originated in the oral tradition are generally considered to be a subset of ballads. Their strength lies in their rhythm and music; their purpose is to give extra vitality to the narrative. They were the first to be collected as oral literature, and to some extent their discovery influenced the search for and collection of other genres.[9]

In short, Beotibar proves that, when narratives transfer from being history to being literature—if they prosper—those *pieces of fiction* will, eventually, become testimonies in the chain of representations; testimonies that may well end up having an impact on history. To put it differently: what literature does is *create* history rather than truthfully reflect it or accurately mirror it.[10] In that same line, it is worth highlighting that the "path of development for oral traditions and legends follows the path of social relationships, with the meaning of a story dependent on the cultural and political context in which it is told.[11] It would not matter if the purpose of the prose of the past were—to quote Basque poet Gabriel Aresti (1933-1975)—*to decorate the future.*[12] Rather, it was Gabriel Celaya, another Basque poet, who most suggestively expressed the power of poetic narrative: *Poetry is a weapon loaded with future.*

THE BATTLE OF BEOTIBAR AS METAPHOR

In 1886 Basque scholar and charter-enthusiast Ramos Azkarate (Tolosa, Gipuzkoa 1847-1904) wrote a play for his fellow Tolosans to perform at the town carnival celebration that year; it was based on the Battle of Beotibar, the historic event which is, partly, our subject of discussion in this volume. Azkarate's fable is *parenetic*. It was written for the will, heart, and inner spirit of the Basques of the time. Its main objective was to recommend and encourage the use of Basque, and to warn people about the language's precarious situation. So, this play by Azkarate can be considered to be an authentic continuation of pro-Basque language tradition from 18th and the first half of the 19th century, and as an example of the new pro-charters and (cultural) nationalist literature of the time: it is based on the rural customs reflected in a large part of traditional Basque literature. The writer chose his symbols, characters and tropes for that purpose: mother (Basque; land; home; loving; strong); stranger (non-Basque;

enemy; foreign; liar); sons (brave Basque-speaking warriors); women and children (afraid of the loss of local traditions).[13] Ramos Azkarate (1847-1904), wrote more than 3,500 verses, stories, and articles in support of Carlism. Antonio Zavala, the ethnographer who recorded most of the writer's work in *Auspoa*,[14] called Azkarate's work a "treasure"[15] of popular Basque literature. Indeed, Azkarate left us a rich chronicle of the Basque language, society, and politics of the 19th century in all his popular literature texts: the chronicle of a passionate, pro-charters Catholic and Carlist. *A rich testimony to* Basque oral literature and of nineteenth-century society in general, even if from a single point of view.

WHEN, WHAT, WHERE, WHO, WHY?

For Azkarate, Beotibar was a blurry past event whose reminiscence and symbolism served an ideological purpose in the late nineteenth century. But what exactly happened in Beotibar in 1321? We can agree on something: seven hundred years ago, *something seems to have happened* in a place called Beotibar near Tolosa (Gipuzkoa). If we were to leave it at that, we would hardly be blamed for committing any wrong or falsehood. However, despite the significance given to the Battle of Beotibar in documents and histories in Castilian and Navarrese archives, the narrative of the historical event was soon clothed with a fantastical epic.

In parallel, the vivid stories that the 1321 event instigated remain testimonies of their own kind to-day—maybe untraceable to any objective historic truth—but certainly not any less influential or significant than the actual historic events to generations of Basques. In fact, the stories, legends, and myths that originated after the actual battle of 1321 became so influential, that they have managed to make the historic veracity of what actually happened in the fields of Beotibar a little less important. Nothing new under the sun, we are aware national imagery is constructed, shaped, and transmitted through such mechanisms.

Obviously, the greater the lack of data, the wider the range of interpretations, and the more unavoidable the risk of ideology taking precedence over professional asepticism. Therefore, *genuine* historians will try to make their *apparent sources* as objective and accurate as possible, if they wish to objectively address the event itself. To do this, historians have their own hierarchies, along with common sense and historiographical techniques. Above all, they will try to get the most reliable information or indications possible from the *facts*. Historians are, therefore, subject to the quantity and quality of documents if they are to be to make *any interpretation*. The first two chapters in this volume choose that path.

In "The Battle of Beotibar (1321). The Genesis of a Legend Over Seven Centuries," the historian Xabier Irujo revisits the Battle of Beotibar of 1321, which, has gone down in history books—and many Basque cultural artifacts—as a fantastic feat of 800 bandits who engaged an army of 60,000 Navarrese infantrymen and caused 10,000 casualties. Irujo's chapter questions that representation and, through the detailed analysis of archival documents, the historian defends that the battle of Beotibar was, in fact, an armed encounter involving the band of cattle rustlers led by Gil Lopez de Oñaz and the forces of the merino (an administrative official) of the Kingdom of Navarre. In short, the chapter analyzes how the historical event became a legend and what reasons lie behind the transition from historical account to mythical story.

A similar historiographic stand is adopted by the historian Idoia Arrieta in her chapter: "1200: A Year of Conquest and Fracture." The scope of this work is also circumscribed by a place and a time: The Basque Country between the years 1200 and 1300. To ensure a better understanding of the historical framework, the first section of the article outlines the main historical events that marked the lifespan of the Kingdom of Navarre (Nafarroa). Arrieta analyzes the events preceding the constitution of a "national" kingdom, the fracture of the year 1200, and the most immediate consequences of the split. More precisely, the contribution focuses on how historiography has overlooked the actions leading to the Basque political rupture as well as its consequences and how this disregard has paved the way for wrong interpretations. Arrieta believes that "historiography is missing the perspectives of different political cultures, anthropological history, and the sociolinguistic analysis of discourse," and, therefore, furnishes her historic research with such foundations.

OTHER STORIES, OTHER ILLUSTRATIONS

Obviously, the editor of this volume wishes good fortune to professional historians— particularly to those whose work is included in this volume—and their scientific quest for objectivity; a mission, we assume, never devoid of frustrations. However, history, stories, tales, and legends do not end with the battle of Beotibar or restrict themselves the realm of the Kingdom of Navarre.

In the past, historic chronicles were often written, performed, and transmitted in verse in the rural Basque Country. Some of these poems were also published in journals throughout the country and were a powerful source of information for many Basque speakers. In his chapter "Gernika and Verdun: a symbol of Basque bipolarity?" the scholar and journalist Eneko Bidegain examines the work of a lesser known Basque poet and chronicler Peio Erramuzpe (1880-1967) of Banka, Nafarroa Beherea (Lower Navarre). Peio Erramuzpe took part in a few impromptu verse competitions but he mostly sang impromptu at family meals or at some village festivities. In 1908 Erramuzpe won the Basque

Assembly award for impromptu poetry singing. His most famous poem, entitled "Euskaldunak eta Gernikako Arbola" ("The Basques and the Tree of Gernika"), was written in support of the unification of Basque provinces and stands out as a powerful nationalistic poetic piece. Bidegain confirms that in the early 20th century it was unusual for such Basque patriotic verses to be written in the continental Basque Country (Iparralde). However, the most striking thing about the poem is not for a farmer from the little village of Banka to express himself as a strong Basque patriot, but rather that a few years later, the same *bertsolari* (poet) composed verses as a converted Frenchman praising France and the country's participation in World War I. A single man, differing ideological perspectives and dual national loyalties. Bidegain's chapter examines these sets of verses and their messages and brings a question to the table: do these two sets of verses confirm the influence of WWI in the Frenchification of Basques in the Continental Basque Country?

Professor Andrea Perales-Fernández-de-Gamboa, from the public University of the Basque Country, examines the historic and mythic figure of Emiliano Zapata (1879-1919), not merely as a historical character, a Mexican revolutionary, or a political leader, but also as a literary and legendary one. In her chapter, Perales-Fernández-de-Gamboa analyzes how the Mexican novelist and script writer Mauricio Magdeleno (1906-1986) contributed to turn Emiliano Zapata into a national agrarian martyr and a national myth. Indeed, even if the long and bloody Mexican Revolution was indisputably won by Venustiano Carranza and Álvaro Obregón, the collective Mexican imagination has bequeathed Pancho Villa and Emiliano Zapata with the glory of victory. In that sense, Perales-Fernández-de-Gamboa's chapter: "Constructing the Agrarian Martyr in Mauricio Magdaleno's Emiliano Zapata: A shared reading between History and Literature" is a brilliant illustration of how defeated heroes, can be turned into myth by popular culture.

The next chapter: "The American Wests: History, Fiction, Myth," abounds in similar topics when addressing the fact that past historical facts "pose the challenge to reconfigure the past to chronicle individual and collective memory." Written by professor Monika Madinabeitia, the chapter delves into the ways in which the human mind copes with unavoidable split between experiencing and remembering an event and the myriad of ways in which such fissures give way to cultural and artistic creativity. Madinabeitia begins her chapter with a compelling reflection about the central subject matter of this volume: How are history and fiction; history and interpretation connected? The scholar believes that both share a common ground, "for history needs narratives and representations to provide plausible explanations and scenarios." Madinabeitia opts to set her reflections within the American West, for that geographic scenario "is a clear example of the interplay between history and literature." By exploring the ways in which different tropes which originated in the American West—individualism, self-reliance-independence—have contributed to fabricate a greater American Epic, Madinabeitia establishes how the dialogue between the Old West and the Mythic West have been formulated and constructed through time.

According to Monika Madinabeitia, "the vessels through which memory is articulated may both illuminate certain episodes and characters and conceal and belittle others." As suggested in her article, those vessels "may also be mechanisms that revisit and combat reductionist views." The editor of this volume aspires for that perspective to have permeated this volume.

RESOURCES

Ayerbe, Mikel. 2012. "Introduction: Testimony and Memory." *In Our Wars*: Mikel Ayerbe (ed.), 9-35. Reno: Center of Basque Studies Press.

Aresti, Gabriel. 2017. *Downhill and Rock & Core*. Reno: Center for Basque Studies Press.

Azkarate, Ramos. 1886/1988 «Beotibarko jatzarraren oroipena Gaon juduaren galerarekin.» *Ijituen kontratuba eta abar: (antzerkiak, ipuinak eta beste)* en, egilea: Ramos Azkarate, 82-127. Lizarra: Etor.

—. 1893 «Tolosa txit noble, leial eta doagaraiari.» *El Cántabro*, 06k 23.

—. 2004. *Galtzaundi berriz ere I*. Edited by Antonio Zavala. Zarautz Auspoa/Gipuzkoako Foru Aldundia.

Azkarate, Ramos. 1886/1988 *Kaleko birunka*. 197. bol., in *Ijituen kontratuba eta abar: (antzerkiak, ipuinak eta beste)*, egilea: Ramos Azkarate, Auspoa liburutegia ek editatuta, 95. Lizarra: Etor.

Barthes, Roland, and Lionel Duisit. "An Introduction to the Structural Analysis of Narrative." *New Literary History* 6, no. 2 (1975): 237–72. https://doi.org/10.2307/468419.

Bidney, David. 1966. "Introduction." *Myth and Literature. Contemporary Theory and Practice*. John B. Vickery (ed.). Lincoln: University of Nevada Press,

Celaya, Gabriel. 1987. *Gaviota. Antología Esencial*. Madrid: Repsol Exploración.

Gallop, Rodney. 1930/1970 *A Book of the Basques*. Reno: University of Nevada Press.

Neulander, Judith S. 1998. "Jewish Oral Tradition." *In Teaching Oral Traditions*: John Miles Foley, 225-238. New York: The Modern Language Association.

Paia, Xabier. 2013. *Anthology of Basque Oral Literature*. Donostia: Etxepare Euskal Institutua.

Perez, Ander. 2016. "Literaturak ez du islatzen errealitatea: sortu egiten du." *Berria*, maiatzak 8.

Sarasola, Ibon. 1982. Historia social de la literatura vasca. Madrid: Akal.

Stoeltje, Beverly J., and Nancy Worthington. 1998. "Multiculturalism and Oral Tradition." *In Teaching Oral Tradition*: John Foley, 423-435. New York: The Modern Language Association.

NOTES

1　The title to the introduction of this volume is directly propped on Basque poet Gabriel Celaya's poem "La poesía es un arma cargada de futuro." Gabriel Celaya (1911-1991), a social poet and confessed communist, was born in Hernani (Gipuzkoa) and wrote in Spanish although his mythical literary work shows an eminently Basque worldview.

2   Barthes, 1975, 237

3   Ayerbe 2012, 9

4   David Bidney (1966,13) defines "myth" as having "a positive value for the ethnologist and folklorist as a record of man's culture history and a means of establishing universal patterns of thought. Myth, like great art and dramatic literature, may have profound symbolic or allegorical value for us of the present, not because myth necessarily and intrinsically has such latent, esoteric wisdom, but because the plot or theme suggests to us universal patterns of motivation and conduct."

5   Ayerbe 2012, 9

6   Neulander 1998, 221

7   Neulander 1998, 226

8   In *A Book of the Basques* (1930/1970) British folklorist Rodney Gallop questions the epic nature of old Basque oral literature. According to Gallop, very few old Basque ballads – "something like Scottish border ballads, long epic poems from Finland, or moving songs from the Balkans."

9   Paia 2013, 96.

10   "Literaturak errealitatea islatu baino gehiago, sortu egiten du." Pérez 2016

11   Stoeltje and Worthington 1998, 427

12   Aresti 2017, 217

13   Azkarate's metaphorical resources are common in the Basque traditional literature of the time. To quote some classics in addition to the many well-known songs that make up the Basque popular heritage, there are similar metaphors in the elegy "Ama Euskeriari agurrak" written by Felipe Arrese Beitia (1879) and in Etienne Decrept's pastoral *Amatxi* (1914).

14   Azkarate 2004

15   Azkarate 2004

1

THE BATTLE OF BEOTIBAR (1321)

The Genesis of a Legend Over Seven Centuries

Xabier Irujo

In 1200, the troops of Alfonso VIII of Castile penetrated the Kingdom of Navarre and conquered a portion of land proportional to the present provinces of Araba and Gipuzkoa. As a result of this operation, an artificial border was drawn, a division that had never existed before, being that the entire territory had been under the rule of the Kingdom of Navarre since its formation in 824. Among other consequences, the creation of the new border helped develop an active network of cattle thieves that would last three hundred years. Livestock rustlers saw a chance to steal cattle on one side and sell it on the other, where the authorities of the Kingdom of Navarre had no jurisdiction. They mainly worked on the nearby valleys of Larraun and Aralar, but occasionally ventured farther, affecting cattle breeders in Arriba-Atallu, Araitz, Areso, Leitza, Basaburua, and more.

As shown in the documents preserved in the Navarrese archives, which have been diligently published and reviewed by multiple authors, between the years 1290 and 1321, the area suffered at least sixty-two acts of cattle theft. The *merino*, in his duties as bailiff, was in charge of chasing down the criminals. During this period, Johan Lopez de Urrotz stood out for his accomplishments in this task: assisted by armies averaging fifty men, Lopez de Urrotz captured and brought to justice a significant number of bandits and recovered a large portion of the stolen cattle, mainly bovine and porcine herds.

Gil Lopez de Oñaz led one of the most infamous gangs, which had been working the border since at least 1309. The first time Johan Lopez de Urrotz is mentioned in the chronicles is, coincidently, in 1309, when he, forty infantrymen, and three horsemen hunted for the "deplorable thief and bandit" Juan Martinez de Oñaz, whom he killed somewhere between Leitza and Ezkurra. That same year, the chronicles mentioned Egidio (Gil) Lopez de Oñaz, brother of Johan Periz de Oñaz and son of Johan Periz, a fifth-degree ancestor of Ignacio de Loiola. Lopez de Urrotz headed off commanding a company of five horsemen, 160 infantrymen, and a contingent formed by locals to confront the group of rustlers, who had entered the valley of Larraun and seized a herd of six hundred pigs from the towns of Etxabe and Agiregi, in Aralar. The *merino* chased them down, recaptured the herd, and returned it to their owners.

The intense level of activity of the Gil Lopez de Oñaz band triggered the events of 1321. That year, the Oñaz band attacked the border town of Gorriti again, and although they very possibly plundered the place, the gang lacked the manpower to storm the castle of Gorriti, let alone to seize it, since the castle was the stronghold of that region of the Kingdom of Navarre.[1] The aggressions perpetrated by the Lopez de Oñaz gang did not go unnoticed by the Navarrese authorities, whose response was proportional to the severity of the crimes committed.

Navarrese chronicler Josep Moret noted that Ponz de Mortagne, the governor of the kingdom, was "greatly" disturbed by the attack, carried out without reason to shatter the peace that had been reigning for years.[2] And since the attacks had been happening yearly for at least the last four decades, Mortagne ordered that an armed contingent be organized with the sole mission of punishing the attackers. He also ordered that troops from the region of Estella join the company, consequently leaving the border with Castile in a modest state of defense,[3] which suggests that the governor was not expecting an attack by Castilian troops through that border. He was not mistaken, since no attack ever happened on that front.

Worried that the *Fueros* (the body of customary Navarrese law built up before 1155) would not allow him to assemble an army to hunt down the Gil Lopez de Oñaz band, the governor lied to the town mayors by telling them the castle of Gorriti had been attacked and had even fallen in the hands of the enemy. Ponz de Mortagne lied because, under the law at the time, if an army invaded Navarre, the mayors had the obligation to send troops and pay for their provisions. Shortly before the army left their hometowns, however, the governor had to admit that the castle had not been lost after all (*Seigneurs, le château de Gorriti n'est pas perdu*).[4] But he argued that the reason to launch the raid should not be only to reclaim the lost castle, but to stop the bandit squads and their trail of murders, thefts, fires, and multiple other evils once and for all, as the king wished to do.

The towns accepted the request, but they clearly stated to the governor that the crown, and not the towns, would bear the expenses, and demanded that the governor "wrote letters," as recorded in the 1323 sentence: "Governor, we are under no obligation to follow the king or the governor beyond the Kingdom of Navarre, if we did, it would be much to our detriment. But, if you wished to give us letters, much like sir Alphonz de Rouroy did when, being governor of the kingdom, he took the people of Puillon, this expedition would harm neither us nor our laws, and we would be glad to join you, because we are well aware of the great harm the Gipuzkoans have caused to Navarre."[5] The governor provided the requested letters, which were written and delivered by the notary of the court, Johan de Caseda, and promised to repay the debt incurred with these towns and cities. In virtue of the letters, the royal treasury would cover the costs, which would later be cause for a lawsuit.

The archival documents at the Comptos Chamber of Navarre (the Navarrese Treasury) establish that the armed force set up by Mortagne, known as the "Gorriti Army," was initially formed by the governor, the mountain *merino*, thirty-nine horsemen and 245 infantrymen.[6] It was later reinforced with nine other horsemen, fifty-five men captained by the *merino* of Estella and the seven squires along with 227 infantrymen, who stayed by the castle of Gorriti for five days. In total, the available documents describe an army of 284 men (thirty-nine horsemen and 245 foot soldiers), plus an unspecified number of infantrymen, on top of some men who were already at the castle of Gorriti and may have joined the force, like the Roiz de Araitz brothers and thirty of their men. If we include Urtubia's sixty men and his squire Ojer Periz de Arronitz, whom we know participated and died at the encounter, the army totals to a minimum of 378 and a maximum of 511 registered men. An unspecified number of infantrymen should be added to the sum and at least fifty men excluded, the ones who signed up for a five-day service at the Castle of Gorriti and never crossed the border into Gipuzkoa. Taking these numbers into consideration, along with data from previous campaigns and the fact that the governor and two *merinos* joined the expedition, it is reasonable to estimate that up to five hundred men took part in the encounter.[7]

As expected, infantrymen formed about 90 percent of the army. This is undoubtedly because of financial reasons, although it also made sense strategically: Beotibar was mountainous and rugged, and the cavalry would, if anything, hinder the operation, rather than play a decisive role in the battle.

The contingent left Pamplona toward Lekunberri on Sunday, September 13, exactly on "the first Sunday after Santa Maria de Setiembre."[8] The expedition lasted nine days. They left Pamplona that day to cover the twenty-seven miles separating them from Gorriti. The troops endured an arduous, almost-three-day journey before seeing the castle. The army from Estella faced a forty-three-mile journey, at least three long days of travel. From Gorriti, they must have needed an additional two days to reach Berastegi, thirteen miles away. At that point, they were left with less than two days to enclose and siege the fortress.

From Lekunberri, the army crossed to Gipuzkoa and arrived in Berastegi on Friday, September 18. Once there, according to historian Juan Martínez de Zaldibia, who wrote his work in the sixteenth century, the Navarrese set fire to Berastegi, and the church was badly damaged.[9] Moret asserts that (the army) charged into the town of Berastegi, entered it forcefully by use of weaponry, sacked it, and finally burned it.[10] There is no written proof of these claims and the *Chronicle of Alfonso XI*, the first documentary source recording the events, doesn't mention these actions. The lack of rigor and credibility of the sources, Zaldibia, Garibai, and Mariana, casts doubt on the historicity of this event, and forces us to wait until archaeological findings provide new information to either confirm or disprove this point. None of the original sources mention these actions, and archival documents show no record of them.

The Oñaz troops retreated inland and lured the Navarrese into the narrow valley of Beotibar, on the way from Berastegi to Tolosa. The Navarrese troops arrived on Saturday, September 19. It is unquestionable that the battle or "façienda de Ipuzcoa," as contemporary sources cite it, took place on that day; "the events happened in Gorriti and Gipuzkoa on September 19."[11]

Beotibar is a neighborhood of Belauntza, in the southeastern corner of Gipuzkoa and close to the Navarrese border. It is on the communication route between Berastegi and Tolosa, and the valley is so narrow that traffic in some sections of the winding path is confined between the sharp slopes of the mountains on one side and the Elduarain River on the other. In the words of Baltasar de Etxabe, the mountains on either side of the path engender the tight and rough passage "known as Veotivar, which means valley of mares."[12]

As I mentioned before, the Navarrese company included about five hundred men, while the Oñaz band, on the other hand, wouldn't have been able to recruit that many members and had to fight with a numerical disadvantage. But what they lacked in number they made up for in knowledge of the land and their advantageous location.

The Elduarain stream blocks the southern end of the passage, so the Navarrese troops had no choice but to go back toward Berastegi. Archers and crossbowmen, positioned at Zelaieta to the south of Elduarain, were then able to assail the army without fear of being counterattacked. This is as stated on the 1323 sentence. From the same text, it can be gathered that, being in the vanguard of the army, the troops of Martin de Oibar were the ones that suffered the offense of the enemy and became isolated from the body of the contingent. When the governor saw that Martin de Oibar had been ambushed, he tried to come to his aid. But the town mayors accused him of not having done enough to rescue Oibar. In his defense, the governor claimed that none of the foot soldiers fighting by his side had wasted any time or retreated. He also claimed that, although he had lost some men, when he arrived, the Oibar troops were still fending off the attack; no men had been killed, injured, or captured yet, which we can learn in greater detail from those who witnessed the battle.[13]

Unable to withstand the offense, however, the governor and his troop eventually retreated to an emplacement defended by Pere Arnalt de Urtubia and his large group of men. Apparently, that was the only retreat route. Their elevated location granted Urtubia's men the advantage of controlling the enemy and avoiding a new strike. Among them were Pere and Ferrand Roiz de Araitz, whose troop didn't amount to more than thirty infantrymen, even after gathering all their available men. It was then, and always according to Governor Mortagne's testimony, that Urtubia told him: "Governor, there is no more you can do here, don't you see our infantrymen are fleeing in terror? If you stay here, you will surely die."[14] So they agreed that Urtubia's men would guard their retreat and the governor and his men would head to the tower of Leitza, where they would regroup and regain strength for the next day's counterattack.

It can be inferred from our records and the lower number of casualties among the infantry that, after the initial attack and the ambush of Oibar's men, the troops simply retreated by retracing their route back to where they came from, without suffering further violence from Gil Lopez de Oñaz's men. When, the same day, the governor and his men stepped into the tower of Leitza, they found no garrison or armors, only a stringless crossbow. Allegedly, the smaller troops of infantrymen had followed the most direct retreat route through Areso and Gorriti to their hometowns, skipping Leitza altogether. Mortagne ordered the infantrymen from the regions of the Ribera and Sanguesa to return, but they never did. Upon realizing that staying at the tower would be fruitless, he set out, probably through Uitzi, to the town of Lekunberri, which he found crowded to the brim with men, to the point of having to lodge at the church. Mortagne still planned to reassemble the troop and retaliate against the Oñaz cattle rustlers, so that night, he ordered the troop members to stay in town. Ignoring his orders, the foot soldiers retreated throughout the night and by sunrise, only a group of horsemen remained. After morning mass, the governor broke camp and left Lekunberri with his company, marching through Sarasa to Pamplona, "as all efforts against our enemies are futile, thanks to the dereliction and noncompliance of the infantrymen from said cities and towns, who have fled or abandoned the battlefield."[15]

Given this is only Mortagne's version of the events, we can't know for certain whether it was the town infantrymen who retreated or the governor and his troop, as the mayors of the chief towns of the kingdom claimed. The court case against the governor was dismissed, and Mortagne never received a sentence.

The *Chronicle of Alfonso XI* records ten thousand casualties in the battlefield, "there were nearly 10,000 dead horsemen and foot soldiers,"[16] which is a far-fetched assertion. Documents at the Navarrese archives show that both *merinos* and the second lieutenant died in the encounter, as well as the three horsemen that were with them, and approximately eighteen infantrymen. The records substantiate the theory that it was the troop in the vanguard of the army, where the second lieutenant and the *merinos* marched, that endured the attack. Records at the Comptos Chamber show that the squires who died in Beotibar were Martin de Oibar, second lieutenant of the kingdom, Johan Lopez de Urrotz, and Ojer Periz de Arronitz, the mountain *merino*.[17] Additionally, six of the ten horsemen escorting Urrotz lost their horses, although we don't know if the owners fled on foot, were captured, or perished. Only four of the six horsemen appear on documents: Garcia Martiniz, Miguel Martiniz de Murillo, Xemen Martiniz de Aiantz, and Yniego Garcia.[18] The documents also show that eighteeen infantrymen lost their loricas; unfortunately, the fate of the men is unknown. The *merino* of Estella, Dru de Saint-Pol, died "along with other army men,"[19] including his squire Lope Ortiz de Monteagudo. We learn of the death of Saint-Pol through a letter, dated June 15, 1322, from King Carlos to Arnalt de Saint-Pol, son of the former. By virtue of this letter, the king allocated a lifetime payment of twenty-five pounds to Arnalt out of the levy of the town of San Cristobal, which "your father Messire Dru de Saint Pol used to receive before losing his life in Gipuzkoa."[20]

In sum, documentary evidence proves the deaths of five squires and of an unspecified number of foot soldiers. Speculative information of the events suggests that an additional four horsemen and eighteen infantrymen died, too. The balance of recorded casualties, including injuries and deaths, totals about thirty men. Particularly unusual was the fact that five squires lost their lives in the encounter, and even more so when two of them were the seneschal of the kingdom, Martin de Oibar, and the *merino*, Johan Lopez de Urrotz. Although it had happened before, like in 1306, when the *merino* Diego Sanchez de Garritz was killed in an ambush, Beotibar's is the deadliest battle on record between 1300 and 1321.

Zaldibia and others after him estimated that the spoils of war amounted to one hundred thousand French pounds, "all the equipment for the beasts and the weapons for the army added up to a hundred thousand pounds."[21] This amount was disproportionate. Documents at the Comptos Chamber reveal that all expenses and compensations paid for by the mountain *merino* totaled 559 pounds and fourteen dineros (pennies): "The *merino* used four pack mules for nine days, and 40 pack mules to carry goods for him and his men for four days. When the ranger left the castle of Gorriti for Gipuzkoa, he carried provisioning for him and the garrison and made payments for "restitutions, compensations and amends" with seventeen bushels of '*pan cocho*.' Each bushel packed six '*robos*' of wheat and each '*robo*' was 12.5 '*cahíces*.' We lost all of them on the nineteenth day when the *merino* was killed in Gipuzkoa. By converting bread to money, where one '*cahíz*' is worth ten *sueldos*, we have 15 '*sueldos*' of 12 pounds."[22]

As mentioned, after the battle, some towns and cities of the kingdom (Auritz, Estella, Larrasoaña, Los Arcos, Olite, Pamplona, Puente la Reina, Sangüesa, and Villava) brought a lawsuit against Governor Ponz de Mortagne deeming him responsible for the Beotibar fiasco.[23] The chronicler of Navarre, Moret, explained that the mayors of these towns believed the battle was lost because, instead of coming to the aid of the Olite troop, in the vanguard of the army, the governor decided to retreat. "A horseman called Garcia Centol, driven by jealousy rather than by caution and common sense," took the governor to court. The parties in the litigation "on the events of Gipuzkoa" were, on the one hand, Garcia Centol, supported by some of the towns and cities of the kingdom; and, on the other, the mayor, the committee, and the council of Olite. But the case was dismissed in Olite, on July 24, 1323, and Mortagne was acquitted of the failures of the expedition.[24]

THE CONCEPTION OF A LEGEND

Fernán Sánchez de Valladolid was the first person to write about this historical event. He did it in chapter 34 of the *Chronicles of Alfonso XI*, "Cómo los navarros con grandes poderes se ayuntaron por entrar e fazer mal e daño en los reynos de Castilla" (How the Powerful Navarrese Assembled to Penetrate and Cause Harm and Havoc in the Kingdoms of Castile). The account is doubly valuable considering that it is the first reference to the battle of Beotibar, and that it was written in 1344, only two decades after the encounter, and, therefore, it can be regarded as a contemporary chronicle of the events.[25]

Since historical narrative standards change over time, we should not judge a medieval text through the lens of the historiographic principles of our century.

Instead, we should extract the bits of truth out of the chronicle to be able to recompose the historical scene. In this case, the nature of the text and its context, however, somewhat distort the events, as the author situates the encounter within an unrelated story and under the wrong circumstances.

The first noticeable issue in the treatment of the events of Beotibar is that the text is part of a royal chronicle. Although it is true that the battle took place within the Kingdom of Castile, the encounter was not the result of any political decision or royal command. Yet, the chronicler chose to disassociate this episode from the stream of historical events comprising the royal chronicle's central narrative, which was the king's life.

The chronicle begins by claiming that when the Kingdom of Navarre learned of the deaths of the regents of Castile, princes Juan and Pedro, in 1319, the Navarrese viewed the weakness of the neighboring kingdom as an opportunity to "take back what they could." To that end, in alliance with the Kingdom of France, they recruited an army to conquer Castile, capture Alfonso XI and "bring him before the king of France." No plan or intention to invade Castile ever existed between 1319 and 1321. Furthermore, the Kingdom of Navarre didn't even plan to reclaim Gipuzkoa until four decades later, in 1368, during the reign of Carlos II. But this license allowed the chronicler to turn an act of banditry into a political episode, in a time of rivalry between the two kingdoms. In addition, the chronicle makes no mention of the attack of the castle of Gorriti, and by omitting this information the author transforms an act of aggression into an operation to defend the territory of Gipuzkoa.

The chronicle misrepresents this episode by painting it as an encounter between the people of Navarre and Gipuzkoa, within a context of confrontation between the kingdoms of Navarre and Castile, which was not the case. The battle of Beotibar was fought between a criminal gang led by Gil Lopez de Oñaz and an "army," assembled by two of the royal *merinos* and aimed at maintaining law and order in the area. In other words, no confrontation arose between the territory of Gipuzkoa and the kingdom, nor was there a war or a declaration of war between the two kingdoms. As noted in previous and later chapters, the town authorities and some members of the Ganboa band cooperated, on multiple occasions, with the troops of the *merino* within the territory of Gipuzkoa, and even worked with the Navarrese to repress the criminals, bandits, and fugitives who acted on either side of the border.

The account goes on to describe the battle, alluding to kitchen pots filled with river stones and restating the involvement of the Navarrese and "other strange people" (the French) in the battlefield, a reoccurring element in the subsequent accounts of the battle. It explains how the Navarrese wanted to "ravage the land" and that, because of the unexpected nature of the attack, "a group of only a few men could be assembled." It is worth remembering, however, that the campaign was not a military one, but a police expedition, therefore, locals would not have had any need to assemble a company to defend the region. Like in most campaigns planned by Johan Lopez de Urrotz, the Navarrese directed their efforts against the criminals and their accomplices.

The battle was described as an ambush, and although the place-name, Beotibar, is not mentioned, references such as kitchen pots filled with river stones or the composition date of the poem confirm the text as a description of the 1321 battle. The author did not specify the number of combatants but affirmed that the Gipuzkoans faced an invading army vastly superior in number and that exactly ten thousand Navarrese men lost their lives in the battlefield: "and just as the story is told, the Navarrese were defeated, and the Gipuzkoans triumphed with great honor, for the Lord bestowed upon them the gift of this honorable victory."[26]

A few years after the chronicle, between January and September of 1348, Ruy Yáñez composed the poem for Alfonso XI.[27] The composition is simply a versified rendition of the chronicle where the text is reproduced line by line. The poem diverts from the chronicle only on few instances, one of the most notable being the allusion to nine thousand deaths (instead of ten thousand) in the battlefield. It is likely a poetic license for rhythm or strophic purposes, "the commander fled [vii] with very few of his men and left nine thousand dead in that mountain."[28]

Centuries went by before the episode was captured on paper again. It was in Juan Martínez de Zaldibia's *Historia Guipuzcoana* (History of Gipuzkoa), later known under the title *Suma de Las Cosas Cantábricas y Guipuzcoanas* (A Compendium of Cantabrian and Gipuzkoan Events), in 1564.[29] As Karmelo Etxegarai, chronicler of the Basque provinces after 1896, explained in a letter to Arturo Campion, Juan Martínez de Zaldibia's was an old and highly respected family in Tolosa. They were a lineage of nobles of the Oñaz band, and many sons of the family served as mayors of Tolosa. The father of the historian, Iñigo Martínez de Zaldibia, was the mayor of Tolosa in 1509. Juan Martínez de Zaldibia, Iñigo's brother and uncle of the historian, became mayor in 1515. Iñigo took office again in 1534, and Juan Martínez, in 1538. Iñigo, once more, in 1542. Historian Zaldibia was elected mayor for the first time in 1541. Then, his dad returned to office in 1551. The historian succeeded him in 1552, and held office twice after that, in 1559, and in 1574, a few months before his death.[30]

Zaldibia is, along with Rodrigo Ximenez de Rada and Carlos, prince of Viana, one of the first Basque historians. He finished *Suma de Las cosas*

Cantábricas y Guipuzcoanas about 1564 and offered the manuscript to the Basque General Assemblies for publication, but it was rejected and remained unpublished until Fausto Arozena sent it to print in 1945. In a letter addressed to the provincial General Assemblies, time-stamped in Tolosa on April 28, 1563, Zaldibia himself presented the aim and contents of his manuscript: "What I did, with effort and humble cleverness, is, by and large, a collection of everything occurred after the Great Flood and the arrival of Tubal in Spain worth adding to the memory of the Basque Nation and of this province, in particular, including the exploits of the province across time."[31]

His account of the battle was in the chapter titled "La Provincia de Gipuzkoa Vino a Ser de Castilla y Se Siguió La Batalla de Beotibar Contra Navarros y Gascones" (The Province of Gipuzkoa Was Annexed to Castile and the Battle of Beotibar Ensued Against the Navarrese and the Gascons) and was riddled with the exaggerations, mistakes, and untruths listed below:

1. Gipuzkoa rejoined the Kingdom of Castile. Zaldibia rewrote history by claiming that "Gipuzkoans returned to their pure condition of Castilians as free people, not conquered or forced to understand the crown of Castile, to which they belonged."[32] He believed that Gipuzkoa was "reannexed" by the crown of Castile because it had already been part of the Visigothic Kingdom of Toledo. Neither claim is historically true and, therefore, no supporting document exists. Gipuzkoa was never part of the Kingdom of Toledo, and the Kingdom of Toledo should not be associated with the Kingdom of Castile.

2. (The Gipuzkoans) "agreed to return to the king of Castile and not the king of Navarre, whom they disliked for the grievances he caused them. So, they communicated with King D. Alonso and handed over their castles and their land. And it must have been so because the king traveled to San Sebastian with only twenty horsemen, and no weapons or fights were involved." Records don't show any kind of dissatisfaction with the king of Navarre in 1200 or any handover of castles. What is more, existing documents and archeological evidence corroborate events of war and armed interventions, because what took place was, in fact, a conquest.

3. Zaldibia avoided referring to the band of Gil Lopez de Oñaz as bandits. Instead, he called them "the Gipuzkoans," suggesting by that name that they represented the Gipuzkoan communities of the early fourteenth century, which was an incorrect assumption. The operation could not have been planned by "Gipuzkoa" or the "province," as declared by Zaldibia, because neither the province nor the brotherhood of Gipuzkoa existed at

the time. The intervention was orchestrated by one of the nobles and no one else in the territory, but Zaldibia seems adamant about presenting a "provincial" body in 1321; he uses the word four times in this brief text about Beotibar.

4. The loss of Gipuzkoa left the Navarrese feeling "bitter" and wanting to destroy all Gipuzkoa: "the only reason why all of this happened was to destroy Gipuzkoa."[33] This is an apocryphal idea taken from the *Chronicle of Alfonso XI*. Existing documents do not support this thesis or such aspirations by the king of Navarre. As a matter of fact, none of the events in or immediately before September 1321 substantiate that the Navarrese had plans to destroy Gipuzkoa. Most importantly, the actions of September 1321 were not at all triggered by how bothered the Navarrese may have felt about the conquest of part of their territory in 1200. The *merinos* Johan Lopez de Urrotz and Dru de Saint-Pol carried out the police raid solely in response to the attack of a criminal group.

5. According to Zaldibia, the Navarrese perpetrated constant attacks, planning "daily assaults, murders and thefts in the province," and ultimately causing the "province" to act. The author meant to turn an aggression planned by a gang of criminals into a defensive war organized by a still-nonexistent province or brotherhood. He even tried to imply that the cattle rustlers were Navarrese and that they acted in Gipuzkoa, which is just as inadmissible as to claim the opposite, that most of the cattle rustlers came from Gipuzkoa and acted in Navarre. Archival documents prove that thief gangs were formed by bandits from multiple territories and that they acted on both sides of the border, in Araba, Gipuzkoa, and Navarre. The study of the sixty-seven campaigns planned by the mountain *merinos* between 1290 and 1320 establishes with a high degree of confidence that the operations by the royal *merinos*, especially those planned by Johan Lopez de Urrotz, were in reaction to the crimes committed by the cattle rustlers of the area. Gil Lopez de Oñaz becomes a recurrent character after 1309, when he tried to steal a herd of six hundred pigs from the town of Larraun.

6. The Navarrese army was formed by men from "Navarre, France and Gascony." Zaldibia strives to highlight the "French" identity of the kingdom, its officials, and its army. But title 1 of chapter 1 of the *Fueros* very clearly states that "If a man from a foreign land, a strange land or a land with a different language happened to become king, no more than five foreign men would be allowed to assist him or serve him."[34] The number of French and Gascon men in the army of 1321 was limited to a few

horsemen belonging to the governor's entourage, like the *merino* of Estella, Dru de Saint-Pol. But even in this case, their names alone would not suffice to determine whether these horsemen were indeed Navarrese or if they had been naturalized.

7. Zaldibia alleges that Mortagne set out from Pamplona "with a crowd of people" and "countless people" and that after a week of "recruiting people" "more than sixty thousand fighters gathered from Navarre, Gascony, and France."[35] Even with the participation of the French crown, which never happened, it would have been impossible for the kingdom to assemble an army of sixty thousand men. As Monteano points out, the 1366 survey of the kingdom counted 16,577 households in the territory's entirety. By adding the clergymen, the enlisted noblemen (exempted from the survey), the floating population, and those who simply evaded the audit, the total number of households would range from eighteen thousand to nineteen thousand.[36] In essence, the documents at the Navarre archives suggest it was a force of about 450 men.

8. Eight hundred Gipuzkoans confronted sixty thousand Navarrese in Beotibar. It is not credible that Gil Lopez de Oñaz's criminal gang would have been able to gather eight hundred men in 1321. It is just as improbable of these ringleaders to have been able to recruit such number of people from the surrounding towns. In Tolosa's case, for instance, population dwindled after the 1282 fire, and to foster growth, the town granted new residents the privilege of 1290. Enlisting and arming eight hundred foot soldiers thirty years after the disaster would have proven to be a difficult task.

9. The death toll provided by Zaldibia contains many mistakes. Zaldibia lists the names of eighteen combatants fallen in Beotibar, but only two of those, the *merino* Johan Lopez de Urrotz and Martin de Oibar, appear as dead in the documents at the Comptos Chamber or in any other archival document. Four others most certainly survived the battle: Martin Baignos de Uriz, Diago Periz d'Esperon, Johan Corbarán de Leet, and Johan Martiniz de Medrano were summoned as witnesses in the case against the governor in 1323, and the latter two were named regents of the kingdom in 1328. Although Moret counts Johan Henrriquiz de Lakarra among the dead of Beotibar, this is a questionable claim because the tally kept at the Comptos Chamber doesn't include his name. There is no written evidence that the remaining eleven men even took part in the encounter, let alone perished there. Although Zaldibia writes about "the governor's brother" and the "lord of Roselen" as if they were two separate people,

it was, in fact, the same person, Joffre de Mortagne, lord of Roseyllon, deputy of the governor of Navarre.[37] These names don't match the names registered on the 1321 books as castle wardens, border guards, noblemen, or the king's guard. As emphasized by Campion, the historian assumed the Navarrese army had been decimated and inflated the death toll with the names of all the warriors he had heard of or imagined.[38] For the same reasons, of the six names documented at the Comptos Chamber, Zaldibia only mentions one.

10. According to Zaldibia, Martin de Oibar died in the battle. His assumption sowed the seed of an old Basque saying: "Beotibar, Beotibar, *hic dia dutac* Martin de Oybar." Just a few lines prior, however, the author contended that Martin de Oibar had been made prisoner and executed three days later. Under these circumstances, it wouldn't come as a surprise if the four-line stanzas cited by the author were his own. To believe or not believe the author is purely a matter of faith.

11. In Zaldibia's account, the Oñaz band took the astronomical sum of one hundred thousand pounds in spoils of war. As mentioned above, documents at the Comptos Chamber reveal that the expenses and compensations paid for by the *merino* amounted to 559 pounds and fourteen dineros (pennies).[39]

12. The reference to a Navarrese document kept in Puente la Reina can count as one of Zaldibia's worst inaccuracies. The author asserts specifically that "what happened in the beginning was written in the days of old at the opening of the old notebook of the province, kept at the church of Puente la Reina, chief town of Navarre."[40] But besides Zaldibia and Garibai, no one has ever seen this document. In words of Etxegarai, the text Zaldibia is referring to is the copy of an unverifiable copy, and he concludes that "this book at the church of Puente la Reina, whose title and contents they omit, is of very dubious nature. It seems that they have heightened the authority of the book to invigorate an account that lacks more reliable testimonies. The copy Father Henao referred to disappeared from the general archives of Gipuzkoa, that is, if it ever was there at all. It is a commonplace procedure among similar cases."[41] Rather than jumping to the conclusion that Zaldibia was an outright liar, we could consider the possibility that he obtained a copy of the sentence of Olite of July. 1323 since Puente la Reina was one of the suing towns. But if that were the case, Zaldibia's wrongdoing would be even more serious because the sentence brings to the reader's attention many of the author's inaccuracies (or falsities, if he actually read the document).

13. A battle of such magnitude, of allegedly sixty-eight thousand warriors, would have had a major impact on the memory of the country's people. To attest to the mark left by the events, Zaldibia includes the first four four-line stanzas of a medieval song, apparently very popular during his time. But he fails to mention that, besides this stanza only he knows about, the events were only recorded in one chapter of the *Chronicle of Alfonso XI* and in the versified interpretation of said chronicle. Similarly, upon analyzing the author's account of the battle, it can be assumed, first, that Zaldibia himself wrote the first four four-line stanzas of the song of Beotibar to lend authority to his story, and, second, that the stanzas were neither of long tradition nor did they belong to a song.

Jerónimo Zurita borrowed from Zaldibia's account to write a brief five-line review of the battle in his *Anales de la Corona de Aragón* (Annals of the Crown of Aragon) of 1585. In his version of the events, the attack of the castle of Gorriti was a defensive operation in response to the "French" Ponz de Mortagne, who incited the Navarrese to go to war against the Gipuzkoans, after tensions over border limits had reignited between the kingdom and the province. There is no written evidence of any of these assertions. In fact, Gipuzkoa and Navarre were not at war either before or after the Gorriti incident, and the governor did not instigate or issue any "command." He was merely defending his borders and his people from a violent attack. On the other hand, as mentioned above, Gipuzkoa would not become a brotherhood or province until the second half of the fourteemth century. Unlike Zaldibia and Garibai, Zurita at least avoided mentioning a throng of men fighting or dying in the encounter.

Esteban Garibai adopted Zaldibia's original account in his *Compendio histo-rial de las chronicas y vniversal historia de todos los Reynos de Espanna* (Historical Compendium of the Chronicles and Universal History of All Spanish King-doms) published in Antwerp in 1571. Jerónimo Zurita wrote his *Anales de la Corona de Aragón* between 1562 and 1580, which explains why Garibai mentioned and quoted him in his 1571 *Compendio Historial*.

Juan de Mariana learned about the events through Garibai's work, and the former included the account in his 1592 Latin American version of *Historia General de España* (General History of Spain). Mariana begins his version by claiming that "the Navarrese, still bound to France, suffered greatly in Vizcaya."[42] As a matter of fact, Navarre was not bound to France, and Guizpucoa was not Vizcaya. Mariana errs again in stating that Mortagne was named governor of Navarre "by the king of France," when it was the king of Navarre who did it.

On top of that, he situates the events within the reign of Carlos I, when actually they happened during the last year of reign of Felipe II. The author incorrectly mentioned Carlos IV the Fair, who was the king of France, but when he reigned in Navarre, he was known as Carlos I the Bald. To make things worse, Mariana argued that Carlos I "*pretended*" to own the castle of "Gorricia" and that the ownership of said castle by Navarre was completely unlawful. He then repeated Zaldibia's version of the sixty thousand Navarrese who clashed with eight hundred Gipuzkoans, and he ended his account by teaming up with Zaldibia and Garibai in contending that the four-line stanzas, still sung in Spanish and Basque, were proof of the battle's popularity.

In the seventeenth century, several authors reproduced Zaldibia's and Garibai's versions of the encounter. Among the most notorious were Baltasar Etxabe (1607),[43] Lope Martínez de Isasti (1625),[44] Andrés Lucas (1633),[45] Francisco García (1685),[46] and Gabriel Henao (1689).[47] Theirs were iterations of the previous versions with small, superfluous, erratic, or false additions.

Baltasar Etxabe Sr., native of Zumaia, published in 1607 his *Discursos de la antigüedad de la lengua cántabra bascongada, compuestos por Balthasar de Echave, natural de la Villa de Çumaya en la Provincia de Guipúzcoa y vezino de México* (Old Speeches of the Basque-Cantabrian Language, Composed by Balthasar de Echave, Native of the Town of Zumaia of the Province of Gipuzkoa and Dweller of Mexico.) The book focused on the Basque language and had the distinction to be the first or one of the first printed books in America to contain some words in Basque. In chapter 20, titled *Como los Cántabros de la Prouincia de Guipúzcoa, venciendo à los Franceses se salieron de la obediencia del Rey de Nauarra, y se encomedaron al Rey de Castilla* (Of How Cantabrians of the Province of Gipuzkoa Defeated the French, Rebelled Against the King of Navarre and Gave Themselves to the King of Castile), the author included a description of the battle, taken mostly from Garibai's work. Needless to say, Etxabe committed the same historiographic inaccuracies.

Lope Martínez de Isasti wrote the *Compendio Historial de la M. N. y M. L. Provincia de Gipuzkoa* (Historical Compendium of the M.N. and M.L. of the Province of Gipuzkoa) in Madrid in 1625–1626. Like Zaldibia, Isasti offered his manuscript to the General Assemblies, but they did not approve it for publication, mainly because the text treated noblemen with special favor. The text was not published until it was sent to print by Ignacio R. Baroja in Donostia in 1850. In it, a short paragraph about the battle is taken from the works of Garibai and Zaldibia, and it replicates their mistakes.

References in Andrés Lucas' and Francisco García's biographies of San Ignacio are brief. We know that García read Garibai because he mentions the seventy thousand combatants, and he must have read Zaldibia, too, by his mentions of an army formed by Navarrese, French, and "Gascon" men. Surprisingly, in García's version, the Navarrese are simply considered "French." García added that Alfonso XI or XII instituted the military Order of the Band in 1332 and awarded bands to the Oñaz family crest for, according to the author, the deeds performed by seven Lopez de Oñaz brothers during the battle.

Gabriel Henao, Jesuit professor of philosophy and theology and dean of the University of Salamanca, wrote a three-volume series titled *Averiguaciones de las Antiguedades de Cantabría* (Discoveries about Old Cantabria) between 1689 and 1691. In chapter 45, "*Batalla, y victoria memorable, que ganaron los Guipúzcoanos y muy principalmente la Compañía militar de Tolosa, en el puesto cercano de Beotibar, siendo Caudillo Gil López de Oñaz y Loyola, hijo de la Casa de Loyola*" (Battle and Memorable Victory of the Gipuzkoans, Thanks to the Military Company of Tolosa, in the Nearby Post of Beotibar, with Commander Gil Lopez de Oñaz y Loyola, of the House of Loyola), Henao digresses to give a long description of the battle peppered with new details, found neither in the texts of the above-mentioned authors nor in archival documents.

In short, rather than an exception, the treatment of historical reality in the case of Beotibar was a sad standard in Spanish-written Basque historiography until well into the nineteenth century. Errozabal, mentioned in Etxabe's text, is another example of the historiographic dismemberment the history of the Basque people endures. In 1704, however, Josep Moret, chronicler of the Kingdom of Navarre, alters this pattern for the first time when he presents, in the third volume of the *Annals of Navarre,* an account of the events based on the archival documents preserved in Pamplona. After Moret, other authors followed suit, mainly, Arturo Campion and Karmelo Etxegarai, in the beginning of the twentieth century. But a great deal of research and analysis is yet to be done.

Ernest Hemingway once said that writing was just a matter of labeling the truth and of capturing in words the greatest truth within ourselves. Abiding by this commandment is not always easy, because, sometimes, the human race has written to escape or to try to escape reality. Writing history to understand reality and writing history to satisfy certain given fantasies is like describing two parallel lines and hoping they never cross in the concave and complex universe that it is the human world. Many have tried and failed, but, unfortunately, their trails always remain, and they are very difficult to rectify.

We could write history to re-create life perpetually. We could write about the past looking to the future, but, by that, we would be betraying the events of both the past and the present and we would lose the ability to distinguish between our temporary future and the rest of possible futures. This is not an advisable strategy, and it doesn't make things any clearer. The historical past has nothing to do with fiction. We will find truth by being sober rather than prodigal, and efficient rather than ascetic. To write history, we only need to refer to specific facts and to detail them as accurately as we can, in the simplest words possible.

RESOURCES

Achón, José Ángel, "Los intereses banderizos en la definitiva configuración de la frontera entre Guipúzcoa y el Reino de Navarra," Nafarroako Historiari buruzko Kongresu Orokorra, Príncipe de Viana, Iruñea, 1986.

Alegría Suescun, David, *Archivo general de Navarra, Sección de Comptos, Registro No. 5 (1291)*, Eusko Ikaskuntza, Donostia, 2000.

Altadill, Julio, *Castillos medievales de Nabarra*, Beñat Idaztiak, Donostia, 1934.

Campion, Arturo, *Gacetilla de la historia de Nabarra, Euskariana. Quinta serie. Algo de historia.* Euskal Erriaren Alde, Iruñea, 1915.

Campion, Arturo, *Gacetilla de la historia de Nabarra. La frontera de malhechores.* Euskal Ikasketen Nazioarteko Aldizkarian: Revue internationale des études basques, Biblioteca de la Gran Enciclopedia Vasca, 1969.

Catalán, Diego, "El Poema de Alfonso XI." Yo Ten Cate (ed.). C. S. I. C., Instituto Miguel de Cervantes, Madrid, 1956.

Ciganda, Roberto (ed.), *Archivo General de Navarra: Sección de Comptos: Registro No. 7 (1300)*, Eusko Ikaskuntza, Donostia, 2006.

Connolly, William E., *The Ethos of Pluralization*, University of Minnesota Press, Minneapolis, 1995.

Díaz de Durana, José Ramón; Fernández de Larrea, Jon Andoni, "Economía ganadera y medio ambiente. Guipúzcoa y el Noreste de Navarra en la Baja Edad Media," Nekazaritzaren Historia, 2002.

Díaz de Durana, José Ramón; Fernández de Larrea, Jon Andoni, "La frontera de los malhechores: bandidos, linajes y villas entre Álava, Guipúzcoa y Navarra durante la Baja Edad Media," Studia Historica. Historia Medieval, no. 23, 2005.

Echave, Baltasar de, *Discursos de la antigüedad de la lengua cántabra bascongada*, Enrico Martínez, Mexico, 1607.

Francisco García, *Vida, virtudes y milagros de S. Ignacio de Loyola*, Iuan García Infanzón, Madrid, 1685.

García Arancón, Raquel, *Archivo General de Navarra (1253–1270). Tomo II. Comptos y Cartularios Reales*, Eusko Ikaskuntza, Donostia, 1996.

Garibay, Esteban de, *Compendio historial de las chronicas y vniversal historia de todos los Reynos de Espanna, donde se escriven las vidas de los Reyes de Navarra: Escrivese tambien la sucession de todos los Reyes de Francia, y Obisspos de la Santa Yglesia de Iruñea*, Christophoro Plantino, Antwerp, 1571.

Garibay, Estevan de, *Compendio historial de las chronicas y universal historia de todos los Reynos de España, donde se escriven las vidas de los Reyes de Navarra. Escrívese también la sucession de todos los Reyes de Francia, y Obispos de la Yglesia de Iruñea*, Sebastián de Cormellas, Barcelona, 1628.

Garibay, Esteban, *Los XI libros del compendio historial de las chronicas y vniuersal historia de todos los reynos de España*, Antwerp, 1571. https://bibliotecadigital.jcyl.es/es/consulta/registro.cmd?id=13294.

Henao, Gabriel de, *Averiguaciones de las antiguedades de Cantabria: enderezadas principalmente a descubrir las de Gipuzkoa, Vizcaya y Alaba, prouincias contenidas en ella por el autor el padre Gabriel de Henao, de la Compañia [de Jesus]*, Eugenio Antonio Garcia, Salamanca, 1689.

Henao, Gabriel de, *Averiguaciones de las antiguedades de Cantabria: ocupadas en explorer sucesos de los cantabros, quando dominaron a España los godos y en los de empresas contra moros, y en defenderse dellos, enderezadas principalmente a descubrir las tres prouincias cantabricas vascongadas, en estos tiempos, y a honor y Gloria de San Ignacio de Loyola, cantabro por padre y madre, y Nacimiento en la una, y por origenes maternos en las otras dos, patriarca y fundador de la Compañía de Jesús, [por] su autor el padre Gabriel de Henao, de la misma Compañía, natural de Valladolid, teólogo y maestro de escritura sagrada en el Colegio real de la misma Compañía, de la Universidad de Salamanca*, Eugenio Antonio Garcia, Salamanca, 1691.

Idoate, Florencio (ed.), *Catálogo de la sección de comptos. Documentos*, Ed. Aramburu, Pamplona, 1974.

Iztueta, Juan Ignacio, *Gipuzkoako dantza gogoangarrien kondaira edo historia*, Euskal Editoreen Elkartea, 1990.

Janin, Erica, "La construcción de Alfonso XI como héroe épico en el Poema de Alfonso Onceno: el caso del asesinato de don Juan el Tuerto", *Letras*, 72, 2015, 121–131, https://repositorio.uca.edu.ar/handle/123456789/3791.

Lema, José Angel, *Los señores de la guerra y de la tierra: nuevos textos para el estudio de los parientes mayores guipuzcoanos (1265–1548)*, Gipuzkoako Foru Aldundia, Kultura, Euskara, Gazteria eta Kirol Saila, Donostia, 2000.

Lucas de Arcones, Andrés, *Vida de San Ignacio de Loyola, patriarca y fundador de la Compañía de Jesús*, Antonio Renè de Lazcano and Bartholome de Lorençana, Granada, 1633.

Mariana, Juan de, *Historia general de España, compuesta, enmendada y añadida por el Padre Juan de Mariana, de la Compañía de Jesús*, Antonio Briasson, Madrid, 1719.

Mariana, Juan de, *Historia general de España, compuesta, enmendada y añadida por el Padre Juan de Mariana, de la Compañía de Jesús*, Marcos Miguel Bousquet, Antwerp, 1737.

Marianae, Io., *Historia de rebus Hispania libri XX*, Petri Roderici, Toledo, 1592.

Martinez de Isasti, Lope, *Compendio Historial de la M. N. y M. L. Provincia de Gipuzkoa compuesto por el doctor Lope de Isasti en Madril año de 1625 y 1626*, Baroja, Donostia, 1850.

Martínez de Zaldibia, Juan, *Historia guipuzcoana*, manuscript, Tolosa, ca. 1560.

Martínez de Zaldibia, Juan, *Suma de las cosas cantabricas y guipuzcoanas*, Gipuzkoako Foru Aldundiko Bulego Tipografikoa, Donostia, 1944.

Martínez Garate, Luis María, "Beotibar: el mito de la batalla," Nabarralde, Iruñea, September 24, 2011.

Moret, Jose de, *Tomo Tercero de los Annales de Navarra*, Francisco Antonio de Neyra, Iruñea, 1704.

Mugueta, Iñigo, "Acciones bélicas en Navarra: La frontera de los malhechores (1321–1335)," Vianako Printzea, year 61, no. 219, 2000.

Recuero Lista, Alejandra, *El reinado de Alfonso XI de Castilla (1312–1350)*, Madrilgo Unibertsitate Autonomoko Filosofia eta Letren Fakultateko Antzinako Historia, Erdi Aroko Historia, Paleografia eta Diplomatikoa Saila. Unpublished doctoral dissertation. Accessed: June 27, 2016.

Soraluze, Nicolás, *Historia general de Guipúzcoa*, Carlos Bailly-Baillière, Madrid, 1870.

Vaughan-Williams, Nick, *Border Politics: The Limits of Sovereign Power*, Edinburgh University Press, Edinburgh, 2012.

Yanguas y Miranda, José, *Diccionario de Antigüedades del Reino de Navarra*, Javier Goyeneche, Pamplona, 1840.

Yanguas y Miranda, José, *Diccionario de Antigüedades del Reino de Navarra*, José Imaz y Gadea, Pamplona, 1840.

Zabalo Zabalegui, Javier (ed.), *Archivo General de Navarra. Sección de Comptos. Registro No. 2*, Eusko Ikaskuntza, Donostia, 2000.

Zabalo, Francisco Javier, "El acoso de guipuzcoanos y alaveses a los ganaderos navarros. La "frontera de los malhechores" entre 1280 y 1349," Vianako Printzea, year 66, no. 234, Pamplona, 2005.

Zabalo, Francisco Javier, "Una encuesta de 1349 sobre bandoleros navarros y guipuzcoanos," Príncipe de Viana, no. 232, 2004.

Zavala Fernández de Heredia, Luis (ed.), *El Castillo de Gorriti. Un pueblo recupera su memoria*, Luis Zavala Fernández de Heredia, Bilbao, 2003.

NOTES

1　Campion, Arturo, *Gacetilla de la historia de Nabarra, Euskariana. Quinta serie. Algo de historia*, Euskal Erriaren Alde, Pamplona, 1915, vol. 3, 317.

2　"sin haberse dado causa para el rompimiento de la paz que años había corría." Moret, Jose de, *Tomo Tercero de los Annales de Navarra*, Francisco Antonio de Neyra, Pamplona, 1704, 344.

3　"en mediano estado dispuesta la frontera contra Castilla." Moret, Jose de, *Tomo Tercero de los Annales de Navarra*, Francisco Antonio de Neyra, Pamplona, 1704, 344.

4　Lema Pueyo, José Ángel *et alia*, *Los Señores de la guerra y de la tierra: nuevos textos para el estudio de los parientes mayores guipuzcoanos, 1265–1548*, Gipuzkoako Foru Aldundia, Donostia, 2000, 109.

5　"Gobernador, no estamos obligados a seguir al rey ni al gobernador fuera del reino de Navarra y, si lo hacemos, esto nos acarrearía graves perjuicios pero, si os place darnos cartas como hizo el señor Alphonz de Rouroy cuando llevó a la gente a Puillon siendo gobernador del reino, de modo que esta partida no nos perjudique ni a nosotros ni a nuestras leyes, marcharemos de buena gana con usted, porque sabemos muy bien que los de Gipuzkoa han hecho y continúan haciendo grandes males en Navarra." Sentence of July 24, 1323, of the lawsuit of the towns of the kingdom against Ponz de Mortagne. En Lema Pueyo, José Ángel *et alia*, *Los Señores de la guerra y de la tierra: nuevos textos para el estudio de los parientes mayores guipuzcoanos, 1265–1548*, Gipuzkoako Foru Aldundia, Donostia, 2000, 110.

6　Archivo General de Navarra, Registros de Comptos. No. 20 (1321), f. 82–84 and 131r.

7　Campion also suggested as many as a thousand men. Campion, Arturo, *Gacetilla de la historia de Nabarra, Euskariana. Quinta serie. Algo de historia*, Euskal Erriaren Alde, Pamplona, 1915, vol. 3, 335.

8　Campion, Arturo, *Gacetilla de la historia de Nabarra, Euskariana. Quinta serie. Algo de historia*, Euskal Erriaren Alde, Pamplona, 1915, vol. 3, 322.

9　Zaldibia, Juan Martínez de, *Historia guipuzcoana*, manuscript, Tolosa, ca. 1560.

10　"cargó sobre la villa de Berastegi, y la entró por fuerza de armas, y después de haberla saqueado, la abrasó." Campion, Arturo, *Gacetilla de la historia de Nabarra, Euskariana. Quinta serie. Algo de historia*, Euskal Erriaren Alde, Pamplona, 1915, vol. 3, 340.

11　"seyendo en Gorriti é en Ipuzcoa atal xix de Septiembre, que fué la facienda." Campion,

Arturo, *Gacetilla de la historia de Nabarra, Euskariana. Quinta serie. Algo de historia*, Euskal Erriaren Alde, Pamplona, 1915, vol. 3, 317.

12   "que se llama Veotivar, que quiere dezir valle de yeguas." Echave, Baltasar de, *Discursos de la antigüedad de la lengua cántabra bascongada*, Enrico Martínez, Mexico, 1607, 75–76.

13   "lo cual podemos saber más ampliamente por aquellos que en la batalla lo vieron." Sentence of July 24, 1323, of the lawsuit of the towns of the kingdom against Ponz de Mortagne. En Lema Pueyo, José Ángel *et alia*, *Los Señores de la guerra y de la tierra: nuevos textos para el estudio de los parientes mayores guipuzcoanos, 1265–1548*, Gipuzkoako Foru Aldundia, Donostia, 2000, 110.

14   "Gobernador, no puede hacer ningún esfuerzo más aquí, observe que los infantes huyen presa del pánico, si se queda aquí solo puede morir." Sentence of July 24, 1323, of the lawsuit of the towns of the kingdom against Ponz de Mortagne. En Lema Pueyo, José Ángel *et alia*, *Los Señores de la guerra y de la tierra: nuevos textos para el estudio de los parientes mayores guipuzcoanos, 1265–1548*, Gipuzkoako Foru Aldundia, Donostia, 2000, 110.

15   "porque ningún esfuerzo podría hacer contra los enemigos por culpa e incumplimiento de los infantes de dichas ciudades y villas que huyeron o abandonaron el campo de batalla." Sentence of July 24, 1323, of the lawsuit of the towns of the kingdom against Ponz de Mortagne. En Lema Pueyo, José Ángel *et alia*, *Los Señores de la guerra y de la tierra: nuevos textos para el estudio de los parientes mayores guipuzcoanos, 1265–1548*, Gipuzkoako Foru Aldundia, Donostia, 2000, 110.

16   "quedaron ay muertos fasta diez mill de cavallo e de pie." Catalán, Diego, El Poema de Alfonso XI. Yo Ten Cate (ed.). C. S. I. C., Instituto Miguel de Cervantes, Madrid, 1956; xlvi + 700 p. (RFE, annex 65), Nueva Revista de Filología Hispánica, XIII, No. 3/4, 1959, 369–370.

17   Campion lists Sancho Sanchiz de Ureta as dead, but I believe he may be the same Sanchez d'Urete who signed the sentence of 1323, along with other signatories. Information about Simon Arnalt de Oroz is unclear. Campion, Arturo, *Gacetilla de la historia de Nabarra, Euskariana. Quinta serie. Algo de historia*, Euskal Erriaren Alde, Pamplona, 1915, vol. 3, 338.

18   AGN, Comptos. Reg. 20, fols. 82 r a 84 r.

19   AGN, Comptos. Reg. 20, fol. 131 r.

20   "Messire Dru de Saint Pol, padre suyo, solia tener á vida ante que moriess en Ypuzcoa." Campion, Arturo, *Gacetilla de la historia de Nabarra*, Revista internacional de los estudios vascos, Eusko Ikaskuntza, Donostia, 1913, 353.

21   "toda la ostilamenta de bestias y armas de la hueste que montava cient mil libras." Martínez de Zaldibia, Juan, *Suma de las cosas cantabricas y guipuzcoanas*, Oficina tipográfica de la Diputación de Guipúzcoa, Donostia, 1944, 36.

22   "El merino tuvo cuatro acémilas a su servicio durante nueve días y además cuarenta acémilas de la tierra, que llevaban lo que él y su compañía necesitaban durante cuatro días. Cuando el merino salió del sitio del castillo de Gorriti, para ir a Ipuzcoa, llevó viandas para la "garnizon" (el abastecimiento de él y de su gente) y hubo pagos por "restitución, compensación, indemnización," de diez y siete cargas de "pan cocho," en las cuales había en cada carga seis robos de trigo: montan veinticinco cahíces dos robos, y "perdidos en el dicho décimo nono día que mataron al dicho merino en Ipuzcoa, convertido el pan á dineros" el cahiz a diez sueldos, monta doce libras quince sueldos." Campion, Arturo, *Gacetilla de la historia de Nabarra, Euskariana. Quinta serie. Algo de historia*, Euskal Erriaren Alde, Pamplona, 1915, vol. 3, 317, 359.

23   Lema Pueyo, José Ángel *et alia*, *Los Señores de la guerra y de la tierra: nuevos textos para*

el estudio de los parientes mayores guipuzcoanos, 1265–1548, Gipuzkoako Foru Aldundia, Donostia, 2000, 107–113.

24 "Un caballero por nombre Garcia Centol, con más celos que prudencia y dirección." Moret, Jose de, *Tomo Tercero de los Annales de Navarra*, Francisco Antonio de Neyra, Pamplona, 1704, 345.

25 Catalán, Diego, El Poema de Alfonso XI. Yo Ten Cate (ed.). C. S. I. C., Instituto Miguel de Cervantes, Madrid, 1956; xlvi + 700 pp. (RFE, annex 65), Nueva Revista de Filología Hispánica, XIII, No. 3/4, 1959, 369.

26 "e desta manera que vos la historia a contado fueron desta vez vençidos los de Navarra, e quedaron los de Lepuzca con gran honra, por Dios que les quiso hazer merçed e dar la honra del vencimiento." Catalán, Diego, El Poema de Alfonso XI. Yo Ten Cate (ed.). C. S. I. C., Instituto Miguel de Cervantes, Madrid, 1956; xlvi + 700 pp. (RFE, annex 65), Nueva Revista de Filología Hispánica, XIII, No. 3/4, 1959, 369–370.

27 Catalán, Diego, El Poema de Alfonso XI. Yo Ten Cate (ed.). C. S. I. C., Instituto Miguel de Cervantes, Madrid, 1956; xlvi + 700 pp. (RFE, annex 65), Nueva Revista de Filología Hispánica, XIII, No. 3/4, 1959, 366.

28 "el caudiello escapó [vil] con muy poca [de] conpaña e dexó bien nueve mili muertos por esa montaña." Catalán, Diego, El Poema de Alfonso XI. Yo Ten Cate (ed.). C. S. I. C., Instituto Miguel de Cervantes, Madrid, 1956; xlvi + 700 pp. (RFE, annex 65), Nueva Revista de Filología Hispánica, XIII, No. 3/4, 1959, 370.

29 Martínez de Zaldibia, Juan, *Suma de las cosas cantabricas è guipuzcoanas* (manuscript) *compuestas por Zalvidea, natural de la Villa de Tolosa, escrita el año de 1564; aumentadas, é aclaradas algunas cosas por Diego de Salvatierra, regidor de la Ciudad de Vitoria en el año de 1585.* http://www.liburuklik.euskadi.eus/.

30 Campion, Arturo, *Gacetilla de la historia de Nabarra, Euskariana. Quinta serie. Algo de historia*, Euskal Erriaren Alde, Pamplona, 1915, vol. 3, 346.

31 "Lo que demás dello, por mi industria y llano ingenio he hecho, es una suma de todo lo que despues del diluvio y venida de Tubal á España es digno de ponerse en memoria de la Nacion Vascongada, y particularmente de esta Provincia, con las hazañas que los de ella han hecho en diversos tiempos." Campion, Arturo, *Gacetilla de la historia de Nabarra, Euskariana. Quinta serie. Algo de historia*, Euskal Erriaren Alde, Pamplona, 1915, vol. 3, 3446.

32 "los guipuzcoanos, después volvieron al prístino estado de ser castellanos, como gente libre y no conquistada y obligada a entender la corona de Castilla de quien realmente ellos eran." Martínez de Zaldibia, Juan, *Suma de las cosas cantabricas y guipuzcoanas*, Oficina tipográfica de la Diputación de Guipúzcoa, Donostia, 1944, 36.

33 "y todo esto no fue por otra cosa salbo por destruyr a Gipuzkoa." Martínez de Zaldibia, Juan, *Suma de las cosas cantabricas y guipuzcoanas*, Oficina tipográfica de la Diputación de Guipúzcoa, Donostia, 1944, 36.

34 "Et si por aventura aviniesse cossa que fuesse Rey ombre de otra tierra, ó de estranio logar ó de estranio lengoage, que non lis adusiesse en essa tierra mas de V en vayllia, ni en servitio de Rey hombres estranios de otra tierra." In *Fuero general de Navarra*, Aranzadi, Pamplona, 1964, 7.

35 "andubieron enrrecogiendo la gente», «se juntaron de nabarros, gascones y franceses vien mas de sesenta mil combatientes." Martínez de Zaldibia, Juan, *Suma de las cosas cantabricas y guipuzcoanas*, Oficina tipográfica de la Diputación de Guipúzcoa, Donostia, 1944, 36.

36 Monteano, Peio, *Navarra de 1366 a 1428: Población y poblamiento*, Príncipe de Viana, 57, no. 208, 1996, 327. As the author notes, some eighteen thousand families lived in Navarre

before the bubonic plague (1348–1351) distributed in about a thousand places within the kingdom's twelve thousand square kilometers (three million acres.)

37   María Itziar, Zabalza Aldave, *Archivo General de Navarra (1274–1321)*. *II*, Eusko Ikaskuntza, Donostia, 1997, 514 (Doc. no. 311).

38   Campion, Arturo, *Gacetilla de la historia de Nabarra, Euskariana*. *Quinta serie. Algo de historia*, Euskal Erriaren Alde, Pamplona, 1915, vol. 3, 358.

39   Campion, Arturo, *Gacetilla de la historia de Nabarra, Euskariana*. *Quinta serie. Algo de historia*, Euskal Erriaren Alde, Pamplona, 1915, vol. 3, 359.

40   "lo que en su entrada subcedio, se sigue aqui según está asentado ab antiguo al principio del quaderno viejo de la Provincia, y se alla scrito en la yglesia de Puen de la Reyna, villa principal de Nabarra." Zaldibia, Juan Martínez de, *Historia guipuzcoana*, manuscript, Tolosa, ca. 1560.

41   "ese libro de la iglesia de Puente la Reina, cuyo título y materia se callan, es muy sospechoso. Tiene aspecto de autoridad forjada para robustecer un relato desprovisto de otros testimonios más fehacientes. La copia a que alude el padre Henao desapareció del Archivo General de Gipuzkoa, si es que en él estuvo de veras. Es procedimiento muy usado en casos análogos." Campion, Arturo, *Gacetilla de la historia de Nabarra, Euskariana*. *Quinta serie. Algo de historia*, Euskal Erriaren Alde, Pamplona, 1915, vol. 3, 346.

42   "los Navarros, que todavia estavan sugetos a Francia, fueron muy maltratados en Vizcaya." Mariana, Juan de, *Historia general de España, compuesta, enmendada y añadida por el Padre Juan de Mariana, de la Compañía de Jesús*, Antonio Briasson, [Madrid], 1719, vol. 5, 517–518. Ver asimismo Mariana, Juan de, *Historia general de España, compuesta, enmendada y añadida por el Padre Juan de Mariana, de la Compañía de Jesús*, Marcos Miguel Bousquet, Amberes, 1737, vol. 5, 517–518.

43   Echave, Baltasar de, *Discursos de la antigüedad de la lengua cántabra bascongada*, Enrico Martínez, México, 1607, 75–76.

44   Martinez de Isasti, Lope, *Compendio Historial de la M. N. y M. L. Provincia de Gipuzkoa compuesto por el doctor Lope de Isasti en Madrid año de 1625 y 1626*, Baroja, Donostia, 1850, 273.

45   Lucas de Arcones, Andrés, *Vida de San Ignacio de Loyola, patriarca y fundador de la Compañía de Jesús*, by Antonio Renè de Lazcano and Bartholome de Lorençana, Granada, 1633.

46   Francisco García, *Vida, virtudes y milagros de S. Ignacio de Loyola*, Iuan García Infanzón, Madrid, 1685.

47   Henao, Gabriel de, *Averiguaciones de las antiguedades de Cantabria: enderezadas principalmente a descubrir las de Gipuzkoa, Vizcaya y Alaba, prouincias contenidas en ella por el autor el padre Gabriel de Henao, de la Compañia (de Jesus)*, Eugenio Antonio Garcia, Salamanca, 1689.

2

1200: A YEAR OF CONQUEST AND FRACTURE

WHY WRITE AN ARTICLE ABOUT THE YEAR 1200?

Idoia Arrieta

TO FIND A BROADER RANGE OF ANSWERS

In 2011, the Nabarralde Foundation published "Donostiaren konkistaren agiri ezkutuaren aurkezpena: ikerketaren ibilbidea eta ekarpen historiko-kritikoa," an article presenting a newly discovered document concerning the conquest of Donostia-San Sebastián, detailing the research process and its contributions to history and academia. Presented with this new piece of evidence, scholars seemingly accepted that Alfonso VIII of Castile had conquered Gipuzkoa (Guipúzcoa) in 1200. But history is obstinate, and this event did not lead to any major shifts.

Since the document did not get the attention it deserved, we would like to seize the opportunity offered by the University of Reno to reintroduce the documents and reexamine their context from a different angle.

The scope of this work is limited to the Basque Country between 1200 and 1300. To ensure a better understanding of the historical framework, the first section outlines the main historical events that marked the Kingdom of Navarre (Nafarroa in Basque, Navarra in Spanish). We analyze the events preceding the constitution of a "national" kingdom, the fracture of the year 1200, and the most immediate consequences of the split.

After the fall of the Roman Empire, a new space arose in Europe.

The former Roman space was reconfigured, and kingdoms solidified their power to form the states that we know today. It is within that context that, first, the Kingdom of Iruñea and then the Kingdom of Navarre were born. However, the bond between the peoples on either side of the Pyrenees has long outlived the kingdom.

The politics of medieval rulers never envisioned the state as the land of Basque speakers—the kings and queens of the time were, in fact, expansionists—but as a feudal monarchy ruling over a group of people with similar cultural and social beliefs. As a matter of fact, the Kingdom of Navarre was created in the era of European feudal states. French politician Jacques Turgot[1] said in 1751 that states are created when people are bound by a governing authority; and nations, on the other hand, are founded in a shared language. In this case, Navarre came to be both a nation and a state, if only for a brief period.[2] Although not intended by the king and the nobility, Basque people began to develop a sense of national identity,[3] much like other Western European peoples in the Middle Ages. It could be argued that our language and traditions survived thanks to ordinary Basque people. But Castile went forth with the blessing of the Catholic Church to conquer, through diplomatic and violent means, the territories comprising the Kingdom of Navarre. These conquests led to the fracture of the political unity of an already shrinking kingdom. With this in mind, the first section of this chapter focuses on the chronological account of such events using research from other authors.

In the new European political landscape, trade was redesigned and cities multiplied. The emergence of new cities and the development of farming, as well as the ability to store and preserve surplus food, went hand in hand. Collaborative actions made trading possible, spurred economic growth and, according to historian Josep Fontana,[4] imbued the participants with a proto-national sentiment, as the interrelations of economic activities fostered a sense of community in people who shared a common culture and language. In Iruñea-Pamplona and its surrounding area, a new trade network flourished, bringing coherence and interdependency to the interactions between guildsmen and traders, and urban and agricultural areas. The Navarrese trade network of the twelfth century was well organized and of great relevance. Castile coveted it. In fact, in the aftermath of the conquest, to assert his power, the king of Castile ratified the municipal charters of the conquered burgs and issued new ones to the towns along the Navarrese border. The second section of this chapter analyzes the burgs of the Kingdom of Navarre, including their dates, relevance, and evolution.

While the first two sections focus on historical events, the third one focuses on historiography. Most academic historians[5] recommend against political readings of the Middle Ages. Given the complexity of the period, they deem the search of any kind of nation-building argument inappropriate because the medieval context can encourage the fabrication of founding myths, ethnic and national identities, and traditions. We agree. This exercise may be anachronistic. But historians have provided a distorted political perspective on the configuration of the territory: they produce fragmented versions of Basque history, often in foreign languages, and they paint the Basques as lacking the will to survive as a people. They are constantly disabling Basque history. To counterweight this position, we studied an event at the core of Basque history's political struggle: the conquest of the western territories of the Kingdom of Navarre.

The documents presented in this chapter entail a break from the prior historical frame of reference. The alteration of the foundation dates of the municipal charters issued to the burgs would not necessarily change the events in any way if it weren't for the fact that the burgs and the trade system alike already existed before Castile's military occupation. The burgs were the engines of a very profitable international trade system and became an irresistible target for Castile.

Two of the documents cited in this chapter attest to the violence exerted by Castile to capture these territories. Additionally, we articulate a possible hypothesis about the material evidence, and we express the need to, at least, further examine them.

Although during our investigation we found undeniable historiographic errors, we realized that they are passing through history unnoticed, maybe because of *pactismo*,[6] so firmly rooted in Basque and Spanish institutions and seemingly invulnerable. The issue lies, of course, in the conquest that took place in the year 1200 and in the pulling force of the traditional approach on the matter.

History has been told from a traditional lens. The aim of this chapter is not to confer prestige to the history of the Kingdom of Navarre nor to lend it legitimacy. We chose to study the Basque community because it is undeniable that the inhabitants of these regions (at least the members of the resistance) must have had a discourse of their own, one built upon popular and religious cultures, and must have lived in groups with different symbolic and emotional elements, which contributed to the complexity of their identities. When defining a community as a mass of people with no political agency, scholars should consider certain cultural aspects, including origin, residence, traditions, and ways of life. Our contribution focuses on how historiography has overlooked the actions leading to the Basque political rupture as well as its consequences and how this disregard has paved the way for wrong interpretations. There are some researchers, however, who have tried to purge historical inaccuracies.[7]

As a result of our research work, we have concluded that historiography is missing the perspectives of different political cultures, anthropological history, and the sociolinguistic analysis of discourse.[8]

THE LOSS OF TERRITORY[9]

The Roman Empire wielded enormous influence in Europe. Many cultures and languages were lost as a result, including those surrounding the Basque language. But it seems like the Basque Country was not entirely Latinized and that the Basques found a way to preserve their language and culture.[10]

As the Roman Empire lost steam, the Basques grew in power in their land. Unlike their neighboring societies, bound by an administrative body, Basque-speaking communities were based on a loyalty system. Chronicles maintain that the Basques had to confront and often reach agreements with incoming new neighbors. The Visigoths and the Franks were in constant battle against the Basques *Deo Auxiliante* (with God on their side).[11]

An elite group of nobles had been actively governing Iruñea-Pamplona since Roman times, during the Visigothic period and even when the Moors conquered the Iberian Peninsula. It was precisely them who, understanding the advantageous location of the city—bordering Al-Andalus and the kingdom of the Franks—created an autonomous polity as soon as the opportunity arose. Thus, in 824, Iñigo Arista was proclaimed head of the land. He reigned over the central regions of Navarre, certain Aragonese valleys of the Pyrenees, and Iruñea-Pamplona, the capital city of the kingdom.

The monarch and his successors forged an alliance with the Muslim forces of Al-Andalus to avoid attacks from Cordoba and maintain their political autonomy. By the end of the ninth century, a series of castles delineated the border between Christian Navarre and the Islamic Al-Andalus.[12]

When the Kingdom of Iruñea was formed in 824, the northern Basque region of the time was under Carolingian suzerainty. During this contentious period, Sancho, as duke of Baskonia [medieval Basque Country], led many uprisings against the Carolingians. No records remain of the alliance between Sancho and Iñigo of Iruñea, but it is reasonable to think they had a close relationship of protection and collaboration.[13]

The Jimena dynasty brought the double games to an end. They resolved to stop paying taxes to the emirs of Cordoba and proclaimed Sancho ruler of an independent Christian kingdom. This is why Sancho I (905–925) is regarded as the first king of Iruñea. But his appointment brought inevitable consequences; the war against the Moors of Al-Andalus caused many grievances. There are no reliable records of this moment in history. Alberto Cañada Juste researches the body of sources from this historical period.[14]

The Kingdom of Iruñea enjoyed the height of its expansion during the reigning years of Sancho III the Great from 1004 to 1035.[15] In the king's own grandiose words: "I, King Sancho, hold full power over Aragón, Iruñea-Pamplona, Sobrarbe [in today's Aragón], Ribagorza [in today's Huesca], Nájera [in today's La rioja], Castile and even Araba [Álava]; same as Sancho VI William rules over Gascony; Count Berenguer over Barcelona; and Emperor Bermudo over Galicia . . ."[16]

The depiction of Sancho the Great's great Kingdom of Baskonia in the world map of Saint-Sever[17] showcases the current Basque regions of Araba, Bizkaia (Vizcaya), Gipuzkoa, and Navarre, as well as the kingdom's expansion into Aragón, La Rioja, and eastern Burgos. To the north, the map shows the Basque County of Gascony, and to the south, Islamic territories.

After the marriage between Sancho the Great and the first daughter of the count of Castile, the two powers grew closer and the border lines between Navarre and Castile were permanently established. The diploma of 1016 certifies that both states confirmed the establishment of the border.

It was a voluntary treaty, signed under no pressure. According to it, the mountain ranges of Neila (in today's Burgos), Urbion (Soria), and Cebollera (La Rioja) constituted natural borders. Additionally, Castile admitted it had no jurisdiction over La Rioja.

This agreement allowed the Kingdom of Iruñea to cement, administer, and expand its reign to surrounding regions. It dilated southward, toward Islamic lands, capturing La Rioja and the Erribera (Rivera) region, even though Tutera (Tudela) and its adjoining area remained Muslim.

During the reign of Sancho III the Great, Araba, Bizkaia, and Gipuzkoa inarguably belonged to Iruñea. The political body[18] was laid out in *tenencias* (districts), which were overseen by the barons of the kingdom *per manum regis* (appointed by the king).[19]

The northern territories, on the other hand, were technically under Frankish rule. But the reality was that the Frankish Kingdom consisted of small autonomous principalities governed by a duke, a marquis, or an authority official of similar rank. In the year 1000, today's Iparralde—the Basque Country to the north of the international frontier between Spain and France—pertained to the Duchy of Gascony. The leaders of the duchy had a close bond with their Iruñea counterparts, and intermarriages between the two circles were common. They also forged strong political ties. To the extent that during the tenth and eleventh centuries, all noble people from Iparralde paid fealty to the crown of Navarre. Historians cannot determine whether their fealty was a form of vassalage.[20] Another indication of their significant political affinity is that nobles on either side of the Pyrenees had representation in the court of Iruñea-Pamplona.

The culmination of the bustling interactions between nobles of both territories throughout the High Middle Ages came with the marriage of Urraka, daughter of King García I of Iruñea, and Sancho William, duke of Gascony. When Sancho acceded to the throne, the bond between the uncle and his nephews and nieces strengthened and the family made a pact pledging the territories of Gascony to the uncle. Lords to the north of the Pyrenees, from Lapurdi (Labourd) to Biarno (Béarn), received feudal estates, honors, and rank promotions for their participation in military operations. Upon Sancho William's passing in 1032, King Sancho III of Iruñea laid claim to his late uncle's land.

Sancho William's death fractured the Basque Country, if ever so slightly. Given that Sancho William died without a successor, the Principality of Baskonia fell under the rule of the Duchy of Aquitaine, and eventually built its life around France. But the Pyrenean regions, nevertheless, continued paying fealty to the king of Navarre.[21]

The Kingdom of Iruñea grew, opened its doors to European influences, and boosted diplomatic relations. The crown respected the unique identities of its territories. According to historian Aitor Pescador,[22] Sancho the Great reigned following a prefeudal model by which none of the crown's regions were stripped of their identities, despite their shared history; furthermore, local nobles preserved their titles and had representation in the court of Iruñea-Pamplona.

When Sancho the Great died, observing Iruñea's customary law, his eldest son inherited the kingdom, and the rest of his children received portions of the royal estate and were appointed to public official positions, under the condition that they swore loyalty to the king. Contrary to what is often claimed, Sancho the Great did not divide up the kingdom among his sons. He applied the Pyrenean law enforced in his kingdom,[23] which established that no territory of the kingdom should be fractionated.

García III of Nájera[24] became heir of the Kingdom of Iruñea. He inherited the king's crown and all the kingdom's territories. In sum, García gained control of the Kingdom of Iruñea; the counties of Araba and Bizkaia; Gipuzkoa; the Nájera Region (in today's La Rioja); and Aragón; as well as all the territories captured by his father: the counties of Sobrarbe and La Ribagorza (both in today's Aragón) to the east, and the county of Castile to the west. From his mother's side, García inherited Old Castile consisting of Trasmiera (Cantabria) and La Bureba (Burgos).

The other three brothers, all vassals of García III, received some lots of land of the king's estate and appointments to public official positions related to such land. Fernando was named count of Castile, but in 1037, he acceded to the throne of León from which he lay the foundation for the Kingdom of Castile. Gonzalo was bequeathed the royal assets of the counties of Sobrarbe and La Ribagorza, and Ramiro, a natural son, received Aragón.

When citing Sancho the Great's legacy, Spanish historians often refer to Castile and Aragón as sovereign kingdoms, when García was, in fact, the sole king of all these territories.

Defending the western border became a hard task, particularly after Fernando was proclaimed king of León. He and his brother started fighting over Castilian territories.

King García was killed because of their disputes at the Battle of Atapuerca in 1054. Although his death dealt a crushing blow to the Kingdom of Iruñea, the loss of territory was minimal; Bizkaia, Gipuzkoa, and Araba were still under Navarrese reign. The crown of Iruñea still governed over the Enkarterris (Biscayan districts) and some land in Cantabria.[25]

During this period, records show Iñigo López, count of Bizkaia, endorsing the king of Navarre, although not as an independent count yet. He was then an administrative representative of the king, to wit, the king still had the power to replace him. The count's appointment was *ad imperandum* (to govern), not *possidendum* (to own).

In 1076, enemy nobles and neighboring kingdoms with enmities for King Sancho IV of Iruñea conspired against and killed him in Peñalen. His murder triggered the temporary disappearance of the Navarrese crown, favoring the unprecedented expansion of the Kingdom of León to limits Alfonso VI would have never imagined.

Once all the direct successors to the Kingdom of Iruñea had escaped or had been forced out, the monarchs of the adjoining kingdoms, namely, King Alfonso VI of Castile and King Sancho Ramírez of Aragón, began capturing Navarrese land, capitalizing on the power vacuum and the climate of uncertainty of the area. On the western front, Alfonso VI of Castile made significant advances into the absent kingdom; he occupied Nájera and submitted Iruñea-Pamplona to his power. The Nájera chronicle reads: "*et in ipsa era venit Alefonsus rex de legion ad Nagera, et Pamplona suo iuri subdidit*" (and at that time king Alfonso came from the legion to Nájera, and subdued Iruñea-Pamplona under his authority).

Alfonso VI of León used the help of local nobles to submit the occupied regions. In return, these nobles were able to preserve or upgrade the social status they had with the Kingdom of Iruñea. Among them were Velázquez-Ayala, Diego Álvarez Lord of Oca, and his son-in-law Lope Íñiguez (son of Íñigo López,[26] who was the former *tenente* [governor of a *tenencia*] of Nájera from 1063 to 1075, and was transferred in 1076, on the same year of his death), *tenente* of Bizkaia and from then on, count of Bizkaia. In his speech for the ratification of the *fueros* (municipal charters granting rights and privileges) of Nájera, Alfonso VI mentioned that Íñigo López and Lope Íñiguez, father and son, "*venit ad me*" (came to me), adding that they had traveled from their homelands to the city of Nájera to pledge fealty and loyalty.

As a result, Alfonso VI of León appropriated even more land, including the *tenencias* of the Enkarterris and of Bizkaia, and distributed them as follows: Sopuerta to Velázquez-Ayala; Karrantza (Carranza) and Lanestosa to Diego Álvarez Lord of Oca; and Trutzioz-Villaverde de Trutzioz-Artzentales (Turcíos, Valle de Villaverde and Arcentales) to Lope Íñiguez.

After Diego Álvarez died in 1087, Lope Íñiguez took over his *tenencia* and under his regency the district took a different direction.

The same year, Sancho Ramírez and the king of Castile began a negotiation that would end in Castile's annexing the lands it had previously occupied: the territories to the west of the Ega River and La Rioja, in other words, Araba, Bizkaia, and a portion of Gipuzkoa. Aragón kept all the territories to the east. Within its realms, the Kingdom of Aragón created the so-called County of Navarre which would pledge vassalage to Castile.

The kingdoms of Iruñea and Aragón shared monarchs until 1134, the last one being Alfonso I the Battler who began his reign in 1104.

Alfonso I married Urraka, daughter of Alfonso VI of Castile and León in 1109. But they never procreated and, because of political issues, their marriage was annulled within a few years. The annulment was a dangerous political move for Aragón; the king risked losing his emperor title and his dynastic rights to the throne of Castile and León. The kingdom eventually had to renounce to its dynastic rights, and the relations between the two houses deteriorated.

In 1113, the king of Iruñea and Aragón reclaimed La Rioja and ousted Diego López I de Haro, Lord of Araba and Bizkaia, from the *tenencia* of Nájera and introduced Fortún Garcés Cajal as his successor. Tensions with Castile didn't defuse. In 1024, Diego López I de Haro, lord in Bizkaia, Araba, and La Rioja, rebelled against Alfonso the Battler.

In 1127, Alfonso VII of Castile and León occupied Burgos and Alfonso the Battler stopped Castilian troops at the Tamara Valley. There, both sides signed the Peace of Tamara, a peace treaty reestablishing the borders of the two kingdoms to their original limits of 1054 and 1076, the years in which the two Navarrese kings died.

Under the new treaty, the Kingdom of Iruñea-Aragón encompassed Trasmiera, Bizkaia, Gipuzkoa, Araba, Pancorbo (in today's Burgos) at the border, Belorado (Burgos, La Bureba, Gobiaran (Valdegovía), Castrojeriz (Burgos), the Mena Valley (Burgos), San Esteban Gormaz (Soria), Nájera, and Soria, with the mountain sides of Demanda at the border. Castile kept Frías (Burgos), Pancorbo, Briviesca (Burgos), Villafranca Montes de Oca (Burgos), Burgos, Santiuste (Guadalajara), Singüenza (Guadalajara) and Medinaceli (Soria).

In his chronicle, San Juan de la Peña described the treaty:[27]

> To avoid future discrepancies between the two kingdoms, they settled on which regions belonged to the Kingdom of Navarre: the piece of land stretching from the Ebro River to the vicinity of the city of Burgos, a region that King Sancho of Castile took by force from his kin Sancho of Navarre (Sancho of Peñalen), son of King Díez Sánchez de Nájera. (…) Documents of the treaty were handed to the monarchs and kingdoms of Castile and Navarre and all of them received signed and sealed letters. (…) And with that, Alfonso of Aragón handed all Castilian lands over to Alfonso of Castile, and refused to be called emperor anymore, but King of Aragón, Iruñea and Navarre, instead.

In the document, the sovereigns conceded to each other's rights. The king of Castile admitted to having forcibly occupied Navarrese lands and relinquished them. The Aragonese, on the other hand, accepted Castile as owner of Castilian land, rejected his title of emperor, and transferred several border burgs to Alfonso VII.

Alfonso I of Navarre and Aragón sieged Baiona (Bayonne) in 1130. The political reasons for this military move are unclear. Academic historian Jon Izaguirre entertains three hypotheses:

> He may have wanted to be a step ahead of the count of Tolosa, who was starting to show support for Alfonso of Castile; but it is also likely that he wanted to reunite all the Basque regions, like Sancho III the Great; or that the siege was a strategy to protect Navarre from the Aquitaine Franks by installing a Navarrese king in a region under French rule. Whatever the reason, Alfonso I lifted the siege in October of 1131 following an attack by the count of Tolosa.[28]

The king wrote his will in 1131, probably while still in Baiona. In it, he named the church his only inheritor: The Knights Templar, the Sovereign Order of Malta, and the Order of the Holy Sepulcher of Jerusalem. He ratified his will at death's door in Sariñena in 1134.

But the local nobility of the Kingdom of Iruñea and nobles from Aragón did not accept the late sovereign's will and resolved to reject his *hilburuko* (Biscayan testament). Lacking a direct successor, the crown of Navarre and Aragón dissolved, and the two kingdoms and their representatives regained their power and sovereignty; in 1134, Navarre recouped its land.

The Aragonese convened in Jaca (in today's Huesca) and anointed Ramiro II the Monk king of Aragón. As for Navarre, the court met in Iruñea-Pamplona to proclaim García Ramírez the Restorer, grandson of Sancho III of Nájera, king of Navarre, and to establish the border that survived until the present day with the Kingdom of Aragón. The Kingdom of Iruñea managed to reunite all the Basque regions once more, except for Baiona.

The Navarrese noblemen brought together the territories of Araba, Bizkaia, and Tutera. Ladrón Íñiguez de Guevara had been the regent of the *tenencias* of Araba, Gipuzkoa, and Bizkaia since 1124. He was a supporter of the king of Iruñea and in 1134 married the king's sister.

By 1147, the Navarrese domains included the Enkarterris, which, at the time, reached the Ason River. A sign of this is that on March 25, 1147, King García of Nájera bestowed immunity and privilege (or land jurisdiction) upon the abbot of the monastery of Santa María del Puerto, in today's Cantabria.

Tutera was already Navarrese territory by then, after Alfonso I the Battler recaptured the region from the Moors in 1119. King García also reclaimed the valley of Erronkari (Roncal).

But the Kingdom of Iruñea lost the portion of land between Erronkari and Jaca to Aragón. And, although Navarre won Logroño (in today's La Rioja) back, Castile took over the remaining land and burgs of La Rioja. Clashes among the crowns continued.

Upon his father's death, Sancho VI the Wise rose to the throne of Iruñea in 1150 and reigned until 1194. After his accession, the land comprising Lapurdi, Zuberoa (Soule), Garazi (Pied-de-Port), Baigorri, Gipuzkoa, Bizkaia, Durango, the Enkarterris, Erriberri (Olite), and Erribera became known as the Kingdom of Navarre.

This new designation eliminated the concept of a nuclear reign in favor of an idea of a more collective kingdom. Reformulating the monarchy enabled the king to project a sense of land sovereignty over specific regions where his authority needed reinvigorating.[29] By that time, the land of the Basques began to welcome languages and people of all origins to foster trade and craftsmanship.

The crowns of Castile and Aragón were amid a generational shift. Alfonso VIII took the throne of Castile in 1159, and Alfonso II became king of Aragón in 1162. The sovereigns were underage, and this brought some respite to the Kingdom of Navarre.

Taking advantage of the circumstances, Sancho VI the Wise tried to recapture the territories lost in the eleventh century. Between 1163 and 1167, King of Navarra Sancho IV the Wise made incursions in the kingdoms of La Rioja and Najera and reappropriated Logroño, Entrena (in today's La Rioja), Navarrete (La Rioja), Ausejo (La Rioja), Autol (La Rioja), Quel (La Rioja). and Resa. He gained the support of the border communities with *fuero* privileges: first, to Guardia (Laguardia), in 1164 and then, to San Vicente de la Sonsierra (La Rioja), in 1172.

When Alfonso VIII of Castile came of age and consolidated his position as head of the crown, he signed a pact of mutual defense with Alfonso II of Aragón.

Border clashes between Castile and Navarre escalated throughout the twelfth century. Castile was after the western territories of Navarre and its trading network.

So, to reclaim his lost territories, the Castilian king launched a military campaign against his Navarrese counterpart, and, to take control of northern Navarre, married Eleanor of Aquitaine, who gave him Gascony in dowry.

Castile waged war against Navarre in 1173. Alfonso VIII attacked La Rioja and La Bureba, and, in 1175, he raided the Enkarterris. A document about Alfonso VIII kept record of the incursion: "*in tempore quo Incartationes introvi* (at the time I entered the Enkarterris)."[30] Castilian troops reached to the Nerbioi River and the castle of Malmasin (Malvecín). The king was assisted in his battles by Diego López de Haro, who seemingly wanted to repossess the Lordship of Bizkaia. At the time, Ladrón Iñiguez governed the *tenencias* of Gipuzkoa and Bizkaia, which were later handed over to his brother, Vélez Ladrón, who simultaneously became the custodian of the castle of Malmasin.

The conflict continued until 1176, when the kingdoms decided to put their border disagreements in the hands of the king of England and comply with his ruling.

The Navarrese wanted to return to the era of king García of Nájera, whereas Castilians sought to recover what Alfonso VI had captured in 1076 after the murder of King Sancho in Peñalen. Both territories intended to reestablish the boundaries set in the eleventh century.

The ruling issued on behalf of King Henry II, Alfonso VIII's father-in-law, ordered that each king must preserve or regain the castles he possessed at beginning of his regency. In sum: the castles of Legin (Leguín), Zabalate (Portilla), and Godin (Lapuebla de Labarca) would remain part of Navarre, and Logroño,

Navarrete, Entrena, Autol, and Ausejo would remain part of Castile. On top of that, Alfonso of Castile would pay Sancho VI an annual sum of three thousand maravedis for ten years, and a previously signed seven-year truce was enforced. The ruling did not satisfy either of the parties. Castile gained control over La Rioja, La Bureba, and a great portion of Bizkaia, confirming that Alfonso VIII's demands took precedence.[31] As part of the deal, the Lordship of Bizkaia, except the Durango Region, went to López de Haro.

Tensions never stopped. The king of Castile immediately started talks with other regents of the peninsula to partition Navarre. On April 15, 1179, King Alfonso VIII forced the king of Navarre to sign an agreement to allocate La Rioja and Bizkaia to Castile; and to Navarre: the Durango Region, Gipuzkoa, Araba (except the Añana salt flats), and the Riojan burgs of Legin and Zabalate. The agreement introduced the Nerbioi River and the Baia River as natural borders and stressed that Itziar (Icíar) and Durango would continue to be under Navarrese reign,[32] meaning Durango was awarded *fuero*. Count Vélez Ladrón from Araba governed the Durango Region. Castile took the castle of Malmasin in the Durango Region and the castle of Morillas in the Baia Valley.[33]

Sancho the Wise pursued good diplomatic relations with the new king of England. On May 12, 1191, Richard I the Lionheart, King of England, Normandy, and Aquitaine, and Count of Anjou, married Berengela, daughter of Sancho VI. Because of the strong Navarrese-English ties, the coastline of Navarre saw an influx of Gascon settlements. Family and trade networks materialized on both sides of the Bidasoa River. In a move to solidify his power and foster trade, Sancho VI formed burgs all along the coast: Donostia-San Sebastián, Getaria (Guetaria), Mutriku (Motrico), Hondarribi (Fuenterrabia); and in Araba: in Vitoria-Gasteiz, Antoñana, and Bernedo.

A document from 1190 kept at the British Museum cites the Navarrese and English borders and hints at the possible interests behind England's decision to divide borders.

It reads: "It is known that the king of England owns all land between the Sea and Hispania all the way to the port of Oiasouna, which establishes the border between the kingdoms of England and Navarre. (...) The domains of the king of Navarre start at the port of Oiasouna and reach Castrourdiales, where they border with Castilian lands."[34]

Over the years, even during the reign of Sancho VII the Strong, the alliances between the kingdoms changed. As a gesture of support, the king of England and Aquitaine transferred Lower Navarre (Nafarroa Behera in Basque, Basse-Navarre in French) to the Kingdom of Navarre and brought Castilian appetencies to a standstill.

The peaceful period between Castile and Navarre came to an end in 1195, when Castile fought the Almohad in the Battle of Alarcos. Alfonso VIII was defeated, and León and Navarre saw their chance to act against him. Although, at the time, Diego López held the title of second lieutenant and was one of the most prevalent noblemen of Castile, he allegedly fled the battlefield and left the king of Castile to fend for himself.

Between 1195 and 1197, King of Navarre Sancho VII the Strong decimated the lands of Almazán (in today's Soria) and Soria, according to historian Rodrigo Jiménez de Rada, and the lands of Logroño, as told in *Chronica Latina*. The king's actions did not go unnoticed; the papal legate in the Iberian Peninsula, Cardinal Gregorio de Sant Ángelo, put the Kingdom of Navarre into question and executed Castile's request for excommunication.[35]

The rest of the kingdoms immediately followed suit. In 1198, King Alfonso VIII of Castile allied with Pedro II of Aragón through the Treaty of Calatayud, where they agreed to the apportionment of the Kingdom of Navarre. They established the Arga River as the dividing line. Simultaneously, the Castilian married his daughter Berengela to Alfonso IX of León. In sum, the crowns of the Peninsula isolated the king of Navarre.

In subsequent military incursions, Castile captured the castle of Inzura and Miranda de Arga, and Pedro II of Aragón, Burgi (Burgui), and Oibar (Aibar). Sancho VII of Navarre had to sign individual treaties with each king to achieve a short-lived period of peace.

The events of the conquest of 1200 are recorded in six medieval chronicles: *De rebus Hispaniae* by Jiménez de Rada; *Crónica de Castilla* by Alfonso VIII; *Chronica Latina Regum Castellae*; *Crónica general* by Alfonso X; *Canónicas de los fechos de España*, written at the beginning of the fifteenth century by García Eugi, bishop of Baiona's diocese; and *Crónica de los Reyes de Navarra*, written by Charles, prince of Viana in 1454. The first few chronicles were almost contemporary to the events, while the rest gradually emerged in the following centuries. The contemporary chronicles mention the conquest only briefly. The later ones, on the other hand, make posteriori interpretations of the events but add little new information.

Some medievalists such as Gonzalo Martínez Díez, Julio González, and Luis Javier Pérez de Ciriza have used contemporized data from said chroniclers. Because of the great relevance of their work for our research, we have decided to consult their literature despite possible political differences.

The Basque population of the twelfth century was distributed along a network of valleys that were sheltered by mountain ranges and massifs, with rivers as natural borders. They lived in small towns or in their ancestral homes.

The Kingdom of Navarre showed interest in modernizing social structures, in transforming the territory, and administering the land. To better manage its realms, the king created a network of urban spaces and implemented the *tenencia* system.

The space that concerns us in this chapter—the city network analyzed in the next section—was structured around the burg of Vitoria-Gasteiz, the administrative area of the Araba plains, and the Navarrese coastal burgs with ports for maritime trade.

The *tenencias* were administrative districts of the Navarrese political space; they all consisted of an urban center or a castle and were part of the kingdom's defense network, having to guard and monitor the surrounding trade routes. Fortresses were able to communicate visually from one to the next. The *tenentes*, most of noble origin, were appointed by the king, and their duties included administering the district, collecting taxes, supervising the royal jurisdiction, and defense planning.

As mentioned earlier, Araba, Gipuzkoa, and the Durango Region needed reconfiguring, especially after the pact of 1179. Castile had already conquered La Rioja and Bizkaia by then, except the Durango Region. So, determined to avoid losing more territory, Navarre went on to reinforce and fortify the burgs and castles bordering Castile and Aragón, focusing mainly on Araba's Vitoria-Gasteiz and Trebiñu (Treviño), and on La Rioja's La Guardia and San Vicente.[36]

Sancho VI split the large *tenencia* of Araba into smaller districts to enhance its defense capabilities; starting in 1181, he created the *tenencias* of Vitoria-Gasteiz and Trebiñu, among others. The *tenencias* on the external border of Araba, in existence since the eleventh century, were divided into three: the *tenencias* of Buradon-Zabalate, controlling the mid-section of the Ebro River; the pivotal *tenencia* of Marañón, managed by the burg of La Guardia and defended by walls and a fortification; and the *tenencia* of Punicastro, encompassing the mountainous area of Araba and the newly formed burg of Antoñana.

The interior of Araba was partitioned in five sections. Today's Trebiñu was split into Trebiñu and Arluzea (Arlucea), along the mountains of Araba following the road to Vitoria-Gasteiz. From the Araba plains emerged three *tenencias*: Zaitegi (Záitegui) on the west; the new burg of Vitoria-Gasteiz in the center; and Aitzorrotz on the east of Araba and the west of Gipuzkoa. The Durango Region must have been located within the latter, but no corroborating records exist. Although the Durango Region was mostly farmland, King Sancho VI of Navarre decided to create a burg in it in 1180.

Present-day Gipuzkoa was not a unified territory at the time and was sectioned in three *tenencias*:[37] the Hernani-Donostia-San Sebastián *tenencia* stretched from Oria (Lasarte-Oria) to Oiartzun (Oyarzun) and expanded to the south to where Tolosa is today. Two fortifications were erected within it: Beloaga, in Oiartzun, and Mendikute, in Oria. Another one was built in the mountain top of Ausa Gaztelu, in the Aralar Valley, and one more in Ataun; the Ipuzcoa *tenencia* began in Deba and ended in Oria and had Getaria as capital city; and the Aitzorrotz *tenencia* spread across the western lands of Gipuzkoa, today's Upper Deba Region.

The Navarrese crown picked the *tenentes* or leaders of their preference and trust to defend the land. The most significant changes were carried out by Sancho VII in the years preceding the conquest.[38]

In 1199, Castilian troops, this time unassisted by Aragón, attacked the western territories of the Kingdom of Navarre: Araba, Gipuzkoa, and the Durango Region. The renowned sixteenth-century chronicler Esteban de Garibay captured Alfonso VIII's plans in his *Compendio*: "Much like his predecessors and his forefathers, the King and Queen, had planned to capture the Kingdom of Navarre, the king of Castile, ignoring the outcome of King Sancho's illness and the successors to the Navarrese throne, don Fernando and don Ramiro, gathered his people and went back to war against Navarre . . . "[39]

The celebrated Basque historian from Arrasate (Mondragón) stated in his book on the king of Navarre that, following the will of his ancestors, the king of Castile wanted to conquer the Kingdom of Navarre, and declared war to it. The reader may be shocked by Garibay's words, considering the historian was a staunch supporter of (the theory of) a voluntary annexation.

On May 6, 1199, the Castilian army set off for Pancorbo, reached Miranda, crossed the Ebro River, crossed the bridge of the Ebro burg toward Ibida (Trebiñu) and, finally, attacked Araba. Alfonso VIII's short-term targets were Trebiñu and the Araba plains, but both Trebiñu and Zabalate resisted the charge. Initially, the Navarrese military forces withstood the attack.

The Castilian troops headed to Vitoria-Gasteiz next and sieged the burg for nine months. The convenient location of the fortress and *tenente* Martin Txipia's battle strategy very possibly helped in resisting the enemy. The siege began before June 5 and on August 31, Alfonso VIII was still there. To deploy Castilian troops in Vitoria-Gasteiz for such a long period of time meant king Alfonso VIII had the city for a solid strategic goal.

Since the city was sieged before the harvest of the Araba plains, starvation spread across the place. Removed from resources and other Christian kingdoms, the Navarrese king resorted to the Almohad for help. Only an Almohad attack on southern Castile would have forced Castile to lift the siege on Vitoria-Gasteiz. They were the only ones who could put Castile in a bind.

So, the Navarrese king set out for Seville to seek help from the Moors. Once in the southern city, he sent emissaries before the Almohad Caliph of Morocco in the hope of securing an agreement. But things did not work out for Sancho VII. The Almohad Caliphate was dealing with its own internal issues. In January 1199, Muhammad ibn Abu Yusuf Yakub, known among Christians as Miramolin ever since his involvement in the Battle of Las Navas de Tolosa, succeeded his late father Abu Yusyf Yakub al Mansur in the throne. Pressing matters in Africa kept delaying Sancho VII's departure from Al-Andalus. The monarch's stay, long and fruitless, yielded nothing more than gifts, money, and the collection of a few cities' income tax, but was not conducive to an Almohad attack against Castile. The Caliphate had just signed a five-year ceasefire with Castile, making it impossible to send troops against the Castilian king.

With Vitoria-Gasteiz still under siege, the Castilian offensive campaign continued north, conquering Araba, Durango, Ipuzkoa, and Donostia-San Sebastián and reaching as far as Baiona by the beginning of the year 1200. Alfonso VIII's troops ravaged their way across Navarre, plundering and destroying any place they went through. As a matter of fact, in 1200, Alfonso VIII awarded privileges to the Monastery of Iranzu as compensation for the stolen cattle and the damages caused to their vegetable gardens.[40]

Back in Vitoria-Gasteiz, the situation took a turn for the worse. The war and the lack of provisions had left the city dwellers and the fighters feeling exhausted, famished, and disheartened. To put an end to the situation, the bishop of Iruñea, Gartzia Fernandez, and a horseman from the sieged garrison successfully negotiated a ceasefire with Alfonso VIII and gathered with Sancho VII to explain the gravity of the situation and to request that he agree to the surrender of the city. Without the king's permission, surrendering would have been considered an act of treason against the king. But Sancho VII supported the capitulation request. He had already lost the Durango Region, Gipuzkoa, and Araba to Castile, although very little information exists about the dates of the conquests.

In the words of Jiménez de Rada: "Castile seized the castles of Donostia-San Sebastián, Hondarribia, Beloaga, Aitzorrotz, Mendikute and Ausa in Gipuzkoa; in the region of Araba: Zaitegi, Arluzea, Atauri, Argantzon, Santa Cruz, Gatzaga, Toro, Antoñana, the castle of Korres and the old town of Vitoria-Gasteiz; and in Navarre: Marañón, Irurita, San Vicente and Orzorroz."[41]

According to Rada, during their campaign, Castile captured, on the one hand, Vitoria-Gasteiz, Ibida (except the castle of Trebiñu, which would later be relinquished in exchange for Insura), Araba, and Gipuzkoa; and, on the other, Donostia-San Sebastián, in the Hernani Valley, Hondarribia and Beloaga, in the Oiartzun Valley, Aitzorrotz, in the Leintz Valley (Léniz), and the castles of Auza, Ataun, and Arzorrotza (today's Mendikute), on the border of Gipuzkoa and Navarre; Zaitegi, Arluzea, Azprozia, the old town of Vitoria-Gasteiz, Marañón, Irurita, and Done Bikendi (San Vicente). Castile would eventually seize Trebiñu and Zabalate, in exchange for Insura and Miranda.[42]

The account in *Chronica Latina Regum Castellae* is even more brief than Rada's and scant in detail:

> In the meantime, however, the king of Castile besieged Vitoria-Gasteiz, and while the siege lasted, he acquired all the neighboring camps: Trebiñu, Arganzon, Santa Cruz, Alchorroza, Old Vitoria, Arluzea, the land called Gipuzkoa, even Donostia-San Sebastián, Marañón, San Vicente and some others. At last Victoria fell, and thus he possessed the whole of the valley and the surrounding lands, and thus returned with the victory to Castile.

The chronicle listed new fortifications: Arganzón (in today's Burgos), and Santikurutze Kanpezu (Santa Cruz de Campezo). But an addition of places does not necessarily mean an expansion of territory. Argantzon, which was granted *fuero* in 1191, was on the way to Vitoria-Gasteiz, and, according to historian Luis Javier Fortún Pérez de Ciriza,[43] Castile must have occupied it before arriving in the burg.

García de Eugui, an Augustinian friar from Navarre, told in his fourteenth-century chronicle: "And then the King D. Alonso took Ipuzcoa and its castles and fortifications . . . and later Donostia-San Sebastián and Hondarribia and Cogitay." The prince of Viana, on the other hand, "said king of Castile marched across Araba, Gipuzkoa and Navarre, and gathered his people and horsemen against the king of Navarre; they sieged Vitoria and other towns and castles for almost a year; the dwellers tried their best to defend themselves, but, eventually, had to surrender unwillingly. And this is how they unjustly took the lands of Araba and Gipuzkoa."[44]

These last two chronicles were written later and do not provide much clarifying information. So, the only documented fact is that, when Sancho VII returned from Al-Andalus hopeless, and with no other aid but money, the Durango Region, Gipuzkoa, and Araba had already been lost to Castile.

Seeing as Navarre could not withstand Alfonso VIII's offensive any longer, both kings agreed to sign truces, allowing Alfonso VIII to exchange the castle of Inzura (in Ameskoa) for Zabalate, and the castle of Miranda de Arga for Trebiñu. The castles of Trebiñu and Zabalate fought back until the day the truces were signed.

Although no records of the capitulation date of Vitoria-Gasteiz have survived, the event must have happened after December 22 and before January 25, as the king of Castile stopped in Belorado that January day on his way to Burgos.

Modern historiographers have tried to explain why these regions joined the kingdom of Castile and claim that they were allured by the idea that Castile had more to offer than the Kingdom of Navarre. But, as explained in the next section, Navarre ran a far more advanced trade network and offered greater economic advantages. According to historian Fortún Pérez de Ciriza, besides reinforcing his power over the entirety of his land, the king of Navarre also replaced the incumbent *tenentes*. The local nobility did not welcome the king's decision and decided to disobey his orders. Although Pérez de Ciriza does not provide any witness accounts, he believes local lords and residents may have forced the *tenentes* out of their fortifications.

Available documents do not detail how Alfonso VIII came to possess the castles. Hegemonic historiography asserts it was a negotiated incorporation, but we found no records supporting this claim. The last section of this chapter goes into more detail on this theme. The *tenentes* did not represent the people but instead represented the king and the queen, who were the only ones with the authority to order the *tenentes* to retreat. That the *tenentes* committed treason against the king lacks credibility because they would have faced harsh consequences had they done so. In view of this, it is telling that the situation abruptly ended when the Navarrese lord authorized the capitulation of the city of Vitoria-Gasteiz.

Documents in our possession show that the *tenentes* kept their oath of fealty to the king. Juan Bidaurreta, the *tenente* of Donostia-San Sebastián (with the castles of Mota, Beloaga, and Hondarribia) continued to govern other *tenencias* at the service of the king of Navarre until 1237.[45] The *tenente* of Vitoria-Gasteiz Martin Txipia performed similar services for the Navarrese kingdom throughout his life. Other *tenentes* had similar experiences: Pedro Garcés from Agoncillo (in today's La Rioja); Gartzia and Gontzalo from the Baztan Valley; and Mattin Enekoitz from Aibar. All of them continued to be loyal to Sancho VII. History lost track of Mattin Ruiz, *tenente* of Zabalate, although the likeliest theory is that he perished at Zabalate, one of the last castles to fall. Similarly, historian Jon Andoni Fernández de Larrea Rojas contends that he has no data to support the argument that any Navarrese *tenente* changed sides to join Castile in 1200; on the contrary, his data confirm that the influential Guevara and Mendoza families continued at the service of Sancho VII.[46] In short, no document indicates that the Navarrese forces surrendered.

The balance of the military campaign was clear. Castile captured the powerful city of Vitoria-Gasteiz; and three well-separated regions: today's Trebiñu, Araba, and Gipuzkoa. According to Fortún Pérez de Ciriza, the Durango Region is not mentioned as captured territory, possibly because it was within the piece of land offered to the *tenente* of Araba and Ipuzcoa, in the district of Aitzorrotz.

Up until the end of the conquest, in January 1200, these regions had belonged to the Kingdom of Navarre. In its latest incursion, Castile reached the Bidasoa River, a crucial milestone in their expansionist strategy that allowed Castile to border Gascony, bringing great future opportunities to Castilians. Alfonso VIII created an inland trade route connecting Burgos to Gascony and France through Miranda, Vitoria-Gasteiz, Agurain (Salvatierra), Segura, Ordizia, Tolosa, Donostia-San Sebastián, and Hondarribia, and joined the Atlantic maritime trade network.

The section about Sancho VII of Navarre explained how the king, faced with the loss of much of his land on returning to his kingdom, demanded justice from Alfonso VIII of Castile and asked him to restore what had been unjustly taken from Navarre. The mighty prince of Castile, however, never answered to his request. Over time, as history tells it, peace settled between them, although much to Sancho VII's and his kingdom's demise. Esteban de Garibay explains the circumstances in his *Compendio*.[47]

Castile's annexation of these regions inevitably altered the course of Basque history; it had significant political consequences on the territorial status and the configuration of the land. At the same time, Navarre strengthened bonds with its neighbors to the north of the Pyrenees. As a result, the remaining population of the Kingdom of Navarre developed a greater sense of cohesion, and all the Basque territories managed to preserve their culture. These shifts depicted a new reality among the kingdoms of the Christian Iberian Peninsula.

After 1200, Alfonso VIII anointed himself "King of Castile, Araba, Bizkaia, Ipuzcoa, and Donostia-San Sebastián."[48]

In return for his assistance in the conquest of these regions, Alfonso VIII compensated Diego López de Haro, Lord of Bizkaia, with *tenencias* in Soria, Nájera, Marañón, and in the newly conquered Donostia-San Sebastián. De Haro, who already was the only lord of the Lordship of Bizkaia and second lieutenant of King Alfonso, took over the management of multiple regions.

Immediately after the conquest, the Castilian king attempted to gain control over the western territories and to that end issued *fueros* to Laredo (in today's Cantabria), Karrantza, Castro-Urdiales (Cantabria). and Frías. He also introduced improvements to the municipalities of Logroño and Haro (La Rioja), even though they were not Castilian territories; they were located within the lordship of Diego López II de Haro. Partly because of family issues, De Haro had to leave Bizkaia and take refuge in Lizarra (Estella). So, the king resolved to divide up De Haro's estate, including La Bureba, the Enkarterris, and his Castilian assets, among other noblemen. In 1201, Castile occupied Bizkaia and controlled it until 1206, when the parties signed the Treaty of Cabreros, and Alfonso VIII returned the land to Diego López. In 1212, in appreciation for his loyalty in the Battle of Las Navas de Tolosa, Castile awarded Durango to López II, who incorporated it to the Lordship of Bizkaia.[49]

The war between Navarre and Castile was of international dimensions. First, because it was a conflict between two sovereign states, and second, because other European crowns needed allies. When Richard Lionheart died on April 6, 1199, his brother, John Lackland, and the king of France waged war against each other. The king of France allied with Alfonso VIII, and John Lackland, with King of Navarre Sancho VII the Strong.

As a result of their alliances, the English took control of the northern Basque territories: Baiona, at the beginning of the twelfth century and, Lapurdi, at the end. Concerning Lower Navarre, the towns of Baigorri, Ortzaize (Ossès), Arberoa (Arberoue), and Garazi, all under Sancho the Strong's newly formed wardenship of Donibane Garazi (Saint-Jean-Pied-de-Port), joined the Kingdom of Navarre with the consent of Richard Lionheart. In 1294, the last viscount of Zuberoa Guillaume Raymond Sault fled his land and sought refuge in Navarre after the English imposed their rule over Zuberoa.[50] Most of the viscount's lineage ended under Navarrese reign.

Alfonso VIII's northern expansion plans faced difficulties. After the kingdom lost access to the sea, Sancho VII allied with the bourgeoisie of Baiona to restrict Castilian entry into Guiena (Guyenne). In similar fashion, the king bowed to protect the realms of the English, opened a new maritime trade route, and entered into a treaty of perpetual peace and alliance with Lackland. A second treaty signed in Angulema (Angoulême) on February 4, 1202, established that all successors of the king of England were bound by the first agreement, and forbade any peace deals with the crowns of Castile or Aragón until the latter two had satisfied the harm inflicted on the king of England. To the bourgeoisie of Baiona, on the other hand, Sancho VII offered protection and the right to enter and travel freely across Navarre in exchange for their refusal to aid his enemy, Alfonso VIII.

The king of Castile tried to claim the title of Lord of Gascony, to which he was entitled through marriage, but failed every attempt to seize the region, unable as he was to penetrate Baiona, Bordeaux. and La Réole. Castile abandoned its northern undertaking in 1205.[51]

Castile and Navarre entered a five-year truce in Guadalajara on October 27, 1207. Restoring relations with Aragón turned out to be a simpler task; Sancho the Wise took some border burgs and castles from Aragón as collateral for a large loan granted to Pedro II of Aragón. Namely Escó (in today's Zaragoz), Peña, Petilla, Gallur (Zaragoza) and Tasmoz (Zaragoza), Burgi, and Erronkari.[52]

In 1212, Alfonso VIII and his bishops led a European propaganda campaign against Islam. The pope, in their support, called for a Holy War. Alfonso VIII decided to send troops to fight the Almohad of Al-Andalus, and the pope forced the rest of the Christian kingdoms of the Peninsula to join Castile in its military efforts against Islam. Threatened with excommunication, Sancho the Wise set off with a scanty army of two hundred horsemen to Las Navas de Tolosa in Jaen.

In the end, the Christian armies prevailed at the battle. In exchange for his assistance, Alfonso VIII returned some fortifications captured between 1198 and 1200 to Sancho of Navarre, including Buradon (Buradón), Toloño (La Guardia), and Marañón. Between 1213 and 1223, the king of Navarre used his purchasing power to acquire multiple other towns such as Buñuel, Cintruénigo, Cadreita, Urzante in the Tutera region, and Elizagorria (Lazagurría), Xabier (Javier), Cárcar, and Resa along the kingdom's border.

But the recovery of a small number of castles did not make up for the tremendous loss Navarre suffered with the conquest of its western territories. Over the centuries, Navarre repeatedly tried to recapture the lands taken by Castile, to no avail.[53] Meanwhile, some captured territories showed interest in returning to the Kingdom of Navarre.

The Navarrese crown repeatedly petitioned for the return of the lost land. At some point, Castile acknowledged Navarre as the genuine head of the territories and even gave its word that they would be returned to Navarre. Some years after the conquest, in 1204, Alfonso VIII, feeling seriously ill, wrote a testament in which he promised the return of all occupied Basque territories to the Kingdom of Navarre.

But his promise was not upheld, and the Kingdom of Navarre never saw its lands back.

What is more, whenever Castilians needed Navarre's support to concoct political conspiracies or strategies, they would use this promise as bait.[54]

Henry III did exactly that in 1234 when he engaged his son Alfonso (later Alfonso X) to Blanche, daughter of Theobald I of Navarre. According to this marriage pact, the Castilian king would return to the king of Navarre: "All of Gipuzkoa, Hondarribia, Donostia-San Sebastián and Mendikute for as long as he lived."[55]

In similar fashion, López de Haro agreed to grant back all lands and castles taken from Sancho VII of Navarre but refused to yield Araba. In the end, neither the wedding nor the pact came to fruition, but the surviving document attests to Castile's intention to return the lands.[56]

In 1256, the king of Castile signed the handover of Donostia-San Sebastián and Hondarribia to Theobald II of Navarre, technically restoring the latter's access to the sea. It appears, however, no such access actually happened. The same year, to affirm his power over the conquered territories, the Castilian king created burgs along the newly formed border between Castile and Navarre, effectively obstructing Navarre's road network.

This political move was an indication of Castile's refusal to comply with its neighbor's demands. These decisions were not without consequences: the new artificial border, known as "the border of crime," triggered clashes and rivalries between brothers.

Since, at the time, the pope was the mediator of the Christian world, the possibility that the Vatican assisted the Kingdom of Castile in its endeavors cannot be ruled out. All actions or ideas contrary to the hierarchy of the church, rooted or not in religious motives, were considered heresy. Certain political acts, too, were judged as such, and were punished accordingly either by leaders fearful of potential future conflicts or by kingdoms covetous of their heretic neighbor's resources, in both cases with the blessings of the papacy.

The Vatican enjoyed a cordial relationship with Castile; not so much with Navarre, presumably, because of the latter's relationship with Al-Andalus and their unfamiliar Basque culture.

In the eleventh century, the Roman Catholic Church emerged from the margins to play a central role in the reformulated feudal system and focused its efforts on fighting the heresy of an egalitarian society, with consequences in medieval politics and historiography.[57]

The Catholic Church was responsible for introducing the Benedictine Rule in the Kingdom of Navarre. The Cluniac reform called for autonomous monasteries adherent of Rome and free from the authority of monarch-appointed bishops. A supporter of the Benedictine Rule, Sancho the Great fostered only the organizational and liturgical aspects of it.[58]

The Gregorian Reform (1073–1085) sought to enforce the authority of the papacy. To that end, clergy used parishes, the quintessential Christian hubs, to infiltrate communities and start organizing the lives and controlling the customs of Christian dwellers, while destroying all other existing cultures in the process.

In the twelfth century, the Saint James Way became a direct expression of the European hegemonic ideology and, as such, played not only a religious role, but political, economic, and social roles, too. By then, historian Joxe Azurmendi argues, Romance languages had branched out from Latin and, with the blessing of the clergy and the church, had started treading a path of their own. Unlike them, the Basque language was unrelated to Latin. Basque speakers were described as barbarians in written chronicles, and Basques and their language were called *barbara limguam blascorum*.

In the same vein, chroniclers of the time, intending to further a specific agenda, described the crossing of the Basque Country as a terribly dangerous undertaking of crusade dimensions. Essentially, the vilification of Basque identities answered to ideological decisions. In this political, cultural, and religious environment, Aymeric Picaud published his *Codex Calixtinus*.[59]

Circa 1135, Picaud, a French clergyman, went on to cross the entire Basque Country, describing the local population in demeaning terms along the way. The medieval world was a Latin and Christian one where a community united by a common, non-Latin language like the Kingdom of Navarre was an oddity. So, travelers felt out of place in such land.

This attitude toward Basque culture preceded these events and took shape during the Third Council of Lateran in 1179, when the Catholic Church declared the ways of the Basque people pagan, *more paganorum*, and decided to wage a holy war against them.[60]

To defend his kingdom, Sancho VII of Navarre allied with the king of León and the Almohad. Upon knowing that the Navarrese king had subscribed an agreement with the Almohad, Pope Celestine III issued a Papal Bull on March 29, 1196. In it, the pontiff exhorted the monarch to get back on the right path, and to accept the cross by abandoning his plans with the Arabs and joining in the crusade against Islam. Sancho VII, however, kept his ties with the Muslim. He later repealed all truces with Castile, which resulted in the papal legate, Cardinal Gregorio, excommunicating the king and putting the kingdom into question.

The Roman Catholic Church took sides with Castile and helped the kingdom advance its border goals with the assistance of the Order of Calatrava.[61]

Alfonso VIII set up special forces on certain parts of his realms to impose and affirm his sovereignty. For the border territories, he used the feudal mechanisms at his disposal: burgs, the church, lordships and, above all, military orders.

The military orders operated in the spirit of *militia Christi*; a life project focused on spiritual combat with the goal of restoring an Earthly Jerusalem on Christian ground. All orders had Islam as their enemy and practiced Cistercian asceticism. In Castile, the Order of Calatrava was the most notorious one.

The crown of Castile and the Order forged a strong connection from the very beginning. Enrique Rodríguez-Picabea,[62] a scholar of the Order of Calatrava, says that Alfonso VIII's decision to offer lordships to members of the Order was not a random one. On the contrary, in placing them across the border, the king was accomplishing social, economic, political, and strategic goals. In other words, the king seemingly used the Order's skills to cement his authority and impose his jurisdiction, especially on the Muslim border. It is worth noting that the Orders set up posts in the border with Navarre, too: in Arrubal (in today's La Rioja), La Rioja, the Ebro Valley, and in Castellum Rubeum.

THE LONG PROCESS OF THE HUMAN CONFLICT (1200-1300)

The conquest of western Navarre was a well planned and calculated systematic military operation performed by Castile. With the war, Castile's authority spread out of its eastern border and into the conquered portion of western Navarre. The political fracture suffered by Navarre because of the military campaign seriously altered the course of life of the Basque community. After the conquest, the western territories of the Basque Country fell under the reign of a different political force. In essence, the geopolitical map had been transformed.

As previously mentioned, Castile's annexation of Bizkaia, Araba, Gipuzkoa, and the Durango Region was a major setback for Navarre. An already small kingdom such as Navarre shrank to an even more vulnerable size after the conquest. In the centuries that followed, the kingdom struggled to withstand the pressure exerted by its neighboring kingdoms, Spain, and France, and the Kingdom of Navarre was conquered in its entirety in 1512.

While the main driving force behind the conquest was political, economic interests played a crucial role, too, as Castile wanted to appropriate Navarre's trade network. Navarre's economic development came to a crashing halt when Castile gained access to the sea; the Kingdom of Navarre could not grow without maritime trade. The campaign was only a stepping stone in the king of Castile's greater goal of establishing a maritime industry and a trade network along the Cantabrian coast and of expanding his reign all the way to Gascony—received in dowry from his wife, Eleanor of Aquitaine.

Alfonso VIII was suddenly in possession of a direct communication route with France, a piece of coastland, a series of well-established trade ports and skilled teams of seamen, blacksmiths, armorers, and shipbuilders. The king was the main beneficiary of this economy. After the occupation of Gipuzkoa in 1200, all the Navarrese ports, which, back then, were internationally renowned trade spots, became Castilian property. To integrate the conquered territories, the king created burgs, granted privileges, confirmed *fueros* or municipal charters, and paid visits, hoping that enhancing these newly incorporated towns would prove profitable later.

In the case of the Basque Country, burgs have been heavily researched.[63] Noteworthy researchers include Beatriz Arizaga Bolunburu, Soledad Tena Díez,

Gonzalo Martínez Díez, José Ángel García de Cortazar, Iñaki García Camino, and García Fernández.[64] Most of them concur with the thesis that maritime trade started in the thirteenth century thanks to Alfonso VIII of Castile.[65]

The goal of this section, however, is to rebut several aspects of this thesis. First, the project for maritime trade had been formulated and developed by the Kingdom of Navarre;[66] second, some burgs already played a part in such strategy; and finally, the burgs received municipal charters earlier than what most researchers claim. Besides wanting to expand their power, Castilians were interested in Navarre's trade network. Following this plan, Castile occupied the western territories of Navarre and dotted the newly established artificial border with burgs, triggering internal wars and family clashes.

Burgs were population areas that had received a municipal charter, also known as foundation letter or *fuero*, from the kingdom or a lord. The creation of the burg occurred with the reception of the charter. The municipal charter or letter was a document written in Latin or a Romance language authorizing the foundation of the burg and enforcing basic rights and responsibilities for its inhabitants. Some burgs were founded on new ground, as was the case for all burgs in Asturias, where municipal charters were extended to create new urban communities.[67] In the Basque Country, however, burgs were founded on already existing towns. After the charter was issued, the town was renovated, reinforced, and expanded as established by the rights contained in the official document. Population areas had legal status; those with municipal charters became burgs; and those without remained outside of the burgs. All burgs, regardless of size, had commonalities: they were normally enclosed by a wall, which had an added symbolic value; they all had at least one street; and while burgs harbored the usual guilds of merchants and craftsmen, most inhabitants were farmers.

The municipal charter or the unique legislation of the burg contained a detailed list of the privileges, freedoms, rights, and responsibilities of their residents. Some of the rights that came with the *fuero* pertained to trade. They included the right to hold a weekly market or annual international fairs and the right to reduce the amount of taxes associated to these activities, such as tariffs. Besides trade safeguards, the charter guaranteed other protections such as basic community rights: self-government powers (mayors, councilors, public employees, scribes), justice, and defense rights. Burgs were assigned a piece of land or district and had rights to use communal land and the water, woods, and fields in it. In exchange, members of the burg paid their lord or monarch a yearly sum of money and a portion of the treasure collected from legal penalties.

In most cases, the *fuero*[68] extended to the burg was not crafted from scratch. Instead, the issuing lord or monarch used a previously written charter as a template and added provisions tailored to the burg in question. The two most popular charters in the Basque Country were the *fueros* of Logroño and Jaca. In the regions of Araba and Bizkaia and inland Gipuzkoa, the *fuero* of Logroño was the most common one. Although it was of Riojan tradition, it originated in the Kingdom of Iruñea. In Navarre and the coast of Gipuzkoa, on the other hand, the *fuero* of Jaca, of Aragonian tradition and Frankish origin,[69] became the most popular.

The burgs of the Kingdom of Iruñea were created after the Jaca *fuero*. The first *fueros* were given along the Saint James Way to promote trade. A second batch was distributed in the south to ensure defense after the conquest of the Erribera Basin. And a third one went to La Rioja, Araba, and Gipuzkoa to reinforce their defensive capabilities against Castile and to boost maritime trade and transportation.

Because the contents of the *fueros* were adapted to the needs of each region, eventually families and subfamilies of *fueros* formed, such as the *subfuero* of San Sebastián in Donostia-San Sebastián, which included additional provisions on trade. The *subfuero* spread from Donostia-San Sebastián to the majority of Gipuzkoan coastal towns: Mutriku, Zumaia (Zumaya), Getaria (Guetaria), Zarautz (Zarauz), Orio, Usurbil (Usúrbil), Hernani, Errenteria (Rentería). and Hondarribia. The Logroño *fuero* disseminated through the burg of Vitoria-Gasteiz reaching Deba (Deva), Itziar, Bergara (Vergara), Ordizia, Tolosa, Segura, Arrasate, Azkoitia (Azcoitia), Elgeta (Elgueta), Leintz Gatzaga (Salinas de Léniz), Zestoa (Cestona), Azpeitia and Urretxu (Villareal de Urrechu), among other towns.

Two types of communities received municipal charters: dwindling communities that existed before the *fuero* that were afterward revitalized and promoted; and new communities of various origins. Some were composed of already existing communities and a castle, a church, or a monastery. Others sprang up on trade routes, passageways, or other new spaces. Most Basque burgs, however, were built upon existing population areas.

Reasons and causes to create a burg vary widely, but four main reasons distinguish and interconnect Basque burgs. First, there was special interest in reinforcing seaports on the Cantabrian Sea coast to foster international relations since these ports were becoming increasingly prominent because of their robust fishing industry. Second, burgs were meant to boost trade and the economy in general. This is why some were created on trade routes and other strategic locations where resources and raw materials were easily accessible to facilitate the production and circulation of goods. Third, burgs marked border lines. And fourth, burgs were created for security; residents worried about their safety, and burgs provided protection.

History can be divided by the foundation of burgs. Of all the cities founded in Roman times the Basque Country, only three important ones survived: Iruñea-Pamplona, Baiona, and Tutera. During the High Middle Ages, the Roman cities of Iruñea-Pamplona (or Pompelo), and Baiona or Lapurdum transformed into the quarters of a bishop, hosting people from all walks of life from local noble families and public officials to servants and laborers. Although Tutera, a small village in Roman times, didn't achieve the relevancy of other Muslim cities of Al-Andalus, it came to be a city of significant importance. All three cities were urban spaces of about three thousand people and joined area trade networks.[70]

In the archeological excavations of the last thirty years, archeologists have found churches and necropolis dating back to the ninth century. These finds have altered historiography's version of what societies looked like before burgs;[71] they point to the existence of commercial relations.

It means that the routes built during the Roman Empire were still in use, although at a lower rate. Long-distance commercial exchanges must have been rare at first. But, as the economy and the population grew in the eighth and ninth centuries, markets blossomed and trade operations became a constant throughout the High Middle Ages. Farming remained the main source of livelihood, but craftmanship and blacksmithing, with its allied sectors, increased.

The monastery in San Millán de la Cogolla (in today's La Rioja) collected taxes from Araba in the form of wrought iron, and from Bizkaia and Gipuzkoa, in heads of livestock. This leads us to believe that the center of the secondary sector in the High Middle Ages was in the Southern Basque Country, specifically in Araba, mid-Navarre, and the Ebro Valley. In the Low Middle Ages, on the other hand, Bizkaia and Gipuzkoa came out ahead with their strong maritime industry.

Most of the Basque population lived in small towns. The current network of towns of the Basque Country was built between the ninth and eleventh centuries. Documents written in 1025 and preserved at San Millán de la Cogolla prove that in Araba, the towns of Vitoria-Gasteiz, Armentia, Arriaga, Berroztegieta (Berrosteguieta), Lasarte, and Erretana (Retana) already existed; on the coast, Plentzia (Plencia), Gorliz (Górliz), Bermeo, Mundaka (Mundaca), Forua (Forúa), Lekeitio (Lequeitio), Getaria, and Zarautz; and inland, the towns of Momoitio, Gerrika, Durango, Tolosa, and Segura are worth a mention. These are the towns whose existence has been corroborated by archeologists. Over time, some of these villages were absorbed into bigger municipalities as small neighborhoods. Others received burg status after the twelfth century.

The Saint James Way was the old trade route of the Middle Ages. It connected Europe to the northern part of the Iberian Peninsula and to Al-Andalus.

Because the route traveled through the Basque Country, the first Basque burgs emerged alongside it. The Kingdom of Iruñea founded more burgs as it expanded and colonized southern territories. The burgs tied to the Way and to the Navarrese repopulation of the south were part of the initial phase of the burg enterprise. The first of these burgs were created by Sancho Ramírez, Pedro I, and mostly by the king of Iruñea and Aragón's Alfonso I the Battler.

The burg of Nájera was founded in this manner; La Rioja belonged to the Kingdom of Iruñea at the time, and the king established himself in the city. Sancho the Great was seemingly the first to grant *fuero* to Nájera. It is reasonable to think that by the time of Sancho the Great, merchants headed to Iruñea-Pamplona were required to pay a tax at the border.

In the twelfth century, European cities underwent a transformation. Europe entered a period of warm weather that dynamized agricultural communities, enabling them to increase their productivity and supply goods to merchants. New street markets and fairs were started, trade maritime routes were energized, and the trade circuits of western Europe came back to life. Today's network of European cities closely resembles the urban map of that time. In the Basque Country, too, city life was gathering steam. Through the concession of *fueros*, the crown began to give legal protection to the foreign communities settling in the Kingdom of Navarre, including to Frankish and Gascon settlements.[72]

The first Frankish communities settled in some burgs of Navarre in the eleventh century. They came in response to the advantageous conditions offered to northern merchants and craftsmen by a kingdom trying to stimulate the economy. This is why the Franks settled in Lizarra. Founded before the year 1090, Lizarra is considered to be the first Basque burg. Navarre recruited craftsmen and merchants, mainly Franks, for the new burg. They were granted privileges and exemptions, including lower taxes, autonomy to appoint their local leader, and special rights to hold trials. Following the example of Lizarra, the crown of Navarre went on to found other burgs: Zangoza (Sangüesa), Gares (Puente la Reina), Atarrabia (Villava), and Iruñea-Pamplona, among others.

As for the Gascon community, it settled along the coast. In the High Middle Ages, most Gascon communities that left the commercial area of Baiona followed the Bidasoa River and established in Hondarribia, Pasaia (Pasajes), Donostia-San Sebastián, Getaria, and the Lower Urola Region. They also chose other emplacements close to fishing.

The decision to establish on the coast revealed the Gascon's great affinity to the sea. Their fondness for the sea was no coincidence. European maritime trade underwent several positive changes during the eleventh and twelfth centuries: for starters, it enjoyed a period of relative calm after pirate incursions ended;

advanced shipbuilding technology became more accessible; the vessels' tonnage or cargo capacity increased; and trade was established among several locations along the main European trade route.

The first records of Basque maritime regions date back to the eleventh century. Apparently, seaports were already being developed, and they had established fluvial and coastal trade relations by then. Maritime merchants of the time faced great obstacles. They couldn't work during the winter and, because of the coastal trade system, had difficulties to set sail at night. To remedy their situation, fishing spots were created in the nearby regions of Baiona, like in Hondarribia, Pasaia, Donostia-San Sebastián, and Getaria. Vessels could drop anchor and stock up on goods in these towns. The nature of the products exchanged in those trade deals was highly diverse.

In the twelfth century, the Saint James Way's importance declined as new trade routes emerged and grew. From then on, in the northern section of the Peninsula, the north-south trade axis prevailed over the east-west one. Navarrese and Aragonian wool and locally sourced iron were channeled through the Basque Country on their way to European manufacturing destinations. Archeological finds have revealed vast iron production in the Basque Country during the twelfth century, which points to the conclusion that the iron industry was directly related to maritime trade.[73] Although the exact date of the beginning of Basque maritime trade remains unclear, the relationship between Donostia-San Sebastián and Baiona was documented as early as the twelfth century in the San Sebastián *fuero*.

The main contributing factor to the second wave of burgs at the end of the twelfth century was precisely the intent to connect the coast to the interior of the kingdom. The *fueros* granted in Gipuzkoa by Sancho VI the Wise and Sancho VII the Strong are clear examples of the endeavor. The *fuero* of Baiona given by the Dukes of Aquitaine and the *fuero* of La Bastide (in today's Nouvelle-Aquitaine) in Lower Navarre issued by the king of Navarre are other examples. In the case of Iparralde, the *fueros* were also meant to affirm the authority of the king in these regions.

The Navarrese monarch implemented a plan of action to promote cities. A large urban space materialized on the coast because of this effort. The *fuero* or privileged law known as San Sebastián regulated the new urban space and functioned as a local government, tasked with the management of its surrounding rural areas. As mentioned above, Donostia-San Sebastián was the chosen town for this role in the area encompassing present-day Gipuzkoa. Before receiving *fuero*, Donostia-San Sebastián already had a well-developed trade system; communities of Gascon merchants had opened permanent establishments there as a result of their lengthy stays in the city. Sancho VI's *fuero* encouraged many residents of Lapurdi to move to Donostia-San Sebastián. King of Navarre Sancho VI the Wise gave Donostia-San Sebastián *fuero* in 1150 or in 1180.

In the twelfth century, the king and queen decided to found a new burg adjoining the old city of Iruñea, or rather, a series of new burgs: the burg of San Zernin (San Cernin), populated by Franks; the burg of San Nikolas (San Nicolás); and the burg of Nafarreria (Navarrería). Each of them was separated by walls from the rest, observed a different body of laws, and elected its own mayors. In times of conflict, they went to war against each other.

The burgs of Vitoria-Gasteiz and Durango[74] were founded in 1181 in similar fashion. The king sought to accomplish two goals with the burgs: to invigorate the economy by creating spaces for craftsmen and merchants, and to form communities of loyalists. The king of Navarre extended the San Sebastián *fuero* to Getaria,[75] Hondarribia, and Mutriku in the twelfth century.

Because of its strategic location midway between France, the Gulf of Biscay, and Castile, Iruñea-Pamplona was the most powerful city in terms of trade in the Kingdom of Navarre. All products ended in Iruñea-Pamplona before being redistributed throughout the kingdom: overseas goods traveled from the Cantabrian Sea through Donostia-San Sebastián and Hondarribia; some products were brought across the Pyrenean municipality of Orreaga; and others were introduced from Castile and Aragón. Local merchants mostly imported fabrics from Flanders and France to resell them among the wealthy. Because Iruñea-Pamplona was home to the Comptos Chamber (the Navarrese Treasury) and the Law Court of the kingdom, the city was home to many public employees and noblemen with great purchasing power. The merchants of Iruñea-Pamplona even loaned money to the crown from time to time.

In Gipuzkoa, the secondary and tertiary sectors were gaining traction. The seaports of Gipuzkoa are mentioned in documents from Bruges of the year 1200. Bizkaia's successful iron industry started taking shape soon after, and eventually came close to monopolizing all trade with Bruges. Both regions were halfway between the Castilian plateau and Northern Europe, making them ideal commercial intermediaries.

Basque ports shipped Basque iron, Castilian wool, and Mediterranean products such as wine to Northern Europe. Conversely, they received fabrics from France and Flanders destined mostly for Castile. Profits generated through their jobs as intermediaries alleviated any food scarcity Basque burgs may have faced. Additionally, they received wheat from Andalucía, France, and other places by sea. Intermediary jobs were divided into two categories: transport of goods (by sea) and buying and selling of goods (trade).

At the end of the twelfth century, the Basque trade system was thriving. The inland trade route started in Baiona and went through Miarritze (Biàrritz), Donibane Lohitzüne (Saint-Jean-de-Luz), Hondarribia, Donostia-San Sebastián, Zarautz, Getaria, Zumaia, Deba, Markina (Marquina), Gernika (Guernica), and Bilbao-Bilbo. Once in Bilbao-Bilbo, the load was split and sent to Portugalete and Balmaseda (Valmaseda). The coastal trade line stretched toward that direction. Some strategic emplacements in the coast came to be the nexus or joints of the medieval communication routes; they functioned as the vital engines of international trade.[76]

Burgs such as Bilbao-Bilbo, Portugalete, Bermeo, Lekeitio, Getaria, Mutriku, Donostia-San Sebastián, Hondarribia, and Baiona housed many merchants and shipment carriers precisely for that reason. Communication routes related to trade became increasingly prominent, to the extent that the Kingdom of Navarre started minting its own coins: gold crowns, silver crowns, white *karlins,* and black *karlins* (small silver coins). However, it still allowed the use of foreign currencies, too.

A wide cleavage separated the kingdoms of Navarre and Castile when it came to trade. According to history professor Gonzalo Martínez,[77] the commercial aspect lagged behind Castile's political consolidation of its territory. Castile founded burgs for military purposes, while Navarre favored commercial operations overall. Proof of this inclination are the burgs of the coast, located along the Cantabrian Sea to benefit from the coastal trade system. By then, the notable Navarrese trade network was in full operation.

As part of his political strategy to weaken Navarre, the king of Castile launched a successful plan to energize the Castilian economic circuit and secure the fealty of fortified communities. When King Alfonso VIII of Castile succeeded to the throne, the only burgs specialized in trade under Castile's rule were along the Saint James Way.[78] The king shifted the then inland-oriented economic policies to the north because he was interested in opening a maritime trade route. Only after the occupation of western Navarre did Castile amp up its power and become an active economic agent of the international trade network.

Castile's water access before the conquest was limited to the coastline of Santander because Asturias was part of the Kingdom of León; López de Haro owned the newly invaded region from the Ason valley to the Nerbioi River;[79] and Count Ladrón governed over the still Navarrese territories of Gipuzkoa and Bizkaia. The port of Donostia-San Sebastián was the peninsula's most important international port. Initially, promoting trade did not seem particularly appealing to the Castilian sovereign;[80] in 1178, he gifted Castro,[81] under Castilian rule since the capture of the Enkarterris in 1175, to the Abbey of Santa

María la Real de Las Huelgas, in Burgos. Similarly, he gave the Sahagun *fuero* to Santander in 1187. A few years later, in 1192, Alfonso VIII of Castile came to his senses and claimed Castro back.[82] The reason behind his decision was the valuable road of the Ason Valley. It linked Burgos to the plateau and was vital to strengthen the ties between the two regions.[83]

Later, in 1199 and 1200, he proceeded with the conquest of Araba, Durango, and Gipuzkoa. The desire to expand to the coast triggered the occupation of Gipuzkoa. Anchoring areas had to be within a short distance of the coast to meet the navigation needs of the time; vessels were powered by sail and would advance a mere fifty-four to eighty-one nautical miles a day, reaching speeds of 2.5 knots.[84]

Immediately after the conquest, Alfonso VIII set in motion a plan to ratify rights and concessions. An important date within the context of the conquest is the date the king issued *fuero* to Laredo. It happened on January 20, 1200, right after the capture of the Basque territories, when the king was on his way back from Vitoria-Gasteiz to Burgos. Later, he ratified *fueros* in the conquered territories of Araba, Gipuzkoa, and the Durango Region, including those of Donostia-San Sebastián (1202), Getaria (1209), Hondarribia (1203), Mutriku (1209), Oiartzun (ca. 1203 or 1204), and Zarautz (1237).

The newly annexed political space was of special interest to Alfonso VIII. The conquest equipped Castilians with a fully operative trade network and boosted their maritime activity, encouraging aspirations to continue invading coastal regions.

In his assessment of Alfonso VIII's reigning years, historian José Ángel García de Cortázar underscores the expansionist ambitions of Castile and points out their military efforts against the Islamic Empire and the kingdoms of León and Navarre.[85]

In the wake of the conquest, Navarre and Castile had to redefine their borders.[86] In 1256, more than fifty years after the invasion, King Alfonso X of Castile, known as the Wise, launched a massive *fuero* campaign to reinforce Castilian borders. He founded several burgs on the Araba-Navarre border, including Korres (Corres), Kanpezu (Campezo), the Done Bikendi Valley, Kontrasta (Contrasta), and Agurain, all of them located on strategic communication spots of Navarre and Araba.[87]

In the same year, Alfonso X issued municipal charters and fortified Tolosa, Ordizia, and Segura, which were very close to the border with Navarre. His fortification efforts spread from the Goierri region (El Goyerri) to the Catabrian watershed.

Navarre gradually lost all communication routes with Araba and Gipuzkoa because of the foundation and fortification of new burgs. Meanwhile, the communication route established between inland Araba and the ports to the Cantabrian Sea proved lucrative for Alfonso X. Likewise, the Castilian king decided to replace Basque place-names with Castilian names: Agurain became Salvatierra; Erraztiolatza became Segura; Ordiazia became Villafranca; and Berasabia became Tolosa. This transition hints at the Hispanicization of the Basque Country.

Alfonso X ordered traffic supervision at the Lizarrate (San Adrián) mountain pass, between Agurain and Segura, to facilitate Castile's trade relations with Europe. He also oversaw traffic on the road from Vitoria-Gasteiz to Arlaban (Arlabán), a route connecting Segura to the seaport of Donostia-San Sebastián through the southern hollow of Gipuzkoa and the Oria Valley. King Alfonso issued charters to the towns of Arrasate and Bergara in the Segura area in 1260 and 1268, respectively. With them, he resumed the Biscayan burg campaign.

The Castilian crown continued to strengthen its trade activity. The Hermandad de las Marismas was a guild created in 1296 to foster and protect the maritime trade relations of its members. The founding document was signed by the coastal cities of Getaria, Donostia-San Sebastián, and Hondarribia along with Bermeo, Santader, Laredo, and Castro-Urdiales. Vitoria-Gasteiz was the only inland signatory.

Alfonso X of Castile founded the burgs of the Basque lands to serve his own interests. A quote about Segura reads as follows: "In 1256, Alfonso X of Castile ordered the foundation of a new burg to serve his interests."[88] It would be the first urban area with *fuero* in the Gipuzkoan region of Goierri.[89]

Multiple complex factors contribute to the foundation of burgs. Some burgs, such as Guardia, Bastida, Urizaharra (Peñacerrada), and Segura in Araba, stood out for their strategic, protective, and defensive attributes.[90] The main reason behind their foundation was to heighten Castile's power in the region and prevail against Navarre. The fortification of burgs pursued two greater goals: to hinder the economic exchanges between Navarre and the sea and divert them to Castile; and to define boundaries between two sovereign states of new creation. As a result of these actions, Castile joined the main international trade networks and took over the iron production of Bizkaia.

Castile, staying true to its goals, created a plethora of burgs from the twelfth to fourteenth centuries in the western section of the Kingdom of Navarre, including twenty-three in Araba, twenty-five in Gipuzkoa, and twenty-one in Bizkaia. Historians argue that the delay in the Biscayan phase was because the long-standing tradition of lordships. While the burg system was introduced by Lope Díaz II de Haro, Lord of Bizkaia, between 1214 and 1236, Balmaseda (1099) and Durango (ca. 1180) preceded this system.[91]

The configuration of border areas first began on the coast when Alfonso VIII ratified the municipal charters of the coastal cities. But, as mentioned earlier, the most consequential restructure of the territory happened in 1256 with Alfonso X's plan to fortify the Gipuzkoa-Navarre border with a chain of burgs. Besides the network of burgs, the king's defensive repertoire also included the castles of Beloaga and Mendikute. Unlike its rival, Navarre did not spare a great deal of effort in reinforcing its borders during the thirteenth century. The defense of Navarrese realms was entrusted to the following castles, from north to south: Gorriti, Ausa, Ataun, Irurita, Orzorroz, and a wooden tower in Leitza (Leiza).

The creation of burgs brought about tensions.[92] This chapter's aim is not to explain the devastating events of the so-called War of the Bands that afflicted the entire Basque Country over a span of almost two centuries; we only intend to investigate conflicts arisen in the interior towns of the Kingdom of Navarre in the wake of the Castilian conquest.

As seen previously, burgs and *tenencias* formed the administrative structure of the Kingdom of Navarre. In all likelihood, the hostility within the realms of the kingdom did not stem from the burg network, a vital piece in the development and organization of Navarrese trade. We are not aware of any existing documents chronicling the confrontations.

The three-hundred-year period following the establishment of the Castile-Navarre civil border in the thirteenth century was distinguished by violence and rivalries in the border areas of the kingdoms. The capture of Araba, Gipuzkoa, and the Durango Region by Alfonso VIII of Castile in 1200 marked the starting point of a conflict that only the conquest of Navarre in 1512 would end.[93]

The reasons behind these events are complicated. Traditional historiography interpreted band wars as strife between noble families and built a narrative based on the violence of the conflict as well as on the legal, political, and administrative aspects of this historical episode. In the last few decades, however, a group of scholars has ventured deeper into the war of bands, producing two research articles cited in the notes section.[94] They have adopted a more social approach to the complex society of the time and point to three factors as the source of such confrontations: the pressures faced by farmers from the ruling class; the clashes between noble families; and the restructuring of the border areas.

The conquest of the year 1200 was a forceful invasion of the land that imposed a new, entirely artificial border. The modification of the border affected all aspects of society, causing social, political, and legal problems, and leading to violent and traumatizing consequences for the entire population. The division of the mountains and valleys of Aralar, Andia, Urbasa, and

Burunda instigated fights between farmers and cattle breeders who had been separated by the new border.[95]

Acts of theft and violence multiplied along the ill-defined borders. From an ordinary shepherd to a preeminent lord, members of all socioeconomic classes perpetrated the crimes, often incited by *ahaide nagusis* (powerful and influential Basque families). An invisible line suddenly split urban areas, forests, mountains, and the bountiful sea, along with the whole of the Navarrese society. Lords and nobles lost much of their possessions without notice, including lands, mills, and mines, and *ahaides* saw an abrupt end to their ties with one another. This means that they were forced to divide their estates between two sovereign kingdoms. Disputes erupted among the upper class of the land of the Pyrenees, who, until then, had held land and rights there. In addition, they tried to misappropriate church assets for each other's kingdoms.

Uprisings became common along the border, particularly at the center, where the borders of all three regions met. The first documented uprising goes back to 1261.[96] That year, the representatives of Araba, Gipuzkoa, and Navarre gathered to assess the damages suffered by border communities. The document, although short, gives an idea of the nature of the crimes. Most of them were related to cattle theft, but some were cases of uprising and even kidnapping. Road banditry and wrongdoing were widespread in the border of Araba, Gipuzkoa, and Navarre during the thirteen and fourteen centuries. The sources describing such crimes could lead to a variety of interpretations.

Border crossing turned crucial for the economic development of burgs because their inhabitants—farmers, craftsmen, ironworkers, shipbuilders, load carriers, and merchants—needed resources and raw materials to perform their jobs. To remedy this situation, many burgs began to monopolize the resources and raw materials within their jurisdictional limits thanks to royal privileges granted by a supportive king.

In Getaria (1270), for instance, the king allowed the population to use as much wood from the surrounding mountains as needed for ship and house building. To keep a tight rein on the noble-born burg detractors, the crown banned them from jeopardizing the use of roads and rivers, the exploitation of royal fields and forests, and the farming of their lands.

As the *fueros* and economic activity of burgs gained traction, the *ahaide nagusis* and landlords devised new schemes to preserve their power and wealth and to increase their income: they seized public spaces such as rivers to fish salmon and other types of fish with basket traps; mountains, to build iron mines or produce coal; and they imposed taxes on the merchandise that passed through their roads.

Throughout the fourteenth and fifteenth centuries, after consistent attempts to regulate the monopoly created by the *ahaide nagusis* on the use of resources and raw materials, the burgs finally succeeded in securing the monopoly in the exploitation of rivers and the sea, and they started renting their use out. Some first-borns of noble origin felt encouraged to relocate to the city to take advantage of the protections granted by the king and profit from the large amount of wealth generated by the cities. The reality is that the rights to exploit resources in the burg remained within the control of a few powerful families. However, burg ordinances regulating the ownership of resources and raw materials proved rather detrimental to many of them, leading to confrontations which involved not only the nobility but also farmers and the bourgeoisie.

In the fourteenth century, Europe became engulfed in a crisis with violent effects on the aristocratic network. The bubonic plague ravaged through the farmer population causing a drop in production and in the income collected by landlords. In their ambition to regain their lost economic status, lords committed all sorts of violent crimes and acts of theft against farmers and individuals of their own class alike. The Basque Country was not spared of this chaos, with the artificial border of Navarre suffering its worst consequences. The border came to be known as "The border of crime."[97]

Historian José Luis Orella Martínez contends that Castile's military operation in the Basque lands shattered the centuries-old fellowship formed among the Navarrese and forever split one shared view of history into two (confronted) views:

> Later, the would-be supporters of the Oñaz band would come to understand Gipuzkoa's involvement in the conquest as a return to the Castilian home it should never have left. (...) The would-be supporters of the Ganboa band, on the other hand, believed that violence should not be rewarded with rights and that Gipuzkoa should maintain its social, political and language ties with Navarre.[98]

CONSIDERATIONS ON HISTORIOGRAPHY AND REVIEW OF DOCUMENTS

In this section, we wish to explore the key aspects surrounding the subject of the conquest by reviewing our own published research.[99] The articles cited in the notes section illustrate how historiography approached the topics presented below during the twentieth century and the first decade of the twenty-first. Some parts of our articles are a verbatim copy of such sources because they provide details of the matter in hand. Since the articles set out on a journey of their own after publication, we will also discuss how new scholars view our work.

This section addresses three key points. The first point is concerned with the foundation dates of some burgs, specifically, the alteration of foundation dates since this may have led to misinterpretations. The second point reveals the ways in which a tightly woven historiography concealed the conquest of the western territories of Navarre. And in the third and final point, we propose a new hypothesis formulated on several artifacts—belt buckles and plaques—found in the chapel of San Prudentzio in Getaria.

The first topic to consider, the alteration of foundation dates, may seem unimportant. After all, a change in dates should not have had an impact on the unfolding of the events. The location of these burgs within one political space or the other would have been inconsequential except for the fact that the realms of the Kingdom of Navarre were defined and united by the language of their inhabitants, the Basque language. or Euskara.

As established in the previous section, the Basque lands had been populated uninterruptedly throughout centuries and millennia.[100] Settlers in these lands created communication routes with each other in their nomadic stage first; later, in Roman times; and through the multiple Saint James ways after the Roman Empire. Coastal settlements established contact through the ports of the coastal trade system. Even when danger was ever-present on the coast and maritime trade shrank, relations with Lapurdum and Baiona continued. This means that trade operations happened throughout the entirety of the High Middle Ages,[101] especially during the eleventh and twelfth centuries, a blossoming period for trade in the Kingdom of Navarre.

The Kingdom of Navarre became a powerful economic actor in the international trade stage. Proof of that are the accounts written by Benjamin of Tudela in his book *Massa'ot* (*The Itinerary of Benjamin of Tudela*) and the documents archived in the city of Bruges,[102] which state that, in 1170, Navarrese ships anchored in European ports and in ports of southern Britain, and that the ships circled around the Iberian Peninsula to enter and sail through the Mediterranean Sea. Both Brugeois record books and English ports mention Navarrese ships arriving at their shores from Deba, Donostia-San Sebastián, Hondarribia, and Baiona, among other places.

The Kingdom of Navarre was on a strategic spot. It was the through route between the peninsula and the continent and the central meeting point for the trade hubs of the Islamic territories, Aragón, Castile, France, and English Guyenne.

Historians agree that, in the twelfth century, King Sancho VI of Navarre issued municipal charters to Vitoria-Gasteiz, Durango, and Donostia-San Sebastián to promote trade.[103] Between 1150 and 1180, Sancho VI granted the San Sebastián *fuero,* which included additional provisions on maritime trade, to the burg of Donostia-San Sebastián. Note that the San Sebastián *fuero* is the first legal code of its kind in the history of European maritime law.[104] The king of Navarre later granted the same *fuero* to Getaria, Mutriku, and Hondarribia. Expert historians have attributed these actions to King Alfonso VIII of Castile.

On the eight hundredth anniversary of the municipal charter given by Alfonso VIII to the town of Getaria celebrated in 2009, we decided to conduct and publish a study, hoping to cast light on such claims.[105] In the article, we were able to demonstrate that Getaria received the San Sebastián *fuero* through Sancho VI of Navarre.

While analyzing *Colección de Documentos Medievales de las villas Guipuzcoanas (1200–1369)*[106] (Collection of Medieval Documents of Gipuzkoan Towns), for instance, we came across a document titled, "Alfonso VIII confirma a Guetaria el fuero de San Sebastián tal como la había sido otorgado por el rey de Navarra Sancho VI" (Alfonso VIII ratifies the San Sebastián *fuero* to Guetaria as it was granted by King Sancho VI of Navarre). This proves that Alfonso VIII of Castile attributed the foundation of Getaria to the Navarrese king; what is more, on September 1, 1209, during the ratification act of the *fuero* in Donostia-San Sebastián, he said, "in the manner in which the King of Navarre gave it to you to have."[107] This document led us to the clear conclusion that Getaria had been a Navarrese burg in origin.

Encouraged by this outcome, we proceeded to analyze the historiography on this event to identify the source of the misinterpretation. We read several texts and chroniclers from different time periods, including historian Lope Martínez de Isasti (1625);[108] a manuscript written by the residents of Getaria for the Royal Academy of Madrid (1786);[109] historian Julio Caro Baroja;[110] and Beatriz Arizaga Bolumburu,[111] an influential medievalist among today's scholars who specializes in Cantabrian burgs and the burgs of the Autonomous Community of the Basque Country. All of them cited *Compendio Historial* as their source, a work written by historian and chronicler Esteban de Garibay and published in Antwerp in 1571.[112]

In his chronicle, however, Garibay stated that it was the king of Navarre who had given *fuero* to Getaria first and Alfonso who ratified it later, "so that they and their descendants enjoyed the benefits of the San Sebastián *fuero* in the mountains, fields and waters, and in all legal cases, the way they used to with the Kingdom of Navarre and as per subscription and ratification of the charter." Later in the book, a quote by the king himself can be found: "This town, whose church was dedicated to Saint Salvador, was founded at a prior time as shown in the *fuero* of the town." Garibay claimed to have held these documents in his hands. We noticed that, in *Conpemdium*, Garibay never rejected what was stated in Alfonso VIII's document.

According to the historian, after Alfonso VIII captured Gipuzkoa, he renovated the burgs of Donostia-San Sebastián, Hondarribia, Getaria, and Mutriku, and he ratified their *fueros* "to repair and expand its coastland, Donostia-San Sebastián, Hondarribia, Getaria and Mutriku, by granting them privileges and ratifying their good customs, traditions and *fueros*."[113] As for Mutriku, the chronicler said, "that King Alfonso VIII, trusted with the governance of this province in 1200, rebuilt the coastal towns of Guetaria and Motrico and fortified them with robust walls and towers, as a way to show appreciation and generosity, and to establish dominance in the Cantabrian Ocean: of this town (of Motrico) only the ruins remained."[114] According to this chronicle, Getaria, like Mutriku, was already a burg, which the king of Castile ordered to level and rebuild from the ground up. In his lecture, published as *Historia de Hondarribia*, historian José Luis Orella Martínez claimed that the burg of Hondarribia, in an area of Gascon name, was also of Navarrese creation.[115]

Before the publication of our article in 2009, Gonzalo Martínez[116] and José Luis Orella were the only historians maintaining that Getaria was a Navarrese burg in origin. The rest based their research on Esteban de Garibay's texts from the sixteenth century and asserted that the Castilian king gave *fuero* to several coastal towns. The new narrative that emerged from their statements was welcomed with open arms.[117] Since then, all historical atlas and encyclopedias, as well as educational articles and audiovisual projects about the Basque Country, and specifically about the burgs of coastal Gipuzkoa, show the burg of Donostia-San Sebastián as the only port founded by Navarre, and credit the economic development of the coast to Castile. Beatriz Arizaga, who specializes in medieval burgs and has open a line of thought in the field, said, "The burg of Donostia-San Sebastián was founded at that time. It was the only burg created by a Navarrese king, as we know that by 1180, the city had been founded with a tailored *fuero*. The second one was founded between 1200 and 1237, a time when the line of Gipuzkoan coastal burgs was being defined. Hondarribia, Getaria, Mutriku and Zarautz were founded by Alfonso VIII."[118]

At this point, we started questioning the research methods used by some historians specialized in the foundation of burgs, seeing as they misquoted Esteban de Garibay; never consulted the sources in their bibliography; and built their theses on false contexts.

Our research indicated that, although no municipal charters have survived, Getaria, Mutriku, and Hondarribia were originally founded by the king of Navarre before the year 1200, and that, thanks to the advantages brought about by the *fueros*, the area grew at an unprecedented rate.

Current researchers who base their work on archival and archeological findings don't fully accept the king of Navarre as the founder of those burgs, although they don't reject the evidence when presented with it. They continue, however, to celebrate the economic growth of the region as Castile's accomplishment: "Things began to change in the twelfth and thirteenth centuries. (. . .) Thanks to the king of Navarre, first, and of Castile, next, Basque seaports entered the European trade system, (. . .) By the beginning of the thirteenth century, Basque ships were already sailing to Mediterranean and Atlantic ports."[119] or "In the thirteenth century, Gipuzkoa prepared to grow northward by fostering trade and reenforcing the iron and shipbuilding industries."[120]

In essence, the hegemonic historiography has depicted Castile as the dominating kingdom of the new era that boosted the economies of the burgs and ports of western Navarre after its conquest. We are intrigued, however, by Gonzalo Martínez Díez's[121] assertion that Basque ports had been witnessing high volumes of import and export traffic for a long time, and that the trade sector of Navarre had outpaced Castile's.[122] By this claim, the interpretations of the above-mentioned historians seem to be incorrect.

Our impression is that Castile made a target of these Basque regions precisely because of their political and economic systems and launched a military campaign to appropriate their trade network. Upon the completion of his plan, the king had successfully conquered the land and removed the local linguistic community from their time and space. He forcefully fractured the Kingdom of Navarre to impose Castile's reign and gain control of the Navarrese trade network.

The second set of observations revolve around the conquest. The documents we presented in 2011 seem to have lost validity within the current interpretive framework.[123] The inability to use current paradigms to interpret evidence compelled us to reintroduce the documents and reformulate our work in a new article.

In said article, we argued that Castilian attacks on Gipuzkoa, Araba, and the Durango Region must have sparked great interest among historiographers, considering the events caused ongoing controversy for more than eight hundred years. This debate indicates, in our opinion, that the theory of a pact between the two kingdoms promulgated by traditional historiography never fully crystallized. In fact, all signs point to the territories having been conquered (documented below); but a series of injustices boosted the theory of a voluntary pact. In our research, as explained next, we delved into the details of this unethical behavior.

Some excellent work was published in the year 2000 to mark the eight hundredth anniversary of the conquest. Two articles stand out among the works of several scholars: *800 aniversario de la conquista de Alava, Guipuzkoa y el Duranguesado* published through the Basque Studies Association Eusko Ikaskuntza;[124] and *Guipuzkoa versus Castilla 1200–2000*,[125] published by the Gipuzkoa Provincial Council. In them, historians analyzed the historiographic production on the conquest from the date closest to the year 2000. We presented a brief overview of their research.[126]

In their work, we identified that all the contributing historians followed Gonzalo Martínez Díez's school of thought[127] and they concurred with his assertion that thirteenth-century chroniclers never argued in favor or against the conquest or the voluntary annexation.[128]

The controversy is in the terms chroniclers used to describe how the land was won: Jiménez de Rada used "obnuit" (obtain in Latin), and in *Chronica Latina Regum Castellae* they used "adquisivit" (acquire in Latin). The above-mentioned historians argued that the terms "obtain" and "acquire" used by the chroniclers of the time were not an explicit reference to the conquest. Additionally, at the end of the sixteenth century, Esteban de Garibay resorted to this semantic detail to promote the theory of the pact, in hopes that it would help justify the *fuero* system. It has been the prevailing theory since then.

This explains why, with few exceptions, most historians endorsed the almost-unrivaled theory of the pact.[129] Among them were Julio González,[130] José Ángel García de Cortazar,[131] Fortún Pérez de Ciriza,[132] and María Rosa Ayerbe.[133] But without any evidence to support their claims, their observations can only be considered opinions. The term "negotiation" took precedence among scholars when Gonzalo Martínez Díez[134] favored it over the term "pact." We are not questioning Martínez Díez's brilliancy as a researcher; we even support his belief that Navarrese lords must have engaged in negotiations when the threat of the conquest started looming over their heads. We only want to state that his true intentions were laid bare in his transcriptions of the documents we present next.

The first step in our research was to consult the document he transcribed. In the 1332 collection *Colección de Documentos Medievales de las villas Guipuzcoanas*, published by the Gipuzkoa Provincial Council, a document titled "Traslado del fuero de San Sebastián sacado a petición del concejo de la villa de Guetaria" (Transfer or copy of the San Sebastián *fuero* as requested by the council of the town of Getaria) reads as follows: "Alfonso of Castile, may God forgive him, who conquered such land"[135]

The next obvious step was to contrast the document he transcribed against the document preserved at the Royal Academy of Madrid. It was titled: "1202–1332 Guetaria SS. Parte del Fuero de S.S. Y en el preambulo se dá por sentada la conquista de S.S" (1202–1332 Getaria SS [Donostia-San Sebastián]. Part of the San Sebastián *fuero*. And the preface acknowledges the conquest of

Donostia-San Sebastián). There was a note on the left margin of the document: "Ojo conquista de S.S." (Attention: conquest of Donostia).

According to this document, in 1332, the inhabitants of Getaria requested a copy of the Latin-written *fueros* of Donostia-San Sebastián ratified by Alfonso VIII. The copy was written by the scribe and notary public Ferrant Martínez. In it, Ferrant Martínez gave account of the request and braved to add: "Alfonso of Castile, may God forgive him, who conquered such land." At the beginning of the nineteenth century, writer, and scholar José Vargas Ponce found the copy at the archives of Getaria and transcribed it. This is the document we presented in our research, side note included, along with the following clarifications.

As we mentioned, the document included a reference to the conquest of Donostia-San Sebastián,[136] and a remark on the event made over a century later blaming the king of Castile for the invasion. The striking side note found in the nineteenth-century copy looks like it was written by Ponce himself[137] as a warning to the reader: "Attention: conquest of Donostia!" A last word on this controversy: current historians who have worked with the physical copy of this document have concealed the word "conquest" appearing in the notable title.

We presented another document of great relevance found in the same collection of texts and related to the conquest of western Navarre. The historians mentioned above were familiar with it. It was penned by King Alfonso XI of Castile, in Zaragoza, on July 9, 1330. It reads:

> Don Alfonso, son of Prince Fernando of Castile and righteous successor to the crown of Castile, has used violence to invade and rob us against the will of God (...) by writing, I salve our and our ancestors' conscience. We know and are aware that the right to own and bequeath the lands of Ypuzcoa, Alava, Rioja and the rest of the lands has belonged and belongs to the Kingdom of Navarre—to the king and queen of Navarre and their successors,—and as long as this man retains (sequesters) these lands against the will of God and reason, he will be usurping them of their right (...).[138]

The text[139] clearly states that Castilian forces exerted violence against Gipuzkoa, Araba, La Rioja, and other lands. The assaultive nature of Castile's annexation of Donostia-San Sebastián has been purposefully covered up and, instead, historians have given preference to the narrative of a negotiated handover.

González Díez interpreted the documents we presented as follows: "With the exception of the long siege of Vitoria-Gasteiz, the incorporation of the rest Araba and of all of Gipuzkoa was not as a consequence of military conquests; their multiple fortifications were relinquished peacefully by their *tenentes*, even though no common agreement or pact existed with them, much less with a non-existent Guipuzcoan Assembly."[140] Martínez, who transcribed the documents himself, contended that the annexation of the territories had not been violent.

We cannot overlook the famous testament of Alfonso VIII, written in 1204 and recovered by historian Father Fidel Fita. It reads: "I also promise that if God gives me health, I will return to the king of Navarre all my properties from the bridge of Araniello to Hondarribia and Santa Cruz de Kanpezu; as well as the castles of Antoñana, Atauri and Portiella Korres. All will I return to the king of Navarre, as I well know it belongs to him, under one condition: that he gives his word that he will not ever harm me or my son." In this popular text, a repentant Castilian king promises, in his 1204 testament, to return some of the land taken through nefarious ways. Although he never fulfilled his promise once in full health, at least he left proof of his confession to the king of Navarre.

In tandem with the king's testament, other evidence help build the case for the theory of a forceful conquest: Esteban de Garibay's claim that the texts he had allegedly held in his hands referred to Alfonso VIII's order to rebuild the burgs of Getaria and Mutriku, this last one lying in ruins; and the remains found in the archeological excavations of the castles of Mendikute, Aitz Txiki, and Aitzorrotz of weapons that were used and spread across the area.[141] This information is clearly indicative of violence.

This collection of evidence brought us to the conclusion that all interpretations of the subject matter are opportunistic interpretations, from those dating back to the time of the events, to those made in the Early Modern Period, and in the present. The conquest has been interpreted to serve selfish interests.

Historians have ignored the evidence we outlined and, instead, used Jiménez de Rada's *De rebus Hispaniae* and *Chronica Latina* to corroborate their theses. Even when Jiménez de Rada indiscriminately used the term "obtinuit" both for the unquestioned conquest of Vitoria-Gasteiz and for Trebiñu, Araba, and Gipuzkoa: "King Alfonso obtained Vitoria-Gasteiz, Trebiñu, Araba and Gipuzkoa." Similarly *Chronica Latina* of the king of Castille says: "while the siege lasted, he acquired all the surrounding land." Here, medievalists saw that Castile won without difficulty.[142]

These medieval chronicles should be understood in context. García de Cortazar himself argues that in the historiographic production of the thirteenth century, there are clear signs that Castile wanted to promote certain cultural models to serve its own interests.[143]

Four chronicles were written in this pursuit: *Najerense*, the only chronicle contemporary of Alfonso VIII; *Chronicon Tudense*, written by Bishop Lucas de Tuy in 1236; *De Rebus Hispaniae*, written by Jiménez de Rada in 1234;[144] and *Chronica Latina regum Castellae* from 1236.[145] The latter two have been crucial sources for the interpretation of Alfonso VIII's period.

Like historian José Antonio Maravall,[146] Cortazar also was of the impression that all four chronicles show a bias toward Castile, with Jiménez de Rada's work being the best embodiment of it. He stated that "the title *De Rebus Hispaniae* itself is indicative of this disposition. Rada was mainly concerned with Spain, and, in his work, he depicted the evolution of this political goal. He portrayed Spain as a historical subject from its inception until the time of the completion of his work. Jiménez de Rada constructed a shared origin for all 'Spaniards' compiling legends, old tales and riddles. And it was the riddles about collective memory that turned the historian into a prominent figure."

Words shape the reality they describe. While it is true that thirteenth-century chroniclers make no mention of the term "conquest," historians seem to have built their narratives around certain words of their choice and have conveniently remained within the interpretive framework established by these chroniclers.

The theses and ideas proposed by the above-mentioned historians have come to form a school of thought immensely popular among former university professors. Recently deceased historian José Ángel Lema construed the document we presented as follows: "A notarized copy of the San Sebastián *fuero* written in 1332, preserved in the nineteenth-century version of it, paints Alfonso VIII as 'one who conquered such burg.' This reference has been interpreted as an act of war, [He cites Arrieta's article in his notes] but 'conquerir' in old Spanish meant 'to obtain' and not necessarily referred to a military operation."[147]

Historians generally avoid taking a stance on the matter. But, although it is accepted that both positions are right and that all postures are valid, scholars almost unanimously agree on the absence of a military campaign over allegations that there are no sources that refer to actions of that nature. This is what historians maintain. But their arguments confuse us, because in the documents we presented the use of the term "conquest" is crystal clear. It is possible that not all noblemen from the *tenencias* acted in the same way, but no conclusive evidence supports the theory of collaboration. Historian Jon Andoni Fernández de Larrea y Rojas, who endorses the theory of the conquest even though he believes the chronicles do not contribute much evidence, provides us with an interesting fact: "There is no record of any *tenente* changing sides and joining

Castile. In fact, the Araban Mendoza and Guevara families remained loyal to King Sancho VII of Navarre."[148]

Because Spanish and French historiographies are driven by the need to forge the identity of their "nations," every piece of text is produced with purpose and intentionality. This is why, in the task of building our own history, even the smallest, simplest piece of evidence found in diplomatic sources should be enough to call our attention.

Basque scholar Manuel de Lekuona posited that a possible obstacle in our historiography is the lack of historical perspective. About the political operation of the thirteenth century, he argued that behind the expression "incorporation into Castile" lay not a "unification" but an action of softer connotations.[149]

Our work has an obvious political scope and that current historiography has lost interest in. It needs to venture deeper than the superficial analysis of events. The lack of our own historical perspective is only part of the problem; today's historiography is just as problematic in that it has provided a linear perspective of history, where each new time period is mechanically interpreted as a developmental stage built upon its predecessor. In the foreword of the book *Gipuzkoaren Historiaren Sintesia*,[150] the Association of Historians of Gipuzkoa Miguel de Aranburu[151] wrote: "In ancient times, Gipuzkoa benefitted from the expansion of Rome adopting its economic and administrative systems and its cultural and religious practices, and joining, for the first time in history, a network of political origins and of global interconnectedness ambitions," and touching on the subject in hand: "Burgs changed the course of Gipuzkoan history, which increasingly projected outwards, especially after the thirteenth century."[152] From the same foreword: "Since the period of the Spanish Catholic Monarchs, Gipuzkoa was immersed in the imperial agenda of the crowns of Castile and Aragón and became a grand supporter of their cause contributing manpower, sailors, weapons, ships, lumber and iron. The province's strategic role was rewarded with a number of substantive privileges which were enforced until the overriding of *fueros* in 1876."[153]

The authors of this text declare that Gipuzkoa's "natural" progression brought benefits to the land and portray a mass of people that was concerned only with survival and had not yet developed a sense of nation. Basque speakers, however, had often banded together as a group in the presence of non-Basque speaking "others." To us, this has a logical explanation: identity. Any researcher interested in approaching the matter from the lens of territorial configuration will understand the conquest as an agent of destruction of a unified Basque society and culture. The Castilian conquests of 1175 and 1200 precipitated the disruption of a shared Basque future. This is an indication of political subjugation and of a fracture in the geopolitical map.

The Basque lands are rarely recorded in medieval documents. But new archeological findings have changed the course of historiographic production. Because archeology has become an invaluable aid to understanding history and memory, institutions increasingly promote excavations. An excavation performed by Zehazten Z. K. (Cultural Services) in 2006 at the chapel of San Prudentzio in Getaria, as part of the project "Gipuzkoako portua 1209–2009" (The Port of Gipuzkoa 1209–2009), produced encouraging results.

Archeologists uncovered material culture of great value. Among the most noteworthy artifacts were coins, most of them from the Middle Ages;[154] and, above all, a metallic assortment of clothing accessories. The archeologists who took part in the excavation hail this collection of more than 150 pieces as one of the most important collections about the Iberian Peninsula of the Middle Ages.[155]

The treasure is made up of belt buckles and plaques. The plaques were decorated in a wealth of styles: some had zoomorphic, armorial, and geometric motifs, while others displayed Christian imagery. Many techniques were used in their production: molding, carving, gilding, and enameling in blue, white, or red.

These types of decorations are linked to the aristocracy of the Middle Ages. Many of these items reportedly feature military and noble coats of arms and similar themes. They were luxury clothing accessories for the rich. The high quality of the pieces, some even gilded or enameled, coupled with their armorial motifs gives us reason to believe that they exclusively belonged to noble families, given that the peasants and farmers who made up the bulk of the population would not have had the means to purchase them.

Aesthetic readings aside, a leather belt found next to one of the plaques was radiocarbon-dated to the end of the twelfth century or the beginning of the thirteenth century, although it seems like the artifacts were buried in the chapel later.

Medicinal rituals, likely pagan in origin but later performed in honor of Saint Prudence, are still celebrated today at San Prudentzio. One of them is meant to relieve headaches and consists of rubbing a rock against the floor. A cross is made on the forehead of the sick person with the rock powder accumulated on the ground. A second ritual uses a special oil to remove warts. A third ritual performed up until the beginning of the twentieth century involved clothes and garments; newborns were placed on the altar along with a ball of yarn as an offering. Archeologists have examined the belt buckles and plaques from an ethnographic lens and suggested the artifacts were most probably offerings.

These pieces, however, are documented in medieval iconography. Sources on the matter point out that belts with armorial motifs appeared in the twelfth century and became a popular accessory in the thirteenth century. People first wore them for identification purposes, which explains the enameling of some of the pieces. Later, fewer buckles were found with inscriptions as society transitioned to wearing them as a status symbol instead of a personal form of identification.[156]

Identifying belt buckles or giving accurate interpretations of what their iconography represents is not within our field of expertise. This analysis should be done by specialists. What calls our attention is that the destruction of the walls of Getaria,[157] the conquest of Gipuzkoa, and the belt buckles and plaques coincide in time. The hypothesis that the plaques were collected after the battle and buried in holy ground would require the use of a different interpretive framework.

Our knowledge on the subject would need to be much deeper to support this hypothesis at face value, but this archeological collection is considered to be among the most significant of the Iberian Peninsula to date. According to what archeologists have determined of it, "it is one of the most notable in Peninsular archeology." This raises two questions: Why have official institutions and other sponsors not promoted it further?[158] And if they have, why have results not been shared with historians?

Many years have gone by since the excavation took place. Try as we might have, we have not been able to see the tests results of the armorial motifs or the absolute chronology. The reports resulting from the archeological excavations have not been made public. Because of their substantial dimensions, these finds deserve further and more thorough research. And since we move in the realm of hypothesis, we would not want to neglect the possibility that the collection of belt plaques could have been spoils of war. Archeology operates around a finish line that is always out of reach. While we cannot pursue our inquiry any further, we can at least propose a hypothesis.

RESOURCES

Agirre, Oiartzabal, Beñi, *Gipuzkoako historia nafarra*, Nabarralde Fundazioa, 2017.

Añíbarro Rodríguez, Javier, *Las cuatro villas de la costa de la mar en la Edad Media. Conflictos jurisdicionales y comerciales*, (Unpublished PhD diss., University of Cantabria, Santander, 2013.)

Aragón Ruano, Álvaro, "Euskal Herria itsastarra lehen mundubiraren testuinguruan," *Elkano eta lehen mundubira: 500 urte geroago*, University of the Basque Country, Summer Course, Donostia-San Sebastián, 2019.

Arizaga Bolumburu, Beatriz (in collaboration), *Bizcaya en la Edad Media*, Haranburu D.L., vol. 4, Donostia-San Sebastián, 1985.

Arizaga Bolumburu, Beatriz, *Castro Urdiales en la Edad Media: La imagen de la villa*, University of Cantabria, Santander, 2001.

Arizaga Bolumburu, Beatriz, *El nacimiento de las villas guipuzcoanas en los s. XIII–XIV*, Sociedad Guipuzcoana de Ediciones y Publicaciones, Donostia-San Sebastián, 1978.

Arizaga Bolumburu, Beatriz, *Gipuzkoako hiri zaharrak*, Gipuzkoako Foru Aldundia, Donostia-San Sebastián, 1994.

Arizaga Bolumburu, Beatriz, *La imagen de la ciudad medieval: la recuperación del paisaje urbano*, Servicio de Publicaciones de la Universidad de Cantabria, Santander, 2002.

Arizaga Bolumburu, Beatriz, *Urbanística Medieval*, Kriseilu, Donostia-San Sebastián, 1990.

Arocena, Fausto, *Guipuzcoa en la Historia*, Biblioteca vasca, Madrid, 1964.

Arrieta Elizalde, Idoia, "Getaria: nafar fundazioa duen hiribildua," *Berria* newspaper, September 8, 2009.

Arrieta Elizalde, Idoia, "Donostiaren konkistaren agiri ezkutatuaren aurkezpena: ikerketaren ibilbidea eta ekarpen historiko-kritikoa," *Euskal lurraldeak eta Nafar Estatua*, Nabarralde Fundazioa, Txertoa argitaletxea, Donostia-San Sebastián, 2011.

Artetxe Fernández, Oihana; Pérez Centeno, Jesús Manuel, "Informe numismático San Prudentzio, Askizu (Getaria) SPA.07," Zehazten Zerbitzu Kulturalak, February 16, 2009.

Ayerbe Iribar, M.ª Rosa, "La incorporación de Guipuzcoa a la corona de Castilla (1199/1200)," *euskonews & media*, no.70, 2000.

Azurmendi, Otaegi, Joxe, *Espainolak eta euskaldunak*, Elkar Argitaletxea, Donostia-San Sebastián, 1992.

Barrena Osoro, Elena, "Segura: hiribilduaren sorreratik eskualdeko hegemoniara," *Segura Historian Zehar*, City of Segura, 2003.

Barrena Osoro, Elena, *La formación Histórica de Guipuzcoa*, Mundaiz, Donostia-San Sebastián, 1989.

Benito Dominguez, Ana María, "La arkeología subacuática en el Pais Vasco: una disciplina emergente," *Itsas Memoria, Revista de Estudios Marítimos del País Vasco*, no. 1, Donostia-San Sebastián, 1996.

Benito Dominguez, Ana María, *Urpeko oroimena Euskal Herriko urpeko arkeologia eta ondarea*, Untzi Museum, Donostia-San Sebastián, 2004.

Cañada Juste, Alberto, "Historiografía navarra de los siglos VIII al X una aproximación a los textos," in "Los Banu Qasi," *Príncipe de Viana*, no. 41, 1980.

Caro Baroja, Julio, *Los Vascos y la historia a través de Garibay*, Caro Raggio, Madrid, 2002.

Crónica Latina de los reyes de Castilla, Cabanes Pecourt, (María Desamparados ed.), Anúbar, Zaragoza, 1985.

Del Castillo, Eneko, *Atlas histórico de Navarra*, Pamiela, Iruñea-Pamplona, 2016.

Descripciones geográfico-historicas de los diferentes pueblos de la Provincia de Guipuzcoa y de la ciudad de Donostia-San Sebastián- San Sebastián y su jurisdición con destino a la Real Academia de Madrid, para el Diccionario Geográfico de España.

Díaz de Durana y Ortiz de Urbina, José Ramón; Fernández de Larrea Rojas, Jon Andoni, "La Frontera de malhechores: bandidos, linajes y villas entre Álava, Guipúzcoa y Navarra durante la Baja Edad Media," *Studia Historica*, no. 23, University of Salamanca, Salamanca, 2005.

Díaz de Durana y Ortiz de Urbina, José Ramón; Fernández de Larrea Rojas, Jon Andoni, *Los señores de la guerra y de la tierra: Nuevos textos para el estudio de los Parientes mayores guipuzkoanos (1265–1548)*, Gipuzkoako Foru Aldundia, Donostia-San Sebastián, 2000.

Díaz de Durana y Ortiz de Urbina, José Ramón, *La lucha de bandos en el País Vasco: de los parientes mayores a la hidalguía universal*, University of the Basque Country, Bilbao-Bilbo, 2002.

Díez de Cortázar, José Ángel, "Cultura en el reinado de Alfonso VIII de Castilla: Signos de un cambio de mentalidades y sensibilidades," II Curso de Cultura-Medieval, Aguilar de Campoo, October 1–6, 1990: 172.

Díez de Cortazar, José Ángel, "La sociedad alavesa medieval antes de la concesión del fuero de Vitoria," City of Vitoria-Gasteiz, Vitoria-Gasteiz, 1982.

Etxezarraga Ortuondo, Iosu, *El laicado y sus institutciones en la configuración religiosa de Gipuzkoa en la Edad Media* (Unpublished PhD diss., University of the Basque Country, 2017.)

Fernández de Larrea Rojas, Jon Andoni: "La conquista castellana de Álava, Guipúzcoa y el Duranguesado (1199–1200)," in "800 aniversario de la conquista de Alava, Guipuzkoa, y el Duranguesado," *RIEV,* no. 45, Donostia-San Sebastián, 2000.

Fontana, Josep, "España y Cataluña: trescientos años de Historia," *Sin Permiso.* Accessed: December 15, 2013, chrome-extension://efaidnbmnnnibpcajpcglclefindmkaj/https:// sinpermiso.info/sites/default/files/textos/fontana.pdf

Fontana, Josep, *Europa ante el espejo,* Crítica, Barcelona, 1994, 2000.

Fontana, Josep, *Historia Análisis del pasado y proyecto social,* Crítica, Barcelona, 1982.

Fortún Pérez de Ciriza, Luis Javier, "La quiebra de la soberanía navarra en Alava, Guipuzcoa y Duranguesado (1199–1200)," *RIEV,* no.45, Donostia-San Sebastián, 2000.

García Fernández, Ernesto, "El mundo urbano," *Nosotros los Vascos, Historia de Euskal Herria,* II, Lur Argitaletxea, Donostia-San Sebastián, 2004.

Garibay y Zamalloa, Esteban de, *Compendio historial de las Chronicas y universal historia de todos los reynos de España, donde se escriven las vidas de los Reyes de Navarra. Escrívese también la sucesión de los Reyes de Francia, y Obispos de la Yglesia de Iruñea (1571),* XII, chapter 32, Sebastián de Comellas, Barcelona, 1628 .

Gipuzkoa versus Castilla. Konkista. Ituna eta eskubide historikoak, 1200–2000, Kaier collection, Koldo Mitxelena Kulturunea, Gipuzkoako Foru Aldundia, Donostia-San Sebastián, 2000.

González Mínguez, Cesar, "La construción de un paisaje historiográfico: el País Vasco en la Edad Media. Balances de las últimas décadas (1983–2003)," *Vasconia* journal, no. 34, Donostia-San Sebastián, 2005.

González, Julio, *El reino de Castilla en la época de Alfonso VIII,* I, CSIC, Madrid, 1960.

Gorosabel, *Cosas Memorables de Guipuzcoa* (1862), La Gran Enciclopedia Vasca, Bilbao-Bilbo, 1972.

Goyhenetche, Manex, "Ipar Euskal Herria Antso Nagusiaren garaian," *Euskal Herria XI. mendean. Antso III.a Nagusiaren erregealdia (1004–1035)* Pamiela, Iruñea-Pamplona, 2004.

I jornada sobre Derecho Pirenaico, Nabarralde Foundation and Martin Ttipia Association, Agurain, 2017.

Izagirre, Ion, "Nafarroa XII. Mendeko Lehen Erdian (1104–1150)," pdf. Internet.

Lacarra, José María, *Historia del Reino de Navarra en la Edad Media,* Nafarroako Aurrezki Kutxa, Iruñea-Pamplona, 1975.

Lekuona, Manuel, "Escollos de nuestra Historiografía," *RSBAP/Euskal Herriaren Adiskideen Elkarteko Boletina,* year XXVII, 1-2 books, Donostia-San Sebastián, 1971.

Lema Pueyo, José Ángel, "De 'ipuzkoa' a la hermandad de villas de Guipuzkoa (ss. VI-XV)," *Gipuzkoaren Historiaren Sintesia,* Gipuzkoako Foru Aldundia, Donostia-San Sebastián, 2017.

Lizana de Salafranca, Joaquín G., "Apliques metálicos de la indumentaria militar medieval aragonesa con emblemas heráldicos," *Emblemata,* no. 3, 1997: 435–438.

Lope Martínez de Isasti, *Compendio Historial de Guipuzcoa* (1625), La Gran Enciclopedia Vasca, Bilbao, 1972.

López de Luzuriaga Martínez, Iñaki, *Euskaldunak eta karolingiar iraultza Akitania eta Baskonian barrena,* Basque Summer University, Bilbao-Bilbo, 2016.

López de Luzuriaga Martínez, Iñaki, *Nafarroako inbasioa (1199–1200),* Nabarralde Fundazioa, 2021.

Maravall, José Antonio, *El concepto de España en la Edad Media,* Centro de Estudios Constitucionales, Madrid, 2013.

Martín Duque, Ángel, "Relaciones financieras entre Sancho el Fuerte de Navarra y los monarcas de la Corona de Aragón," *Príncipe de Viana,* Cultura Navarra.es.

Martínez Díez, Gonzalo, "El descontento rural por las villas hace que Guipúzcoa se incline por Castilla," *La Voz de España* newspaper, Donostia-San Sebastián, February 27, 1974: 19.

Martínez Díez, Gonzalo, "Fueros locales en el teritorio de la provincia de Santander," *Anuario de Historia del Derecho Español*, Madrid, 1976.

Martínez Díez, Gonzalo, *Alfonso VIII, rey de Castilla y de Toledo*, Burgos, 1995. Newer edition: Martínez Díez, Gonzalo; *Alfonso VIII rey de Castilla y Toledo (1158–1214)*, Trea argitaletxea, Gijón, 2007.

Martínez Díez, Gonzalo; González Díez, Emiliano; Martínez Llorente, Félix, *Colección de Documentos Medievales de las Villas de Guipucoa (1200–1369)*, Gipuzkoako Foru Aldundia, Zarautz, 1991.

Martínez Díez, Gonzalo, *Guipuzcoa en los albores de su historia (Sglos X–XII)*, Gipuzkoako Foru Aldundia, Donostia-San Sebastián, 1975.

Monreal Zia, Gregorio, "1200, una fecha significativa en la evolución de Vasconia," in "800 aniversario de la conquista de Alava, Guipuzcoa, y el Duranguesado," *RIEV*, no. 45, Donostia-San Sebastián, 2000.

Monsalvo Antón, José María, *Los conflictos sociales en la Edad Media*, Síntesis Editorial, Madrid, 2016.

Nosotros los Vascos. Gran Atlas histórico de Euskal Herria, Lur argitaletxea, Donostia-San Sebastián, 1995.

Orella Unzué, José Luis, "La gasconización medieval occidental del Reino de Navarra," *Lurralde*, no. 33, Donostia-San Sebastián, 2010.

Orella Unzué, José Luis, "La hermandad de frontera entre el Reino de Navarra y la provincia de Guipúzcoa siglos XIV–XV," *Príncipe de Viana*, no. 46, 1985.

Orella Unzué, José Luis, "Los orígenes de la hermandad de Guipúzcoa (Las relaciones Guipúzcoa-Navarra en los siglos XIII-XIV)," *Vasconia*, no. 3, Donostia-San Sebastián, 1984.

Orella Unzué, José Luis, "Gipuzkoa eta Nafarroaren arteko harremanak 1200. Urtean," *Gipuzkoa Versus Castilla*, Gipuzkoako Foru Aldundia, Kaier collection, Koldo Mitxelena kultugunea, Donostia-San Sebastián, 2001.

Orella Unzué, José Luis, "Historia de Hondarribia en la Alta y Baja Edad Media: desde la fundación hasta finales del siglo XIII," Conference at Zuloaga Etxea, Hondarribiko Historiaren Lagunen Elkartea, Hondarribia, November 2003.

Ortega Villoslada, Antonio, "Viajes a Flandes e Inglaterra ¿Cabotaje o Recta Vía?" *Espacio, Tiempo y Forma*, Series III, in Historia Medieval, no. 16, Universidad Nacional de Educación a Distancia, Madrid, 2003.

Pérez Bustamante, Rogelio, "Privilegio del rey Alfonso VIII otorgando al monasterio de San Juan de Burgos, los Díezmos de la villa de Castro Urdiales," Eguaras T. I. Collection, 219, Biblioteca Municipal de Santander, 1980.

Pérez Centeno, Jesús María; Esteban Delgado, Milagros; Alberdi Lonbide, Xabier; Getaria, "Puerto de Gipuzkoa 1209–2009. Avance preliminar de Resultados, 2007 San Martín de Askizu y San Prudencio de Askizu y San Antón Getaria," University of Deusto and Zehazten, Gipuzkoako Foru Aldundia, Donostia-San Sebastián, foreword of December 19, 2007.

Pescador Medrano, Aitor, "Antso Nagusiaren ondarea," *Euskal Herria XI. mendean*, Pamiela, Iruñea-Pamplona, 2004.

Pescador Medrano, Aitor, "Tenentes y tenencias del Reino de Pamplona en Álava, Vizcaya, Guipúzcoa, La Rioja y Castilla (104–176)," *Vasconia*, no. 29, Donostia-San Sebastián, 1999.

Ríos, María Luz, *Introducción a la Historia Medieval de Álava, Guipuzcoa y Vizcaya en sus Textos* Txertoa argitaletxea, Donostia-San Sebastián, 1979.

Rodríguez-Picavea Matilla, Enrique, "Monarquía castellana: Alfonso VIII y la orden de Calatrava," II curso de cultura Medieval, Aguilar de Campoo, 1990.

Ruiz Fernández, Amanda; Agirre García, Jaione; *Hiribilduen sorrera Euskal Herriko Erdi Aroaren Historiarako dokumentu idatzi eta grafikoen iruzkin-ereduak*, Basque Summer University, Bilbao-Bilbo, 2006.

Sagredo Garde, Iñaki, *Navarra. Castillos que defendieron el Reino*, Pamiela, bk. III, Iruñea-Pamplona, 2007.

Sánchez Mora, Antoni, "Diego López de Haro," Real Academia de la Historia, https://dbe.rah. es/biografias/43950/diego-lopez-de-haro.

Sarasola Etxegoien, Nerea; "El poblamiento medieval de Gipuzkoa. Revisión crítica del registro arqueológico," *Munibe*, no. 61, Donostia-San Sebastián, 2010.

Serrano Izko, Vicente, *Nafarroa Historiaren Hariak*, Euskara Kultur Elkargoa, Iruñea-Pamplona, 2005.

Soria Sesé, Lourdes, "La historiografía castellana sobre la incorporación de Guipuzcoa a Castilla," *Gipuzkoa versus Castilla*, Gipuzkoako Foru Aldundia, Kaier collection, Koldo Mitxelena kulturgunea, Donostia-San Sebastián, 2001.

Tena Díez, Soledad, *La sociedad urbana en la Guipúzcoa costera medieval: San Sebastián, Rentería y Fuenterrabía: 1200–1500*, Fundación Social y Cultural Kutxa, 1997.

Torregarai Pagola, Elena; Aragón Ruano, Álvaro (ed.) *Gipuzkoaren Historiaren Sintesia*, Gipuzkoako Foru Aldundia, Donostia-San Sebastián, 2017.

Urzainqui, Tomas, *La Navarra Marítima*, Pamiela (sixth edition), Iruñea, 2010.

Ximenez de Rada, Rodericus; *Historia de rebus Hispaniae sive Historia Gothica*, Turnhout, 1987.

Zabala, Mª José, "La creación de villas en el señorío de Bizkaia: Los fueros y las cartas pueblas," in "Cuadernos de Sección, Historia y Geografía," *Eusko Ikaskuntza*, no. 23, Donostia-San Sebastián, 1995.

NOTES

1 Fontana, Josep, "España y Cataluña: trescientos años de Historia," *Sin Permiso*. Accessed: December 15, 2013, chrome-extension://efaidnbmnnnibpcajpcglclefindmkaj/https://sin-permiso.info/sites/default/files/textos/fontana.pdf.

2 The nation-state was formed within the Kingdom of Iruñea during the era of Sancho III the Great when all Basque lands were united under the same ruler. Although it was a short chapter for Iparralde (Northern Basque Country, to the north of the international frontier between Spain and France), the political ties between the regions remained tight.

3 Basques referred to others as non-Basque speakers.

4 Fontana, Josep, *Europa ante el espejo*. Crítica, Barcelona, 1994, 2000: 54.

5 González Mínguez, Cesar, "La construcción de un paisaje historiográfico: el País Vasco en la Edad Media. Balances de las últimas décadas (1983–2003)," *Vasconia*, no. 34, Donostia-San Sebastián, 2005: 117–138.

6 Pactism: The nature of the system based on the defense of the pact. The connection to the Castilian crown is understood from the point of view of the treaty, and not from the point of view of conquest. According to them, in the year 1200, the western territories of Navarre voluntarily and by means of the treaty entered the crown of Castile, which made it possible

to maintain the statutes, customs, and freedoms, that is, to maintain its legal-political system. This view of the sixteenth century was the basis of the classical foral tradition, and they say that it has been maintained as a special feature in our territories.

7   Aitor Pescador Medrano, in "Antso Nagusiaren Ondarea," states that, during the 1970s, historians José María Lacarra and Antonio Ubieto Arteta tried to stop historiographic inaccuracies of historical events. Other researchers are working on the same task. Medievalists of particular interest include Manex Goyhenetche, José Luis Orella, Roldán Jimeno, Aitor Pescador, Tomás Urzainqui, Beñi Agirre, and Iñaki López de Luzuriaga.

8   Monsalvo Antón, José María, *Los Conflictos sociales en la Edad Media*. Síntesis Editorial, Madrid, 2016. In this synthesis work, Monsalvo compiles traditional and more modern perspectives.

9   This study is included in an unpublished research project we conducted with Beñi Agirre.

10   References to these political phases can be found in multiple publications: *Nosotros los Vascos. Gran Atlas histórico de Euskal Herria*. Donostia-San Sebastián: Lur argitaletxea, 1995: 81–112. Lacarra, José María, *Historia del Reino de Navarra en la Edad Media*, Nafarroako Aurrezki Kutxa, Iruñea-Pamplona, 1975. This is a classic work among its kind, and it provides a deeper understanding of these phases. Barrena Osoro, Elena, *La formación histórica de Guipuzcoa*. Mundaiz, Donostia-San Sebastián, 1989. Ríos, María Luz, *Introducción a la Historia medieval de Álava, Guipuzcoa y Vizcaya en sus Textos*, Txertoa argitaletxea, Donostia-San Sebastián, 1979. Del Castillo, Eneko, *Atlas histórico de Navarra*, Pamiela, Iruñea-Pamplona, 2016. And, particularly, the large body of work by José Ángel García de Cortázar and Beatriz Arizaga Bolunburu.

11   Azurmendi, Otaegi, Joxe, *Espainolak eta euskaldunak*, Elkar argitaletxea, Donostia-San Sebastián, 1992: 75.

12   Iñaki Sagredo Garde published an inventory and analysis of the castles of all the territories that once belonged to the Kingdom of Navarre under the title: *Navarra. Castillos que defendieron el Reino*. It is a five-volume work published through Pamiela.

13   López de Luzuriaga, Martínez, Iñaki, *Euskaldunak eta karolingiar iraultza Akitania eta Baskonian barrena*. Basque Summer University, Bilbao-Bilbo, 2016: 147–179.

14   Cañada Juste, Alberto, "Historiografía navarra de los siglos VIII-al X una aproximación a los textos, Los Banu Qasi (714–924)," in "Los Banu Qasi" *Príncipe de Viana*, no. 41, Iruñea-Pamplona, 1980.

15   For this section, I consulted: Goyhenetche, Manex; Jimeno, Roldán; Pescador, Aitor; Urzainqui, Tomás, *Euskal Herria XI. Mendean*. Pamiela, Iruñea-Pamplona, 2004.

16   "*Nik, Antso erregeak, botere guztia baitut Aragoin, Iruñean, Sobrarben, Ribagortzan, Naiaran eta Gaztelan eta Araban, nola Antso Gilenek Gaskoinian eta Berenguer kondeak Bartzelonan eta Bermudo enperadore jaunak Galizian . . . ,*" Pescador Medrano, Aitor, "Antso Nagusiaren ondarea," *Euskal Herria XI. Mendean*. Pamiela, Iruñea-Pamplona, 2004: 148.

17   Goyenetche, Manex, "Ipar Euskal Herria Antso Nagusiaren garaian," *Euskal Herria XI. Mendean*. Pamiela, Iruñea-Pamplona, 2004: 86–87.

18   *Tenencias* were the administrative divisions of a kingdom. They were mostly along borders and played military roles. Although it was the king or the queen who appointed the *tenentes*, the consolidation of certain families ended in the establishment of a succession system. The succession system was predominant in Bizkaia.

19   Pescador Medrano, Aitor, "Tenentes y tenencias del Reino de Pamplona en Álava, Vizcaya,

Guipúzcoa, La Rioja y Castilla (104–1076)," *Vasconia*, no. 29, Donostia-San Sebastián, 1999: 107–144.

20 Goyhenetche, Manex, "Ipar Euskal Herria Antso Nagusiaren garaian," *Euskal Herria XI Mendean. Antso III.a Nagusiaren erregealdia (1004–1035)*. Pamiela, Iruñea-Pamplona, 2004.

21 Del Castillo, Eneko, A*tlas histórico de Navarra*. Pamiela, Iruñea-Pamplona, 2016.

22 Pescador Medrano, Aitor, "Antso Nagusiaren ondarea," *Euskal Herria XI. Mendean*. Pamiela, Iruñea-Pamplona, 2004: 148.

23 The conference *I Jornada sobre Derecho Pirenaico* in Agurain in 2017, organized and later edited by the Nabarralde and Martin Ttipia cultural foundations, offers an interesting viewpoint of the Pyrenean Law.

24 For this section, I consulted: Pescador Medrano, Aitor; "Antso Nagusiaren ondarea," *Euskal Herria XI. mendean*, Pamiela, Iruñea-Pamplona, 2004: 137–148.

25 Today's Bizkaia was divided in four regions after the eleventh century: The Enkarterris, between the Ason River and the Arlantzon Valley; Central Bizkaia, lodged between the Nerbioi and Deba rivers; Urduña; and the Durango Region. While Urduña and the Durango Region were fairly homogeneous, the other two regions were formed of smaller units: the region to the west of the Nerbioi River, known as the Enkarterris after the twelfth century, comprised the valleys of Sopuerta, Karrantza, Somorrostro, Artzentales, Gordexola, and Salcedo, and, most likely, the Vecio Valley, too, between the Ason and Nerbioi Rivers; and Central Bizkaia was sectioned in rural districts and territories.

26 Iñigo López, likely of Navarrese origins, was the lord and *tenente* of Bizkaia and owned inherited land in Bizkaia. In 1054, he stood in favor of King García of Navarre. We know from a 1076 document, in which he offered the town of Camprovín (in today's La Rioja) to the monastery of San Millán de la Cogolla, that he pledged fealty to the King of Navarre, Sancho IV of Peñalen, even though the reigning king at the time was Alfonso VI. Upon his death, his son Lope Iñiguez pledged fealty to Alfonso VI and claimed ownership of the *tenencias* of Araba, in 1081, and of Bizkaia and Gipuzkoa. In the document, however, he is mentioned as count of Bizkaia.

27 "*Para que en adelante no surgiere ninguna disención entre ambos reinos se decidió que tierra era reino de Navarra, es decir, desde el río Ebro hasta cerca de la ciudad de Burgos, que el rey Sancho de Castilla había arrebatado con violencia a su pariente el rey Sancho de Navarra (Sancho el de Peñalén), hijo del rey Díez (Díez Sanchez de Nájera)." "De lo cual se extendieron documentos entre ambos reyes y reinos de Castilla y de Navarra y cada uno de ellos recibió cartas suas firmatas et bene valladas." Entonces Alfonso de Aragón entregó toda la tierra de Castilla a Alfonso de Castilla, y en adelante no quiso que se llamara emperador, sino rey de Aragón, Pamplona y Navarra,*" Urzainqui, Tomás, *La Navarra Marítima*. Pamiela, Iruñea-Pamplona, 2010: 105–106.

28 "*baliteke Tolosako kondearen mugimenduei aurreratu nahi izatea, Gaztelako Alfontsoren alde jartzekotan zegoen eta; posible da Antso III.a Nagusiaren antzera lurralde baskoi guztiak batu nahi izatea; edota Akitaniako frankoengatik babesteko asmoz errege nafarra jarri nahi izatea frantsesak agintzen zuen tokian. Dena dela, 1131. urteko urrian setioa altxa zuen Alfontso I.ak Tolosako kondearen eraso baten ondorioz,*" Izagirre, Ion, "Nafarroa XII. Mendeko Lehen Erdian (1104–1150)," pdf. Internet.

29 Fortún Pérez de Ciriza, "La quiebra de la soberanía navarra, en Álava, Guipúzcoa, y el Duranguesado. (1199–1200)," *RIEV*, no. 45, Donostia-San Sebastián, 2000.

30   Quote from: González, Julio, *El reino de Castilla en la época de Alfonso VIII*. CSIC, vol. II, Madrid, 1960: 152.

31   Del Castillo, Eneko. *Atlas histórico de Navarra*. Pamiela, Iruñea-Pamplona, 2016: 154.

32   *Gipuzkoa versus Castilla. Konkista. Ituna eta eskubide historikoak, 1200–2000*. Kaier collection, Koldo Mitxelena Kulturunea, Gipuzkoako Foru Aldundia, Donostia-San Sebastián, 2000: 27.

33   Fernández de Larrea, Joséba Andoni, "La conquista castellana de Álava, Guipúzcoa y el Duranguesado (1199–1200)," *RIEV*, Donostia-San Sebastián, 2000: 431.

34   Del Castillo, Eneko. *Atlas histórico de Navarra*. Pamiela, Iruñea-Pamplona, 2016: 68. Reference from *La Navarra Marítima* by Tomás Urzainqui.

35   Fernández de Larrea, Joséba Andoni, "La conquista castellana de Álava, Guipúzcoa y el Duranguesado (1199–1200)," *RIEV*, Donostia-San Sebastián, 2000: 431.

36   Garibay y Zamalloa, Esteban de, *Compendio historial de las Chronicas y universal historia de todos los reynos de España, donde se escriven las vidas de los Reyes de Navarra. Escrívese también la sucesión de los Reyes de Francia, y Obispos de la Yglesia de Iruñea (1571)*. Sebastián de Comellas, XXIII, Barcelona, 1628: 164.

37   Barrena Osoro, Elena, *La formación Histórica de Guipuzcoa*. Mundaiz, Donostia-San Sebastián, 1989.

38   Fortún Pérez de Ciriza, Luis Javier, "La quiebra de la soberanía navarra en Alava, Guipuzcoa y Duranguesado (1199–1200)," *RIEV* no. 45, Donostia-San Sebastián, 2000: 463–470.

39   " (. . .) *El rey de Castilla continuando los pretensión antiguos suyos, y de los Reyes sus progenitores de la obtención del reyno de Navarra, sin aguardar aun al suceso de la enfermedad del Rey don Sancho, ni mirar, que a falta suya quedavan por herederos, los infantes don Fernando y don Ramiro, congrego sus gentes y volvió a la guerra contra Navarra…*" Garibay y Zamalloa, Esteban de, *Compendio historial de las Chronicas y universal historia de todos los reynos de España, donde se escriven las vidas de los Reyes de Navarra. Escrívese también la sucesión de los Reyes de Francia, y Obispos de la Yglesia de Iruñea (1571)*. Sebastián de Comellas, XXIII, Barcelona, 1628: 169.

40   González, Julio, *El reino de Castilla en la época de Alfonso VIII*. CSIC, vol. II, doc. 690, Madrid, 1960.

41   "*Obtinuit itaque Rex nobilis Aldefonsus Victoriam, Ibidam, Alavam eta Guipuscoam, et earum terrarum munitiones et castra, preter Trevennium quod fuit postea commutatione Inzurae datum sibi. Mirandam etiam dedit commutatione simili pro Portella, Sanctum Sebastiánum, Fontem Rapidum, Beloagam, Zeguitagui, Aizcorroz, Asluceam, Arzorociam, Victoriam Veterem, Maranionem, Aussam, Athavit, Iruritam et Sanctum Vicentium acquisivit,*" Larrea, Joséba Andoni, "La conquista castellana de Álava, Guipúzcoa y el Duranguesado (1199–1200)," *RIEV*, Donostia-San Sebastián, 2000: 434.

42   *Gipuzkoa versus Castilla. Konkista. Ituna eta eskubide historikoak, 1200–2000*, Kaier collection, Koldo Mitxelena Kulturunea, Gipuzkoako Foru Aldundia, Donostia-San Sebastián, 2000: 37.

43   Fortún Pérez de Ciriza, Luis Javier, "La quiebra de la soberanía navarra en Alava, Guipuzcoa y Duranguesado (1199–1200)," *RIEV*, no. 45, Donostia-San Sebastián, 2000: 480.

44   "*Et entonces priso el rey D. Alonso Ipuzcoa con sus castillos et sus fortalezas … e la hora gano Sant Sebastián e Fontarrabia et Cogitay …*" Eta Bianako Printzeak "*el dicho rey de Castilla, corrió toda la tierra de Alava, é Guipuzcoa é Navarra; é como el poder de la gente suya, e caballería,*

fuese con el dicho rey de Navarra; e como quiera que Vitoria tobieran sitiada cerca de una año; e otras villas e castillos, e ficieron todo su esfuerzo de ser defender; pero finalment, mas non lo pdiendo facer, hobieronse de render por fuerza, e ansi tomaron la tierra de Alava é la de Guipuzcoa injustament," Arocena, Fausto, *Guipuzcoa en la Historia.* Biblioteca vasca, Madrid, 1964: 74.

45   Sagredo, Iñaki, *Navarra: Castillos que defendieron el Reino.* Pamiela, Iruñea-Pamplona, 2007: 19.

46   Fernández de Larrea, Joseba Andoni, "La conquista castellana de Álava, Guipúzcoa y el Duranguesado (1199–1200)," *RIEV*, Donostia-San Sebastián, 2000: 437.

47   GARIBAY Y ZAMALLOA, ESTEBAN DE, *Compendio historial de las Chronicas y universal historia de todos los reynos de España, donde se escriven las vidas de los Reyes de Navarra. Escrívese también la sucesión de los Reyes de Francia, y Obispos de la Yglesia de Iruñea (1571).* Sebastián de Comellas, XXIII, Barcelona, 1628: 171.

48   "*regnante in Castella … et in Alava, et in Bicaya et in Ypuzcoa et in Sancto Sebastiáno.*" This text shows the array of titles held by Alfonso VIII. Martínez Díez, Gonzalo, *Guipuzcoa en los albores de su Historia (Siglos X–XII).* Donostia-San Sebastián: Gipuzkoako Foru Aldundia, 1975: 156–158.

49   Sánchez Mora, Antonio, "Diego López de Haro" Real Academia de la Historia. URL: https://dbe.rah.es/biografias/43950/diego-lopez-de-haro#:~:text=L%C3%B3pez%20 de%20Haro%2C%20Diego.%20%3F,(esposa%20del%20citado%20Monarca).

50   Serrano Izko, Vicente; *Nafarroa Historiaren Hariak.* Euskara Kultur Elkargoa, Iruñea-Pamplona, 2005: 128.

51   Lacarra, José María, *Historia del Reino de Navarra en la Edad Media.* Caja de Ahorros de Navarra, Iruñea-Pamplona, 1975: 118.

52   Martín Duque, Ángel, "Relaciones financieras entre Sancho el Fuerte de Navarra y los monarcas de la corona de Aragón" *Principe de Viana*, no. 227, cultura navarra. es.

53   Tomás Urzainqui lists Navarre's attempts to recover the lands in *La Navarra Marítima.* Pamiela (sixth edition), Iruñea-Pamplona, 2010: 259–262.

54   Barrena Osoro, Elena, "Segura: hiribilduaren sorreratik eskualdeko hegemoniara," *Segura Historian Zehar*, City of Segura, 2003.

55   "*Totam Ypuzkoam, Fontem Rabiam, Sanctum Sebastiánum et castrum de Montis Acuti, las cuales poseerá mientras viviere,*" Martínez Díez, Gonzalo; González Díez, Emiliano; Martínez Llorente, Felix, *Colección de Documentos Medievales de las Villas de Guipucoa (1200–1369).* Gipuzkoako Foru Aldundia, no.7 .dok, Zarautz, 1991.

56   Martínez Díez, Gonzalo; González Díez, Emiliano; Martínez Llorente, Felix, *Colección de Documentos Medievales de las Villas de Guipucoa (1200–1369).* Gipuzkoako Foru Aldundia, no.19 .dok, Zarautz, 1991.

57   Fontana, Josep, *Historia Análisis del pasado y proyeco social.* Crítica, Barcelona, 1982.

58   Pescador Medrano, Aitor; "Antso Nagusiaren ondarea," *Euskal Herria XI. Mendean.* Pamiela, Iruñea-Pamplona, 2004.

59   Azurmendi, Otaegi, Joxe, *Espainolak eta euskaldunak.* Elkar argitaletxea, Donostia-San Sebastián, 1992.

60   Azurmendi, Otaegi, Joxe, *Espainolak eta euskaldunak.* Elkar argitaletxea, Donostia-San Sebastián, 1992.

61   The Order of Calatrava helped define the jurisdiction of the Kingdom of Castile especially on the Islamic border but also on the Navarrese one. The fortification *Castellum Rubeum* in Arrubal, in the Ebro Valley, La Rioja, can be considered an example of their efforts.

62 Rodríguez-Picavea Matilla, Enrique, "Monarquía castellana: Alfonso VIII y la Orden de Calatrava" II curso de cultura Medieval, Centro de Estudios del Románico, Aguilar de Campoo, 1990: 361–378.

63 In the last few years, literature on burgs has multiplied. Javier Añibarro Rodríguez outlines these publications in his article "Las cuatro villas de la costa de la mar en la Edad Media. Conflictos jurisdiccionales y comerciales" (Unpublished PhD diss., University of Cantabria, Santander, 2013.)

64 The subject of burgs has been extensively researched, so we will only refer to a few publications. Arizaga Bolumburu, Beatriz, *El nacimiento de las villas guipuzcoanas en los s. XIII–XIV*, Sociedad Guipuzcoana de Ediciones y Publicaciones, Donosita-San Sebastián, 1978. Arizaga Bolumburu, Beatriz, *Urbanística Medieval*. Kriseilu argitaletxea, Donostia-San Sebastián, 1990. Arizaga Bolumburu, Beatriz, *La imagen de la ciudad medieval: la recuperación del paisaje urbano*. Servicio de Publicaciones de la Universidad de Cantabria, Santander, 2002. Tena García, Soledad, *La sociedad urbana en la Guipúzcoa costera medieval: San Sebastián, Rentería y Fuenterrabía: 1200–1500*. Fundación Social y Cultural Kutxa, 1997. García Fernandez, Ernesto, "El mundo urbano," *Nosotros los Vascos, Historia de Euskal Herria*, Lur argitaletxea, Donostia-San Sebastián, II, 2004.

65 Iosu Etxezarraga Ortuondo shares this perspective. "El laicado y sus institutciones en la configuración religiosa de Gipuzkoa en la Edad Media" (Unpublished PhD diss., September 6, 2017: 128.)

66 Martínez Díez, Gonzalo, *Alfonso VIII rey de Castilla y Toledo (1158–1214)*. Ediciones Trea, Gijón, 2007: 211.

67 "*In Asturias a municipal charter constitutes an official act of creation. In the Basque Country, a municipal chapter is issued when the new urban space is already under development,*" Zabala, MªJosé, "La creación de las Villas en el Señorío de Bizkaia: Los fueros y las Cartas Pueblas," in "Cuadernos de Sección. Historia y Geografía" no. 23, *Eusko Ikaskuntza*, Donostia-San Sebastián, 1995: 9–29.

68 The *fuero* families have been researched by Amanda Ruiz Fernández and Jaione Agirre García in "Hiribilduen sorrera Euskal Herrian: Foruen Familiak Mapa Batean," *Euskal Herriko Erdi Aroaren Historiako dokumentu idatzi eta Grafikoen iruzkin-Ereduak*, Basque Summer University, Bilbao-Bilbo, 2006.

69 "*There are 'smaller' towns with fuero privileges whose role was to surveil the border. These fueros were issued by the crown of Aragón: Sancho Ramírez (1076–1094), Pedro I (1094–1102) and Alfonso I the Battler (1102–1134),*" Ruiz Fernández, Amanda; Agirre García, Jaione, "Hiribilduen sorrera Euskal Herrian: Foruen Familiak Mapa Batean," *Euskal Herriko Erdi Aroaren Historiako dokumentu idatzi eta Grafikoen iruzkin-Ereduak*, Basque Summer University, Bilbao-Bilbo, 2006.

70 Navarrese burgs are reportedly the oldest in the Iberian Peninsula, with some recorded in documents of the ninth and tenth centuries. Santa Cara or Cascante, for instance. They were Roman cities in origin and, although they survived, their relevance subsided. Zabala, Mª José, "La creación de las villas en el señorío de Bizkaia: los fueros y las cartas pueblas," Cuadernos de Sección. Historia y Geografía, no. 23, *Eusko Ikaskuntza*, Donostia-San Sebastián, 1995: 9–29.

71 Sarasola Etxegoien, Nerea; "El poblamiento medieval de Gipuzkoa. Revisión crítica del registro arqueológico," *Munibe*, no. 61, Donostia-San Sebastián, 2010: 339–393.

72 Orella Unzué, José Luis, "La Gasconización Medieval occidental del Reino de Navarra" *Lurralde*, no. 33, Donostia-San Sebastián, 2010: 177–208.

73 In his thesis, Etxezarraga argues that the first record of maritime routes is in 1237 from Gipuzkoa, when Donostia-San Sebastián signed agreements with various ports of the English Channel. Etxezarraga Ortuondo, Iosu, "El laicado y sus instituciones en la configuración religiosa de Gipuzkoa en la Edad Media," (Unpublished PhD diss., University of the Basque Country, 2017.)

74 Many hypotheses have formed around the missing document of the municipal charter of Durango. Recent hypotheses suggest the burg received its municipal charter at the end of the thirteenth century; José Ángel García de Cortázar proposes the year 1290; whereas Esteban de Garibay states it was Sancho VI the Wise who granted *fuero* to Durango (Garibay y Zamalloa, Esteban de, *Compendio historial de las Chronicas y universal historia de todos los reynos de España, donde se escriven las vidas de los Reyes de Navarra. Escrívese también la sucesión de los Reyes de Francia, y Obispos de la Yglesia de Iruñea (1571)*, Sebastián de Comellas, XXIII, Barcelona, 1628).

75 The next section gives details on this topic.

76 The Coastal Way is already mentioned in the twelfth-century chronicle *Historia Compostelana*. García Fernández, Ernesto, "El mundo Urbano," *Nosotros los Vascos. Historia de Euskal Herria*, Lur argitaletxea, II, Donosita-San Sebastián, 2004: 256.

77 Martínez Díez, Gonzalo, "Fueros locales en el territorio de la provincia de Santander," *Anuario de Historia del Derecho Español*, Madrid, 1976: 546–555.

78 Martínez Díez, Gonzalo, *Alfonso VIII rey de Castilla y Toledo (1158–1214)*, Ediciones Trea, Gijón, 2007: 211.

79 We believe that to boost trade and urban life, López de Haro, who was then *tenente* of Nájera, La Rioja, Old Castile and Trasmiera, founded Castro and gave it the Logroño *fuero* in 1163. Alfonso VIII would have been only five years old at the time.

80 Martínez Díez, Gonzalo, *Alfonso VIII rey de Castilla y Toledo (1158–1214)*, Ediciones Trea, Gijón, 2007: 211–212.

81 No trace of the original document, of any copies or of any copy requests of the Castro municipal chapter have been found to this date. The date of March 10, 1163, proposed by Henao is generally accepted, although he didn't mention the sources or documents he used to support his claim. It is certain that Castro had the Logroño *fuero* and that, in 1200, the burg of Laredo was granted the same law as the Franks.

82 Castro was taken over by Alfonso VIII in 1192 after successful negotiation talks with the Abbess of Huelgas, who would collect a yearly sum of 400 aureos (gold coins) in tithe payments from the salt mines in exchange for the *"villam et castrum de Portu de Urdiales."* Pérez Bustamante, Rogelio, "Privilegia del rey Alfonso VIII otorgando al Monasterio de San Juan de Burgos, los diezmos de la villa de Castro Urdiales," Eguaras T. I. Collection, Biblioteca Municipal de Santander, 219, 1980: 237.

83 We believe that to boost trade and urban life, López de Haro, who was then *tenente* of Nájera, La Rioja, Old Castile and Trasmiera, founded Castro and gave it the Logroño *fuero* in 1163. Alfonso VIII would have been only five years old at the time.

84 Ortega Villoslada, Antonio, "Viajes a Flandes e Inglaterra ¿Cabotaje o recta vía?" *Espacio, Tiempo y Forma*, Series III, in Historia Medieval, no. 16, Universidad Nacional de Educación a Distancia, Madrid, 2003.

85 García de Cortázar, José Ángel, "Cultura en el reinado de Alfonso VIII de Castilla: signos

de un cambio de mentalidades y sensiblidades," II curso de cultura medieval, Centro de Estudios del Románico, Aguilar de Campoo, October 1–6, 1990: 172.

86 Navarre had to define its border with the foundation of these burgs: San Vicente de la Sonsierra (1172), La Guardia (1164), Labraza (1196), Los Arcos, Lizarra and Inzura (1201), and La Burunda (1208). Castile had to capture its way to the sea.

87 In 1242, Fernando III ratified the *fuero* given to Bastida by King of Navarre Sancho VII the Wise, and in 1254, the *fuero* of Trebiñu, which was a Navarrese burg possibly founded in 1161.

88 "*Alfonso X de Castilla mandó en el año 1256 fundar una nueva villa para su servicio*," quote by Josè Joaquín de Gorosabel in *Cosas Memorables de Guipuzcoa*, 1862, La Gran Enciclopedia Vasca, Bilbao-Bilbo, 1972: 495.

89 Tolosa received *fuero* when the burg campaign in the large territory of Gipuzkoa spread across the interior. Martínez Díez, Gonzalo; González Díez, Emiliano; Martínez Llorente, Félix, *Colección de Documentos Medievales de las Villas de Guipucoa (1200–1369)*, Gipuzkoako Foru Aldundia, Zarautz, 1991.

90 Barrena Osoro, Elena, "Segura: Hiribilduaren sorreratik eskualdeko hegemoniara" *Segura Historian Zehar*. City of Segura, Segura, 2003: 118.

91 Zabala, Mª José, "La creación de las villas en el señorío de Bizkaia: los fueros y las cartas pueblas," in "Cuadernos de Sección. Historia y Geografía" no. 23, *Eusko Ikaskuntza*, Donostia-San Sebastián, 1995: 9–29.

92 Extensive historiography exists around the social issues of the Early Middle Ages, as shown in Ricardo Córdoba de la Llave's article "Conflictividad social en los reinos hispánicos durante la Baja Edad Media," *Vínculos de Historia*, 3, 2014. Córdoba recommended the research work by Durana and Fernández de Larrea for our own work. They studied the historiography on this topic in "De la lucha de bandos a la hidalguía universal. El País Vasco a fines de la Edad Media" Conference in Vitoria-Gasteiz, June 26-28.

93 Díaz de Durana Ortiz de Urbina, José Ramón; Fernández de Larrea Rojas, Jon Andoni, "La Frontera de malhechores: bandidos, linajes y villas entre Álava, Guipúzcoa y Navarra durante la Baja Edad Media" *Studia Historica*, no. 23, 2005.

94 In the last few decades, however, a group of scholars has ventured deeper into the war of bands producing two research articles as a result. Díaz de Durana Ortiz de Urbina, José Ramón, *La lucha de bandos en el País Vasco: de los parientes mayores a la hidalguía universal: Guipúzcoa, de los bandos a la provincia (s. XIV-a XVI)*, University of the Basque Country, Biblao-Bilbo, 2002. Díaz de Durana y Ortiz de Urbina, José Ramón; Fernández de Larrea Rojas, Jon Andoni, *Los señores de la guerra y de la tierra: nuevos textos para el estudio de los parientes mayores gipuzkoanos (1265–1548)*, Gipuzkoako Foru Aldundia, Donostia-San Sebastián, 2000. A more recent article written along the lines of the prior two is Iosu Etxezarraga Ortuondo's "El laicado y sus institutciones en la configuración religiosa de Gipuzkoa en la Edad Media" (Unpublished thesis, University of the Basque Country, 2017.)

95 Orella Unzué, José Luis, "La hermandad de frontera entre el Reino de Navarra y la provincia de Guipúzcoa siglos XIV-XV," *Príncipe de Viana*, no. 46, Iruñea-Pamplona, 1985.

96 Orella Unzué, José Luis, "Los orígenes de la hermandad de Guipúzcoa (Las relaciones Guipúzcoa-Navarra en los siglos XIII–XIV)" *Vasconia*, no. 3, Donostia-San Sebastián, 1984.

97 Díaz de Durana, José Ramón; Fernández de Larrea, Jon Andoni, "La frontera de malhechores: bandidos, linajes y villas entre Álava, Guipúzcoa y Navarra durante la Baja Edad Media," *Studia Historica*, no. 23, University of Salamanca, Salamanca, 2005: 171–205.

The purpose of these articles was to analyze the borders between Araba, Gipuzkoa, and Navarre at the end of the Middles Ages.

98 *"Gero oinaztarrak izango zirenen ikuspuntutik, gertatutakoa gipuzkoarrek sekula utzi behar izango zuten Gaztelako etxera bueltatzea izan zen. (…) Beste batzuek, berriz, gero ganboatarrak izango zirenek, indarkeriak ezin duela inolako eskubiderik ekarri uste zuten, eta gipuzkoarrek nafarrekin zituzten loturak -hizkuntza, gizarte eta politikan- izaten jarraitu beharko zutela,"* Orella Unzué, José Luis, "Gipuzkoa eta Nafarroaren arteko harremanak 1200. urtean" *Gipuzkoa Versus Castilla*, Conference at Koldo Mitxelena Kulturunea, October 2–4, 2000, Gipuzkoako Foru Aldundia, Donostia-San Sebastián, 2001.

99 Arrieta Elizalde, Idoia, "Donostiaren konkistaren agiri ezkutatuaren aurkezpena: ikerketaren ibilbidea eta ekarpen historiko-kritikoa," in "Euskal lurraldeak eta Nafar Estatua," *Nabarralde Fundazioa*, Txertoa argitaletxea, Donostia-San Sebastián, 2011: 227–248. Arrieta Elizalde, Idoia, *"Getaria: nafar fundazioa duen hiribildua,"* *Berria* Newspaper, September 8, 2009.

100 In the last few years, the Arkeolan Foundation and Zehazten Cultural Services have carried out several archeological projects in the town of Getaria. Both groups have confirmed Getaria as an ongoing populated area since Roman times.

101 These publications provide an interesting perspective on the subject at hand: the journals *Aranzadiana* and *Arkeoikuska*, published since 1987; Benito Domínguez, Ana María, "La arqueología subacuática en el Pais Vasco: una disciplina emergente," *Itsas Memoria, Revista de Estudios Marítimos del País Vasco*, 1, Donostia-San Sebastián, 1996: 277–309; Benito Domínguez, Ana María, *Urpeko Oroimena Euskal Herriko urpeko arkeologia eta ondarea*, Untzi Museum, Donostia-San Sebastián, 2004.

102 Urzainqui Mina, Tomás; Olaizola Iguiñiz, Juan M.ª; *La Navarra marítima*, Pamiela (sixth edition), Iruñea-Pamplona, 2010: 222.

103 Orella Unzué, José Luis, "Historia de Hondarribia en la Alta y Baja Edad Media: desde la fundación hasta finales del siglo XIII," Conference at Zuloaga Etxea, Hondarribiko Historiaren Lagunen Elkartea, Hondarribia, November 2003: 25.

104 Urzainqui Mina, Tomás; Olaizola Iguiñiz, Juan M.ª; *La Navarra marítima*, Pamiela (sixth edition), Iruñea-Pamplona, 2010: 170.

105 Arrieta Elizalde, Idoia, "Donostiaren konkistaren agiri ezkutaren aurkezpena: ikerketaren ibilbidea eta ekarpen historiko-kritikoa," "Euskal lurraldeak eta nafar Estatua," *Nabarralde Fundazioa*, Txertoa argitaletxea, Donostia-San Sebastián, 2011: 227–248. Arrieta Elizalde, Idoia, *"Getaria: nafar fundazioa duen hiribildua,"* *Berria* newspaper, September 8, 2009.

106 Martínez Díez, Gonzalo; González Díez, Emiliano; Martínez Llorente, Félix, *Colección de Documentos Medievales de las Villas de Guipuzcoa (1200–1369)*, Gipuzkoako Foru Aldundia, Zarautz, 1991.

107 *"eo modo quo rex Navarre illud dedit vobis habendum."* The document is included in the aforementioned collection, on page 21. Martínez Díez, Gonzalo; González Díez, Emiliano; Martínez Llorente, Félix, *Colección de Documentos Medievales de las Villas de Guipuzcoa (1200–1369)*, Gipuzkoako Foru Aldundia, Zarautz, 1991: 21.

108 Lope Martínez de Isastiren, *Compendio Historial de Guipuzcoa* (1625), La Gran Enciclopedia Vasca, Bilbao-Bilbo, 1972.

109 *Descripciones geográfico-historicas de los diferentes pueblos de la Provincia de Guipuzcoa y de la ciudad de Donostia-San Sebastián- San Sebastián y su jurisdición con destino a la Real Acadeemia de Madrid, para el Diccionario Geográfico de España 1785–1786.* See section about Getaria.

110 Caro Baroja, Julio, *Los Vascos y la historia a través de Garibay*, Caro Raggio, Madrid, 2002: 40–45.

111 This historian specializes in burgs and is a prolific author on the topic. In this article, I mention only the works she published in Basque, and I cite a few others. Arizaga Bolumburu, Beatriz, *Gipuzkoako Hiri Zaharrak*, Gipuzkoako Foru Aldundia, Donostia-San Sebastián, 1994. Arizaga Bolumburu, Beatriz, *El nacimiento de las villas guipuzcoanas en los s. XIII–XIV*, Sociedad Guipuzcoana de Ediciones y Publicaciones, Donostia-San Sebastián, 1978. Arizaga Bolumburu, Beatriz, *Urbanística Medieval*, Kriseilu, Donostia-San Sebastián, 1990. Arizaga Bolumburu, Beatriz, *Castro Urdiales en la Edad Media: La imagen de la villa*, University of Cantabria, Santander, 2001. Arizaga Bolumburu, Beatriz, *La imagen de la ciudad medieval: la recuperación del paisaje urbano*, Servicio de Publicaciones de la Universidad de Cantabria, Santander 2002. Arizaga Bolumburu, Beatriz (collaboration), *Bizcaya en la Edad Media*, Haranburu D.L., vol. 4., Donostia-San Sebastián, 1985.

112 Garibay y Zamalloa, Esteban de, *Compendio historial de las Chronicas y universal historia de todos los reynos de España, donde se escriven las vidas de los Reyes de Navarra. Escrívese también la sucesión de los Reyes de Francia, y Obispos de la Yglesia de Iruñea* (1571), XII, chapter 32, Sebastián de Comellas, Barcelona, 1628: 734.

113 "*reparar y acrecentar en las marinas della, a las villas de San Sebastián, Fuenteravia, Guetaria y Motrico, dándoles privilegios y confirmaciones de sus buenos usos, costumbres y fueros.*" Garibay y Zamalloa, Esteban de, *Compendio historial de las Chronicas y universal historia de todos los reynos de España, donde se escriven las vidas de los Reyes de Navarra. Escrívese también la sucesión de los Reyes de Francia, y Obispos de la Yglesia de Iruñea (1571)*, XII, chapter 29, Sebastián de Comellas, Barcelona, 1628: 142.

114 "*que el Rey D. Alonso el octavo (a quien se encomendó esta provincia el año 1200) queriendose mostrar grato y remunerador a ella, reedifico en las marinas las villas de Guetaria y Motrico, las cuales fortificó con muy buenas murallas y torres, queriendo predominar en el Oceano Cantábrico: de las de esta villa (Mutrikuren inguruan ari da) solo parecen las ruinas,*" Lope Martínez de Isasti, *Compendio Historial de Guipuzcoa* (1625), La Gran Enciclopedia Vasca, Bilbao-Bilbo, 1972: 586. Garibay y Zamalloa, Esteban de, *Compendio historial de las Chronicas y universal historia de todos los reynos de España, donde se escriven las vidas de los Reyes de Navarra. Escrívese también la sucesión de los Reyes de Francia, y Obispos de la Yglesia de Iruñea (1571)*, XXIV, chapter 17, Sebastián de Comellas, Barcelona, 1628: 201.

115 Orella Unzué, José Luis, "Historia de Hondarribia en la Alta y Baja Edad Media: desde la fundación hasta finales del siglo XIII," Conference at Zuloaga Etxea, Hondarribiko Historiaren Lagunen Elkartea, Hondarribia, November 2003: 25.

116 In this article, the author states that Donostia-San Sebastián and Getaria were the only two burgs of Navarrese origin. Martínez Díez, Gonzalo; "El descontento rural por las villas hace que Guipuzcoa se incline por Castilla," *La Voz de España* newspaper, Donostia-San Sebastián, February 27, 1974: 19.

117 In *Los vascos y la historia a través de Garibay*, Julio Caro Baroja provided the wrong foundation dates for Getaria and attributed the creation of the burg to the king of Castile. My impression is that, given the prestige of the author, many other scholars assumed Baroja's was an accurate rendering of Garibay's words, and have reproduced the mistake until today. The copy I read was funded in part by the Gipuzkoa Provincial Council and published on the thirtieth anniversary of the first edition. Caro Baroja, Julio, *Los Vascos y la historia a través de Garibay*, Caro Raggio, Madrid, 2002: 40–45.

118 *"Garai horretan fundatu zen Donostiako hiria, errege nafar batek sortutako hiri bakarra, hain zuzen, bai baitakigu 1180. urterako bere foru propioekin fundatuta zegoela. Bigarrena 1200etik 1237ra bitartekoa da eta aldi horretan Gipuzkoako itsasertzeko hirien lerroa markatzen da. Hondarribia, Getaria, Mutriku eta Zarautz Alfonso VIII.ak fundatu zituen,"* Arizaga Bolumburu, Beatriz *Gipuzkoako Hiri Zaharrak,* Gipuzkoako Foru Aldundia, Donostia-San Sebastián, 1994.

119 *"XII eta XIII. Mendeetan gauzak aldatzen hasi ziren. Nafarroako erregeak, lehendabizi, eta Gaztelakoak, ondoren, euskal kaiak Europako merkataritza ardatzetan sartu zituzten, Mendearen hasieratik hasiko gara ikusten euskal itsasontziak Mediterraneo eta Atlantikoko portuetan,"* Aragón Ruano, Álvaro, "Euskal Herria 'itsastarra' lehen mundubiraren testuinguruan," *Elkano eta Lehen Mundubira: 500 urte geroago,* Mundubira 500 Elkano Fundazioa, University of the Basque Country-Summer Course of 2009, Donostia-San Sebastián, 2020: 79–80.

120 *"XIII. mendean Gipuzkoan kanpoaldera proiektatzeko aldaketak gauzatu ziren: burdingintzan, itsasgintzan eta merkataritzan."* In the words of Lema Pueyo: "The first [wave of burgs] took place between 1203 and 1237 with the municipal charters of Hondarribia, Getaria, Mutriku and Zarautz, in areas where the presence of human settlements has been documented to prior dates. As we saw in the case of Getaria, King Alfonso VIII's endeavor built upon a prior Navarrese initiative." Lema Pueyo, José Ángel, "De "Ipuzkoa" a la hermandad de villas de Guipuzkoa (ss. VI-XV)" Gipuzkoako Foru Aldundia, Donostia-San Sebastián, 2017: 208.

121 "We omit in this article all references to the most important Gipuzkoan document among all those before 1200; the *fuero* of San Sebastián (1150–1164) issued by King Sancho the Wise to a town that, by then, was witness to heavy commercial and maritime trade, a sign that it must have been at least several decades old." Martínez Díez, Gonzalo, *Guipuzcoa en los albores de su Historia,* Foru Aldundia, Donostia-San Sebastián, 1975: 147.

122 Martínez Díez, Gonzalo, *Alfonso VIII, rey de Castilla y de Toledo,* Burgos, 1995; berriagoa da Martínez Díez, Gonzalo, *Alfonso VIII rey de Castilla y Toledo (1158–1214),* Ediciones Trea, Gijón, 2007: 211.

123 I first presented the documents about the conquest of Donostia-San Sebastián on April 8, 2011, in the article "Ezkutatu diguten: Donostiaren konkista" published in *Berria.* The conferences, presentations and interviews came later. Find more information of the presentation and story of the documents in: Arrieta Elizalde, Idoia, "Donostia-San Sebastiánren Konkistaren Agiri Ezkutatuaren Aurkezpena: Ikerketaren Ibilbidea eta Ekarpen Historiko-Kritikoa" in "Euskal Lurraldeak eta Nafar Estatua," *Nabarralde Fundazioa,* Txertoa argitaletxea, Donostia-San Sebastián, 2011: 229–248.

124 *800 aniversario de la conquista de Alava, Guipuzkoa, y el Duranguesado,* RIEV, no. 45, Donostia-San Sebastián, 2000.

125 *Gipuzkoa versus Castilla. Konkista. Ituna eta eskubide historikoak, 1200–2000,* Kaier collection, Koldo Mitxelena Kulturunea, Gipuzkoako Foru Aldundia, Donostia-San Sebastián, 2000.

126 Arrieta Elizalde, Idoia, *"Donostiaren Konkistaren Agiri Ezkutatuaren Aurkezpena: Ikerketaren Ibilbidea eta Ekarpen Historiko-Kritikoa,"* in "Euskal Lurraldeak eta Nafar Estatua," *Nabarralde Fundazioa,* Txertoa argitaletxea, Donostia-San Sebastián, 2011: 229–248.

127 These publications by Gonzalo Martínez have set a general trend and defined the main line of research among medievalists. Martínez, Díez, Gonzalo, *Guipuzcoa en los albores*

de su historia (siglos X-XII), Gipuzkoako Foru Aldundia, Donostia-San Sebastián, 1975. Martínez Díez, Gonzalo, *Alfonso VIII, rey de Castilla y de Toledo*, Burgos, 1995; or a newer edition Martínez Díez, Gonzalo, *Alfonso VIII rey de Castilla y Toledo (1158–1214)* Ediciones Trea, Gijón, 2007.

128 They are these six chronicles, only one of them is Navarrese: *Chronicon* written by Bishop Lucas de Tuy in 1236; *Anales Toledanos Primeros* or *Crónica de Veinte Reyes*; *De rebus Hispaniae*, written by the then Archbishop of Toledo Rodrigo Jiménez de Rada in 1243; the anonymous *Chronica Latina regum Castellae* from 1236; *Primera Crónica General*; and the collection of diplomatic documents of Alfonso VIII published by Julio González, as well as the collection of documents of King Sancho VII of Navarre. All six chronicles can be found in: Fernández de Larrea, Jon Andoni, "La conquista castellana de Álava, Guipúzcoa y el Duranguesado (1199–1200)," *800 aniversario de la conquista de Alava, Guipuzkoa, y el Duranguesado, RIEV*, no. 45. A deeper analysis of some of them can be found in Lourdes Soria Sesé's article "La historiografía castellana sobre la incorporación de Guipúzcoa a Castilla," *Gipuzkoa versus Castilla. Konkista. Ituna eta eskubide historikoak, 1200–2000*. Kaier collection, Koldo Mitxelena Kulturunea, Gipuzkoako Foru Aldundia, Donostia-San Sebastián, 2000: 111.

129 Labayru and Ortueta, for instance, argued that Gipuzkoa's was a military conquest, based on the testament of Alfonso VIII, which was rescued from history by Father Fita. In fact, a repentant Castilian king requested, in his 1204 testament, that some of the land taken through nefarious ways be returned. Monreal Zia, Gregorio, "1200, una fecha significativa en la evolución de Vasconia," *800 aniversario de la conquista de Alava, Guipuzkoa, y el Duranguesado, RIEV*, no. 45.

130 González, Julio, *El reino de Castilla en la época de Alfonso VIII*, CSIC, vol. I, Madrid, 1960.

131 García de Cortazar, J. A., "La sociedad alavesa medieval antes de la concesión del fuero de Vitoria." *City of Vitoria-Gasteiz*, Vitoria-Gasteiz, 1982.

132 Fortún Pérez de Ciriza, Luis Javier, "La quiebra de la soberanía navarra en Alava, Guipuzcoa y Duranguesado (1199–1200)," *RIEV*, no. 45, Donostia-San Sebastián, 2000.

133 Ayerbe Iribar, M.ª Rosa, "La incorporación de Guipuzcoa a la corona de Castilla (1199/1200)", Euskonews & Media, no.70, 2000: 10–17.

134 Martínez Díez, Gonzalo, *Guipuzcoa en los albores de su historia*, Gipuzkoako Foru Aldundia, Donostia-San Sebastián, 1975.

135 *"(. . .) Don Alfonso de Castillea, que Dios perdone, que la dicha villa conquiso (. . .)" Traslado del fuero de San Sebastián sacado a petición del concejo de Guetaria.* In *Donostia-San Sebastián, on March 4, 1332.* Martínez Díez, Gonzalo; González Díez, Emiliano; Martínez Llorente, Félix, *Colección de Documentos Medievales de las Villas de Guipucoa (1200–1369)*, Gipuzkoako Foru Aldundia, Zarautz, 1991: 173.

136 As far as I am concerned, the document has never been brought forward.

137 I lack the skills to certify that the note was indeed produced by Vargas Ponce himself, but, to me, it looks like his own handwriting.

138 *"(. . .) don Alfonso, fijo del infante don Fernando de Castiella, a qui el drecho del rregnar los rregnos de Castiella por drecha sucessión entegrament partanesce como quiere que de fecho nos lo tenga otro por violencia ocupados et usurpados contra Dios (. . .) riendo descargo las conciencias de nuestros predecessores et nuestra conoscemos et di(zimos) dat que el drecho de auer et heredar la propiedad de las tierras de Ypúzcoa et de Alava et de Rioja et de toda la otra tierra que ha seydo et es del rregno de Navarra es (del rey et de la rreyna de Navarra et de lures sucessores et quanto*

tiempo las ha hombre tenidas (embargadas son) tenidas contra Dios et rrazon et usurpándoles lur drecho (...)," El príncipe Alfonso de Castilla, hijo del infante Fernando de la Cerda, formula un reconocimiento sobre el derecho de propiedad y posesión de las tierras de Guipúzcoa, Álava y Rioja que asiste a la corona de Navarra. En Sangüesa, el 9 de julio de 1330; Martínez Díez, Gonzalo; González Díez, Emiliano; Martínez Llorente, Félix, *Colección de Documentos Medievales de las Villas de Guipucoa (1200–1369),* Gipuzkoako Foru Aldundia, Zarautz, 1991: 169–170.

139   Tomás Urzainqui refers to the document and even transcribes a piece of it but omits the acts of violence. Urzainqui, Tomás, *La Navarra Marítima*, Pamiela (sixth edition), Iruñea-Pamplona, 2010: 260.

140   *"Fuera del largo y prolongado asedio de Vitoria, la incorporación del resto de Álava y de toda Guipúzcoa no fue el fruto de conquistas militares; las numerosas fortalezas le fueron entregadas por sus tenentes pacíficamente, aunque no existiera nungún acuerdo ni pacto colectivo con los mismos, y mucho menos con una supuesta junta guipuzcoana inexistente."* Martínez Díez, Gonzalo, *Alfonso VIII rey de Castilla y Toledo (1158–1214),* Ediciones Trea, Gijón, 2007: 86.

141   Sagredo, Iñaki, *Navarra: Castillos que defendieron el reino,* Pamiela, vol. III, 19, 2007.

142   *"Obtinuit itaque Rex nobilis Aldefonsus Victoriam, Ibidam, Alavam et Guipuscuam."* *"Chronica Latina regum Castellae* reads *"dum duraret obsedio castra omnia circum adiacentia acquisivit ..."* Martínez Díez, Gonzalo, *Guipuzcoa en los albores de su historia (Sglos X-XII),* Gipuzkoako Foru Aldundia, Donostia-San Sebastián, 1975: 152.

143   García de Cortázar, José Ángel, "Cultura en el reinado de Alfonso VIII de Castilla: Signos de un cambio de mentalidades y sensibilidades," II Curso de Cultura-Medieval, Agilar de Campoo, October 1–6, 1990: 172.

144   Ximenez de Rada, Rodericus; *Historia de rebus Hispaniae sive Historia Gothica,* Turnhout, 1987.

145   Cabanes Pecourt, María Dolores, *Crónica Latina de los reyes de Castilla,* (thirteenth century) Anúbar, Zaragoza, 1985: 29–30.

146   Maravall, José Antonio, *El concepto de España en la Edad Media,* Centro de Estudios Constitucionales, Madrid, 2013: 32–35.

147   *"Donostiako foruko kopia notarial batek, 1332an erredaktatuak, XIX. mendeko bertsio batean gordeak, aipatu egiten zuen Alfonso VIII.a: "que la dicha villa conquisó." Aipamen horretan, gerra-ekintza bat ikusi nahi izan da"* (Arrietaren artikulua aipatzen du oharretan) *Halere, conquerir gaztelaniako aditz arkaikoak ez du zertan adierazi eskurapena besterik, eta ez derrigorrean manu militari."* Lema Pueyo, José Ángel, "De 'Ipuzkoa' a la hermandad de villas de Guipuzkoa (ss. VI–XV)," *Gipuzkoaren Historiaren Sintesia,* Gipuzkoako Foru Aldundia, Donostia-San Sebastián, 2017: 206.

148   *"ez dela ezagutzen Nafarroako tenenteen artean Gaztelako bandora pasa zen tenenteen izenik. Aldiz Nafarroako Antso VII. Ari leial mantendu zirela Arabako Gebara eta Mendoza familiak,"* Fernández de Larrea, Jon Andoni, "La conquista castellana de Álava, Guipúzcoa y el Duranguesado (1199–1200)" *RIEV,* Donostia-San Sebastián, 2000: 437.

149   "Another possible obstacle in our historiography, as a result of the lack of historical perspective, is hidden in the trite phrase '[Gipuzkoa's] incorporation into Castile.' This is an easy hurdle to hit if we allocate, without much questioning, the modern meaning of 'union' or 'fusion' to expressions about a political operation of the thirteenth century." I am unable to say which historian used the term 'incorporation" for the first time to refer to this historical event, but he or she certainly used it to express something more moderate than a union or a fusion." Lekuona, Manuel, "Escollos de nuestra Historiografía," *RSBAP/Euskal Herriaren Adiskideen Elkarteko Boletina,* XXVII, 1, 2 books, Donostia-San Sebastián, 1971.

150 Edited by Torregarai Pagola, Elena and Aragón Ruano, Álvaro, *Gipuzkoaren Historiaren Sintesia*, Gipuzkoako Foru Aldundia, Donostia-San Sebastián, 2017.

151 The project launched by the Association of Historians of Gipuzkoa Miguel de Aranburu in 2010 included historians coming from the University of the Basque Country and from private companies specialized in the management of Culture and History.

152 *"Antzinatean, Erromaren hedadurak mesede egin zion Gipuzkoari, eta inperioaren eredu administratibo, ekonomiko, kultural eta erlijiosoak hartzeak onura ekarri zion, sartu baitzen lehenengo aldiz historian konektibitate globalaren bokazio zuen politikoki sorrarazitako sare batean"* "Hiribilduek markatu zuten Gipuzkoako etorkizuneko historia, gero eta gehiago, XIII. mendetik kanpora proiektatzen zena," Lema Pueyo, José Ángel, "De 'Ipuzkoa' a la hermandad de villas de Guipuzkoa (ss. VI–XV)" *Gipuzkoaren Historiaren Sintesia*, Gipuzkoako Foru Aldundia, Donostia-San Sebastián, 2017: 205.

153 *"Errege Katolikoen erregetzaz gero Gaztelako eta Aragoiko koroaren programa inperialean murgilduta, Gipuzkoa egitasmo horren aldezkari nabarmena izan zen gizonak, marinelak, armak, itsasontziak, egurra eta burdina ekarriz. Rol estrategiko horrek zenbait pribilegio garrantzitsu ekarri zizkion probintziari ondorio gisa, zeinak gorde egin ziren foruak deuseztatu arte 1876an,"* edited by Torregarai Pagola, Elena, Aragón Ruano, Álvaro, *Gipuzkoaren Historiaren Sintesia*, Gipuzkoako Foru Aldundia, Donostia-San Sebastián, 2017.

154 Artetxe Fernández, Oihana and Pérez Centeno, Jesús Manuel; "Informe Numismático San Prudentzio, Askizu (Getaria)," SPA.07, February 16, 2009, Zehazten Zerbitzu Kulturalak.

155 Pérez Centeno, Jesús María, Esteban Delgado, Milagros; Alberdi Lonbide, Xabier, "Getaria: Puerto de Gipuzkoa 1209–2009. Avance preliminar de Resultados, 2007 San Martín de Askizu y San Prudencio de Askizu y San Antón Getaria," University of Deusto and Zehazten Z. K., Gipuzkoako Foru Aldundia, Donostia-San Sebastián, foreword of December 19, 2007.

156 Lizana de Salafranca, Joaquín, "Apliques metálicos de la indumentaria militar medieval aragonesa con emblemas heráldicos," *Emblemata*, 3, 1997: 435–438.

157 It is a fact that Castile forcefully invaded Gipuzkoa in 1200 and that it destroyed Getaria. As stated by Esteban de Garibay, chronicler of King Felipe II: "rebuilt the coastal towns of Getaria and Mutriku, and fortified them with robust walls and towers as a way to prevail in the Cantabrian Ocean." He said the wall of Getaria had to be rebuilt, implying it had to have been previously destroyed.

158 The Gipuzkoa Provincial Council sponsored this project along with the City of Getaria.

3

GERNIKA AND VERDUN

A SYMBOL OF BASQUE BIPOLARITY?

Eneko Bidegain

At one time, reflections, and chronicles were written and performed in verse in the Basque Country, as in the cases of Bilintx, Iparragirre, Xenpelar, Elizanburu, Txirrita, and Xalbador. But many others were not so well known. Sets of verses were published in journals, prizes were awarded at the Floral Games, and the Basque Assembly had its own competition, won in 1908 by *bertsolari* (poet-singer) Peio Erramuzpe of Banka (Nafarroa Beherea [Lower Navarre]). His verses were entitled *Euskaldunak eta Gernikako Arbola* (*The Basques and the Tree of Gernika*), and it was unusual for the time for such patriotic verses to be written in the Northern Basque Country. But the most striking thing is not that a farmer from Banka in the early twentieth century was a Basque patriot, but rather that a few years later, the same *bertsolari* composed verses as a Frenchman praising France: *Gerla Haundia* (*The Great War*), about World War I (WWI; 1914–1918).

A single person, perspectives of two different countries, dual loyalties. How is this possible? Here, we will examine these two sets of verses and their messages, and we will try to understand how the same person can be politically both Basque and French at the same time. But we will also bring another hypothesis to the table: do these two sets of verses confirm the influence of WWI in the Frenchification of Basques in the Northern Basque Country?

PEIO ERRAMUZPE

The author of our two sets of verses, Peio Erramuzpe, nicknamed *Manexene*, was born in Banka on October 30, 1880, and died on June 23, 1967, at the age of 86.[1] He was a farmer by trade but earned his name as a *bertsolari*. He got his start at family meals and a few village festivals. However, his emerging ability to write verses was noted by his friends, among them priests, writers, and *bertsolaris* Jean Elizalde (nicknamed *Zerbitzari*) and Jules Moulier (*Oxobi*).[2]

The city council of Banka compiled some of these verses in a small volume that included chronicles of certain events: *Uholdea* (*The Flood*; although undated, it is believed to be about the flood in the Baztan and Baigorri area in 1913),[3] *Kristof Colombo Ameriketako lurretan* (*Christopher Columbus in the Americas*), *The Basques and the Tree of Gernika*, and *The Great War*.

WWI AND THE BASQUE COUNTRY

WWI began on July 28, 1914, when the Austro-Hungarian Empire declared war on Serbia, after which more and more countries joined the war daily. On August 1, France mobilized and drafted all men between the ages of twenty and forty-nine. Soldiers from the Northern Basque Country became all too familiar with battlefields near Charleroi (Belgium) in August and September 1914 and with the trenches near the Ladies' Road in the department of Aisne during most of the war. They also took part in the Battle of Verdun in 1916.

Much has been written in the Basque Country about this war, in the press (in the weekly *Eskualduna*[4] and in *Euzkadi*), in verse and in literature. Piarres Xarriton compiled the chronicles of priest and soldier Jean Saint-Pierre,[6] and of Jean Etxepare,[7] both of whom wrote on site. The chronicles written by Zerbitzari for *Eskualduna* were not collected at the time but were compiled by Patri Urkizu[8] a few years later. Barbier's books were published shortly after the war: *Piarres I*[9] and *Piarres II*,[10] war chronicles to some extent though, as Toledo[11] says, books that are not exactly journalism, nor historical works, nor novels, nor chronicles.

The above authors were all fully sympathetic to WWI and to France. They approved of the war, took great care to be good soldiers, praised France, and presented themselves as French.[12]

Within this pro-France stance, however, there are certain subtleties, as there is a strong bond with the Basque language and the Basque Country in texts by Oxobi[13] and in Barbier's books.[14] This is also the case in the chronicles by Evaristo Buztintza (*Kirikiño*) and Juan Bautista Bilbao (*Batxi*); the latter compiled by Koldo Izagirre and Iñigo Aranbarri in their 1997 book, *Hau mundu arrano hau*.[15]

The verses by Matxin Irabola of Senper received special recognition around the centenary of WWI. Irabola fought in the war, but his verses were nothing at all like those of his contemporaries. He criticized the war and its authorities without mincing words.[16]

Patri Urkizu[17] compiled a great number of verses and letters from WWI during the centenary. His collection includes verses by Txirrita, Kirikiño, Etxahun-Iruri, Zerbitzari, Kepa Enbeita, Luis Ligetx, and various other authors.

More critical accounts of the war in song and in literature date from recent decades. Gorka Knörr's song *Azken agurraren negarra*,[18] for example, is written from a patriotic Basque point of view. In it, a soldier going to war sings, "I am called to take up arms for the French" ("armen hartzera deitzen naute frantsen aldera") and "Leaving the Basque Country and going abroad ..." ("Eskualerritik urrunduz, ta atzerrira joanak ..."). Knörr points out that these Basque soldiers saw France as a foreign land; but this as yet unanalyzed song is not a chronicle of war, but rather an examination from the point of view of the Basque patriotism that reemerged in the 1970s but was rarely mentioned until the centenary. In the Basque Country, the Spanish Civil War (1936) has received much more attention. Outside the Basque Country, WWII overshadowed WWI. On the centenary, however, many new works came out: in music, punk band Kaleko Urdanga's *Morts pour la Patrie (Dead for the Fatherland)*,[19] and in literature, Peruarena's novel, *Su zelaiak (Fields of Fire)*,[20] and Montoia's novel *Hezur gabeko hilak (The Boneless Dead)*,[21] published a few years earlier.

THE NORTHERN BASQUE COUNTRY IN FRANCE

Six thousand Basques from the Northern Basque Country died in WWI, and many others were wounded. This war seems to have been a step toward uniting the Basques of the Northern Basque Country with France. In previous decades, France made great efforts to Frenchify its citizens. In 1870, when France the Third Republic was formed, it was made a priority for all citizens to learn not only the French language[22] but also French history and geography, and French patriotism.[23] Schoolchildren and young people in the military service were also prepared for a possible war of revenge against Germany.[24]

According to Weber, at the end of the nineteenth century, citizens still had no national awareness or ties to the homeland. Townspeople knew their town, but did not see that town as part of a nation, and French city dwellers saw the rural people as uncivilized.[25] The process of urbanization was in conflict with the rural world, and the peasant was a symbol of a backward society, the city of a progressive one.[26] Caron and Vernus state that the retreat of the rural world and the rise of European nationalisms occurred together—the destruction of the rural world created a need for other solidarity networks, such as the nation.[27] On the road to "civilization," the Basques' first contact with a nation or homeland was with France.[28] Elias,[29] Kirsch,[30] and Thiesse[31] also mention the preeminence of France and the French.

According to this account, when the Basques of the Northern Basque Country made the leap from a rural environment to an urban one, they likewise leapt from a Basque identity to a French one. But as Altzibar[32] found, in the late nineteenth and early twentieth centuries, there was also strong support in the Northern Basque County for the Basque homeland, the unity of the seven provinces, and the Basque language. However, in the movement in favor of the Basque language, there was also a move back toward tradition (the Basques joined the conservative French nationalists[33] mentioned by Caron and Vernus).

This suggests that the Basques of the Northern Basque Country had no national awareness until the arrival of French teachings. The Basque patriotism that was spreading at the same time apparently did not reach the farms of Nafarroa Beherea, Lapurdi (Labourd), or Zuberoa (Soule).

TWO SETS OF VERSES

The issues of national awareness that arose in the late nineteenth and early twentieth centuries are reflected in the two sets of verses analyzed below. We will analyze their content and see how the union of Basques from the Northern Basque Country with the French nation is reflected in *The Great War*. Although the verses are not dated, there is a gap of at least ten years between *The Great War* and *The Basques and the Tree of Gernika*. We will first look at the more recent verses to see whether they are consistent with the theory that WWI Frenchified the Basques.

We will then examine the verses in honor of the tree of Gernika. Our aim is not only to compare these with the political stance in the verses about war, but also to see whether Basque peasants felt a connection with the Basque nation before they developed their identification with the French nation.

THE GREAT WAR

These verses are about WWI and were written after the war.

GERLA HAUNDIA[34]

Tune: "Kailla kantuz ogi petik"

I

Hemeretzi ehun eta hamalauko urtean
Agorrilaren lehena atsalde apalean
Ezkila errepiketan aditu nuenean
Ikara bat eman zautan boz harek bihotzean

2
Ezkilak huna zer zion bere boz ozenean
Frantzia gertatzen zela hertsamendu gaitzean
Ene haurrak orai xuti guziak bat batean
Alemana jazarri zaut ero bulta tzarrean

3
Nola primaderan dohan urtzo papo _abarra
Airez aire hegaldatuz hegotik iparrera
Halaber laster joan ginen Alemanen bidera
Haren oldar eroaren nolazpait trabatzera

4
Beljika ttipia zuen lehertu zangopetan
Gu laster xehakatzeko iraganik handikan
Batzu gure alde eta bertzeak heiekilan
Europa gehiena zen ixtante jarri sutan

5
Lehenbiziko guduan nagusitu zitzaukun
Orduan gu ihesari Pariseri ez urrun
Hango armada bat jin zen Marnerat gure lagun
Gudu bakar oste bera izan ote da nehun

6
Marnen garraitu ginuen bainan hark ez etsitu
Bertze gisa batera zen handik goiti jokatu
Satorrek bezala zuen lur azala zilatu
Holaxet nahi gintuen bera gordez garraitu

7
Gu ere hura bezala sartu ginen lurrean
Burdin harizko hesiak emanik aintzinean
Nork erran zer pairatu den zilo heien barnean
Lotseria bat lotzen zaut oraino orroitzean

8
Frantzia buru batean holaxet zen hetsia
Nolazpait gibel aintzinka lau urtez atxikia
Etsaiak ez utzi nahi hartu zuen pozia
Ortzantza iduri ari burdinazk'erauntsia

9
Auhenik eta nigarrik baizik etzen orotan
Herriak gizonetarik hustu ziren bet betan
Emazteak eta haurrak zaharrekin etxetan

Berri txarraren beldurrez zaudelarik gogoetan

10

Gerla itsaso gainean gerla itsaso pean
Lur gainean lur barnean bait'ere airean
Herioa marrumaka beti gure aldean
Ginion: ifernua da jarri orai lurrean

11

Verdungo inguruetan metaka hil gaixuak
Hobirik gabe lurrean iguzkiak belztuak
Asko gorputz ezin erran nola xehakatuak
Biziak heien aldean ja hil bilakatuak

12

Azkenean Jainko Jauna zitzaukun urrikaldu
Ama Birjinak baitzuen guretako otoiztu
Ziloetarik ihesi etsaia abiatu
Bere lurretan sartzean hark bakea galdetu

13

Jondoni Martin goizean lau urteren burian
Su izigarria hil zen eguerdi aintzinean
Foch haundia buruzagi jarri ondar urtean
Harek gidatuz garraitu ginuen azkenean

14

Hamabortz ehun mila hil frantses gizonetarik
Bertze hainbertze mainkertu betikotz ahuldurik
Aita amak nigarretan beren haurrak galdurik
Asko haur gaixo orobat ez dutenak aitarik

15

Gerlan hilez orroit gaiten orai bake denboran
Herriarentzat baitute beren odola eman
Heier esker gure lurra guretako da izan
Jainkoa otoitz dezagun bere ganat har ditzan

THE GREAT WAR

1

In the year nineteen hundred and fourteen
At nightfall on the first of August
When I heard the bell tolling
Its call gave my heart a shiver

2

The bell tolled loudly to say
France is hard pressed
My children, stand together as one now
Germany strikes in a vicious mad attack

3
As in the spring the first crocus shoots
Rise through the air from south to north
So we soon made our way to Germany
To impede its mad aggression

4
They trampled little Belgium under their feet
To then crush us in a great invasion
Some on our side and others on theirs
Most of Europe burst into flames

5
You prevailed over us in the first battle
Then we fled to nearby Paris
An army came from there to the Marne to help us
Has any place seen such a host in a single battle?

6
We were victorious in the Marne but they did not give up
From then on it was conducted a different way
Like moles they dug in the earth
Wanting to defeat us by hiding

7
Like them we also went into the ground
Iron wire fences before us
Who could say what was suffered in those trenches?
Fear grips me even now when I remember

8
France was sorely besieged on one side
Advancing and retreating for four years somehow
Blocking the enemy with a good will
The iron storm sounded like thunder

9
Sobbing and sorrows all around
The villages were emptied of men
Wives and children at home with the elderly
Minds prey to fear of bad news

10
War on the sea war under the sea
On the ground, under the ground and in the air
Death ever howling by our side
And we said surely hell has come to earth
11
Mounds of the piteous dead around Verdun
Lying without graves, blackened by the sun
Who could say how these countless bodies were torn apart
Survivors dying at their sides
12
In the end, the Lord God took pity on us
The Virgin Mary prayed for us
The enemy abandoned the trenches and fled
Back in their own land they begged for peace
13
Four years later in the morning of Saint Martin's day
The terrible fire was quenched before noon
The great Foch made commander in the final year
In the end we were victorious under his leadership
14
Fifteen hundred thousand Frenchmen killed
So many others wounded, forever crippled
Fathers and mothers weeping for their lost children
And so many poor children fatherless
15
Now in times of peace let us pray for our war dead
They gave their blood for our country
Thanks to them our land is still ours
Let us pray that God will take them unto Himself

A CHRONICLE OF WAR

Erramuzpe's *The Great War* is first and foremost a chronicle of WWI. He narrates the war chronologically, in fifteen verses, highlighting particular events.

The first half of these verses are about the beginning of the war. Another three provide general information. One verse is devoted to the Battle of Verdun. The twelfth and thirteenth verses are about the end of the war, and the last two assess it.

The verses begin with the declaration of war. The first two lines of the first verse give the date ("In the year nineteen hundred and fourteen / At nightfall on the first of August"; "Hemeretzi ehun eta hamalauko urtean /Agorrilaren lehena atsalde apalean"), though saying only that bells were heard ("When I heard the bell tolling"; "Ezkila errepiketan aditu nuenean"), and that the sound of the bells was terrible ("Its call gave my heart a shiver"; "Ikara bat eman zautan boz harek bihotzean"). The second verse states that conflict has broken out between Germany and France, but does not use the word "war," saying instead that France is "hard pressed" and Germany launches a "vicious mad attack" whose result is the need to mobilize. The *bertsolari* himself calls on people to mobilize: "My children, stand together as one now" ("Ene haurrak orai xuti guziak bat batean").

The third verse portrays the soldiers going to war ("we soon made our way to Germany"; "laster joan ginen Alemanen bidera"), while the fourth gives geostrategic details: Germany invaded Belgium, attacked France, and divided Europe in two— "Some on our side and others on theirs" ("Batzu gure alde eta bertzeak heiekilan"). The war then spreads throughout Europe ("Most of Europe burst into flames"; "Europa gehiena zen ixtante jarri sutan").

The fifth, sixth, and seventh stanzas are about the first two months of the war. In only two lines of the fifth stanza does Erramuzpe recount war movements and the retreat of the French army. Without going into the details of the massacre suffered by the French army near Belgium ("You prevailed over us in the first battle"; "Lehenbiziko guduan nagusitu zitzaukun"), the second line briefly mentions that the French retreated to Paris ("Then we fled to nearby Paris"; "Orduan gu ihesari Pariseri ez urrun"). More lines are devoted to France's victory in the Battle of the Marne than to the failure of France and its allies: "Has any place seen such a host in a single battle?" ("Gudu bakar oste bera izan ote da nehun") (end of the fifth stanza), and "We were victorious in the Marne but ..." ("Marnen garraitu ginuen bainan ...") (beginning of the sixth).

Two full stanzas are devoted to the trench warfare that began after the Battle of the Marne, mentioning only its beginning, even though trench warfare was a tactic used throughout most of the four years of the war.

Erramuzpe touches on general war information. He describes the four-year "advance-and-retreat" war in the eighth stanza. In the next, he discusses the suffering and the strife at home caused by the war. The tenth stanza describes the extent of the war ("War on the sea war under the sea / On the ground, under the ground and in the air"; "Gerla itsaso gainean gerla itsaso pean / Lur gainean lur barnean bait'ere airean").

Although Erramuzpe notes the importance of Marne, only one other battle is discussed, the Battle of Verdun, in the eleventh stanza. Verdun became a symbol of WWI because it was a long (February 21 to December 18, 1916) and especially violent battle. The French army lost 163,000 soldiers, and Germany lost 143,000. All regiments of the French army took part in the battle, in turns. Some six hundred Basque soldiers died at Verdun, 10 percent of those who died throughout the war.[35]

The next two stanzas present the end of the war as God's decision ("In the end, the Lord God took pity on us / The Virgin Mary prayed for us;" "Azkenean Jainko Jauna zitzaukun urrikaldu / Ama Birjinak baitzuen guretako otoiztu"). The thirteenth stanza recounts the armistice of November 11, 1918, and the final two stanzas sum up the war: how many dead and wounded, and the resultant circumstances at home. The author closes with political consequences: "Thanks to them our land is still ours" ("Heier esker gure lurra guretako da izan").

THE DARK SIDE

Erramuzpe also deals with the dark side of war, which did not appear often in wartime chronicles and verses. Those published in *Eskualduna*, for example, always bore messages of hope. Of course, information was censored during the war, so that Germany would have access to as little information as possible about the French army and so that people would not be alarmed.[36]

Erramuzpe's verses date from after the war, so he was able to report what had happened freely and more realistically. There was no mention in the daily news that Germany had defeated France in Belgium, but Erramuzpe states clearly that the Germans had "prevailed" and that they remained strong after the Battle of the Marne (fifth stanza).

Wartime chronicles suggest that soldiers went happily to the front, thinking they would win easily and return home soon. Erramuzpe reflects this initial optimism with a metaphor in testament to their innocence: "As in the spring the first crocus shoots / Rise through the air from south to north / So we soon made our way to Germany" ("Nola primaderan dohan urtzo papo abarra / Airez are hegaldatuz hegotik iparrera / Halaber laster joan ginen Alemanen bidera"). Nevertheless, he confesses that the bell announcing the war "gave [his] heart a shiver" ("ikara bat eman" ziola "bihotzean").

Living conditions in the trenches also appeared rarely in chronicles. Although there were some descriptions, there were few complaints about the harshness of the conditions. Erramuzpe, however, uses the words "suffer" and "fear": "Who could say what was suffered in those trenches? / Fear grips me even now when I remember" ("Nork erran zer pairatu den zilo heien barnean / Lotseria bat lotzen zaut oraino orroitzean") (seventh stanza).

This situation could be understood as heroic (as perhaps suggested in soldiers' letters that were published), but Erramuzpe also offers a bleak reading of
the human consequences of war (eleventh and fourteenth stanzas). He provides
details about Verdun that were kept quiet at the time: "Mounds of the piteous
dead . . . / Lying without graves, blackened by the sun / Who could say how
these countless bodies were torn apart" (" . . . metaka hil gaixuak / Hobirik gabe
lurrean iguzkiak belztuak / Asko gorputz ezin erran nola xehakatuak"); and calls
war "hell" (tenth stanza): "And we said surely hell has come to earth" ("Ginion:
ifernua da jarri orai lurrean").

In the fourteenth stanza, Erramuzpe states that 150,000 Frenchmen died,
and is disturbed at the thought of their families: "Fathers and mothers weeping for their lost children / And so many poor children fatherless" ("Aita amak
nigarretan beren haurrak galdurik / Asko haur gaixo orobat ez dutenak aitarik").
In the ninth stanza, he describes their grief ("Sobbing and sorrows all around";
"Auhenik eta nigarrik baizik etzen orotan" and "Minds prey to fear of bad news";
"Berri txarren beldurrez zaudelarik gogoetan"), as well as his own sorrow at the
emptiness of the villages and houses ("The villages were emptied of men /
Wives and children at home with the elderly"; "Herriak gizonetarik hustu ziren
bet betan / Emazteak eta haurrak zaharrekin etxetan").

UNITED WITH FRANCE

Erramuzpe clearly takes one side of the war, not as an outside observer, but as
a participant. Specifically, he almost always uses the first-person plural in references to France and the French army: "To then crush us" and "Some on our
side" (fourth stanza); "you prevailed over us," "Then we fled" and "to the Marne
to help us" (fifth); "We were victorious in the Marne" and "wanting to defeat
us" (sixth); "Like them we also . . ." (seventh); "by our side" (tenth); "took pity
on us" and "prayed for us" (twelfth); "we were victorious" (thirteenth); and "our
land is still ours" (fifteenth).

When he speaks about France using the first person, this indicates that
he feels himself to be part of France. *Eskualduna* used the same technique
in its published chronicles, news items, and verses about WWI.[37] Erramuzpe
also demonstrates a pro-France stance in calling for the defense of France
and for praise for those who have died for France: "My children, stand
together as one now." ("Ene haurrak orai xuti guziak bat batean") he says in
the second stanza, true to the mobilization. Finally, he calls for a prayer for
the dead: "let us pray for our war dead" ("gerlan hilez orroit gaiten"), and
"Let us pray that God will take them unto Himself" ("Jainkoa otoitz dezagun bere ganat har ditzan").

His loyalty to France is also evident in how he speaks about France vs. how he speaks about Germany. In the second stanza, France is the victim ("France is hard pressed"; "Frantzia gertatzen dela hertsamendu gaitzean"), and Germany the aggressor ("Germany strikes in a vicious mad attack"; "Alemana jazarri zaut ero bulta tzarrean"). And he links the Germans with insanity in the third stanza ("its mad aggression"), describes their aggression in the fourth ("They trampled little Belgium under their feet"; "Beljika ttipia zuen lehertu zangopean"), and later compares them to moles ("Like moles they dug in the earth"; "Satorrek bezala zuen lur azala zilatu"). He also mentions the Germans' stubbornness and strategy in the sixth stanza: Germany did not give up after the Battle of the Marne and hoped to defeat France by moving into the trenches.

At the same time, Erramuzpe praises the French army. In the thirteenth stanza, he describes General Foch as "great" and writes that victory was achieved under his guidance. In contrast, he portrays the Germans' humiliation at the end of the war: "The enemy abandoned the trenches and fled / Back in their own land they begged for peace" ("Ziloetarik ihesi etsaia abiatu / Bere lurretan sartzean hark bakea galdetu").

In the fourteenth stanza, Erramuzpe mentions only how many Frenchmen were killed; he shows no interest in the dead of other nationalities. Furthermore, as his French account is in the first person, it is thought that he numbers the Basques who died among those Frenchmen. In the final stanza, he makes it clear that he considers the Northern Basque Country part of France: "Thanks to [those who died in the war] our land is still ours" ("[gerlan hil diren] haier esker gure lurra guretako da izan").

THE BASQUES AND THE TREE OF GERNIKA

Did Erramuzpe always feel this link with France? The verses he wrote six years before WWI began might raise some doubts since, according to these verses, which won him an honorable mention in the Basque Assembly's 1908 competition in Atharratze, he was loyal to the Basque Country. He clearly praises the Basque Country in *The Basques and the Tree of Gernika*. Speaking about the Tree of Gernika in his first stanza, he wrote, "You tell the world about / The bond among the seven great Basque peoples" ("Zeren zaukun hedatzen orotarat ari / Zazpi Eskual Herri ederren lokarri").

These verses have patriotic themes: the brotherhood and unity among all Basques, that even in death the tree survives, criticism of subordination to France, and loyalty to the Basque language.

ESKUALDUNAK ETA GERNIKAKO ARBOLA[38]

(honorable mention at the Euskaltzaleen Biltzarra awards in Atharratze in 1908)

Tune: "Gitarra xahar-xahar bat dut nik ene laguna"

1

Eskualdunek ohore egun Gernikari
Hango arbola eder xoragarriari
Zeren zaukun hedatzen orotarat ari
Zazpi Eskual Herri ederren lokarri

2

Elgar maitatzen dugu Eskualdun guziek
Anaiatasun batez haundi'ta ttipiek
Nahiz bi aldetarat gauzkaten mendiek
Gernikako haritza lokarri zazpiek

3

Orok erraiten zuten eroria zela
Eskualdunak betikotz galduak ginela
Bainan laster berri bat etorri zaukula
Hil badare umeak azkar dituela

4

Mil urte iraganik azkenean hil zen
Gur'arbaso zaharrak harat ziren biltzen
Eskualdunen zuzenak handikan beiratzen
Elgarrekin suharki hantxet hitz egiten

5

Españan Gernikako arbolaren pean
Frantzian Uztaritzen Haitzeko gainean
Ikusgarriak ziren bat ala bertzean
Beren zuzenen alde mintzo zirenean

6

Uztarizko biltzarra aspaldi galdua
Seietan hogoi urte badu hurbildua
Orhoitzapenak dauku arintzen gogoa
Estekan dugulakotz geroztik lepoa

7

Oraino irauten du Gernikan biltzarrak
Han dire bateratzen Eskualdun zuhurrak
Odol asko zainetan bihotzez suharrak
Inoiz ez du baratu etsaien beldurrak

8

Arbola saindu hura bizi zelarikan
Ordaina utzi zuen bere hazitikan
Ama hila aldean han da geroztikan
Haundi ta azkar doha beti indarretan

9
Mende hunen hastean haitz gazte hartarik
Zazpi ezkur zituzten ezarri erainik
Eskual Herri bezanbat hola berexirik
Agertu ote dira zazpiak sorturik

10
Zazpi erainetarik bortz dira agertu
Biga lurrean dira sort'gabe gelditu
Biga galtze hortarik zer ote da heldu
Nahiago ginuke ez balire galdu

11
Landare hetarikan bat guri igorri
Orduan bozkarioz oro gira jarri
Bihotzez amodio ezpainetan irri
Uztaritze Haitzean landaturik zarri

12
Oi Gernikaren ume parerik gabea
Atsegin da guretzat zure ikustea
Zu zira orai gure kontsolatzailea
Libertate sainduko arbola maitea

13
Arbola saindua du orai Uztaritzek
Ohora dezagula Frantses Eskualdunek
Besta gaitzak eginez hortako guziek
Pilota dantza eta bertsuak zonbaitek

14
Hori zen lehenago toki hautatua
Hor egiten baitzuten biltzar aipatua
Haundi ta azkar zaite arbola saindua
Gutaz izanen zira beti maitatua

15
Toki horren gainean gure aitek lehen
Orhoit gaiten guziak zer egiten zuten
Batasunean zuten suhar hitz egiten
Eskualdunen zuzenak oso egon ziten

16
Gizon bedera zohan herri bakotxetik
Biltzar denbora zuten iragaiten xutik
Ororen buruzagi zena zen bakarrik
Harrizk'alki batean egoiten jarririk
17
Ikusgarri ederrak ziren denboretan
Orhoitzapena dugu orai bihotzetan
Odolikan duguno guhaurek zainetan
Eskualdun izan gaiten hitz eta obretan
18
Ez bagir'Eskualdunak lehen bezain handi
Apaldu gabe xutik beden gaiten geldi
Gernikako arbola dugula lokarri
Beti tink atxikiak bihotzez elgarri
19
Eskuarazko hizkuntza atxikiz mihian
Berdinikan ez baitu lurraren gainian
Lehengo fede bera horrekin batean
Zeruan izaiteko eternitatean

THE BASQUES AND THE TREE OF GERNIKA
1
Basques honor Gernika today
Its beautiful splendid tree
You tell the world about
The bond among the seven great Basque peoples
2
All Basques love one another
In brotherhood, big and small
Though the mountains split us in two
The oak of Gernika binds all seven
3
Everyone said it had fallen
We Basques were lost forever
But soon a new one came to us
Even in death its young were strong
4
It died after a thousand years

Our ancient ancestors used to gather there
Looking after the Basques' rights
Speaking with each other ardently there

5
In Spain under the tree of Gernika
In France on the Rock of Uztaritz
They were spectacular in one place and the other
When they spoke up for their rights

6
The Uztaritz assembly is long gone
Lost nearly six score years ago
Memory eases our minds
Our necks have been in the yoke ever since

7
The Gernika Assembly endures
There wise Basques gather
Blood strong in their veins and brave of heart
Our enemies' fears never ceased

8
While that sacred tree lived
It left a replacement in its seeds
Since the mother tree died it has been there
Growing big and strong in her strength

9
At the beginning of this century from that young rock
Seven acorns were planted
As special as the Basque Country
Would all seven sprout and appear?

10
Of the seven sown five appeared
Two remained in the ground without growing
What happened to the two that were lost?
We would have preferred that it were not so

11
One of these plants was sent to us
Then we rejoiced all around
With love in our hearts and a smile on our lips
Arisen from the Uztaritz Rock

12

Oh incomparable child of Gernika
We are delighted to see you
You are now our consolation
Beloved tree of holy liberty

13
Uztaritz now has a holy tree
Let all French Basques honor it
all of us from there celebrating
With pelota, dancing and verses

14
That was the place chosen earlier
Where our assembly was held
Grow be strong, holy tree
You will always be loved by us

15
Our fathers before us at that place
Let us all remember what they did
Speaking ardently in unity
For the full rights of the Basques

16
One man from each of the peoples
Stood at assembly time
Only the leader of them all
Seated on a bench of rock

17
These were beautiful sights in their time
We hold the memories in our hearts now
We ourselves have the blood in our veins
In the words and deeds that make us Basque

18
If we are not as great as the Basques were before
At least set us stand tall
The tree of Gernika is our bond
Ever binding our hearts together

19
Safeguarding the Basque language on our tongues
There is nothing else like it on earth
With the same faith as before
May it hold its place in heaven for all eternity

A LOOK AT HISTORY

In contrast to *The Great War*, these verses are not written as a chronicle, nor do they follow chronological order. However, as in other sets of verses, Erramuzpe shows his interest in history. In the sixteenth stanza, he says that the tree of Gernika has survived for a thousand years, and that "our ancient ancestors" ("gur'arbaso zaharrak") used to gather there.

His next reference to history is to the lost Uztaritz Assembly in the sixth stanza, whose third line notes the importance of history: "Memory eases our minds" ("Orhoitzapenak dauku arintzen gogoa"). That is, remembering our past can lift our spirits; we need to know history to know who we are. Erramuzpe refers to memory again in the seventeenth stanza, after describing the assemblies in the fifteenth and sixteenth stanzas.

Erramuzpe does not mention democracy, but we are given to understand from his description that these structures focused on assembly rather than on authoritarianism. Specifically, the assemblies were gathering places and places for discussion: "Speaking with each other ardently there" ("Elgarrekin suharki hantxet hitz egiten") (fourth stanza); "Where our assembly was held" ("Hor egiten baitzuten biltzar aipatua") (fourteenth); and "Speaking ardently in unity" ("Batasunean zuten suhar hitz egiten") (fifteenth). In the seventeenth stanza, he says that the assemblies were "beautiful sights" ("ikusgarri ederrak"), and in the sixteenth he explains that they consisted of representatives of each of the seven peoples ("One man from each of the peoples"; "Gizon bedera zohan herri bakotxetik").

RIGHTS AND FREEDOM

In his description of these assemblies, Erramuzpe praises the charters that the Basques once had. Each province of the Basque Country had its own assembly and its own autonomy, until these were gradually lost in the eighteenth and nineteenth centuries. He emphasizes repeatedly that these assemblies guaranteed the rights of the Basques. The Tree of Gernika "[looked] after the Basques' rights" ("euskaldunen zuzenak [...] beiratzen") he writes in the fourth stanza. In the next stanza, he applauds defending those rights, in both Gernika and Uztartiz: "They were spectacular in one place and the other / When they spoke up for their rights" ("Ikusgarriak ziren bat ala bertzean / Beren zuzenen alde mintzo zirenean"). In the fifteenth stanza as well, he explains that the Basques' ancestors had spoken in those places, "For the full rights of the Basques" ("Eskualdunen zuzenak oso egon ziten").

Erramuzpe considers these rights to be extremely important and describes the tree of Gernika as the "Beloved tree of holy liberty" ("Libertate sainduko arbola maitea") (twelfth stanza).

Lapurdi, Nafarroa Beherea, and Zuberoa lost their assemblies and autonomy in 1789 as a result of the French Revolution. Erramuzpe refers to this in the seventh stanza ("The Uztaritz assembly is long gone"; "Uztarizko biltzarra aspaldi galdua"), explaining that the loss had occurred almost "six score years" ("seietan hogoi urte") earlier and that the Basques were then oppressed: "Our necks have been in the yoke ever since" ("Estekan dugulakotz geroztik lepoa").

Given that loss, Erramuzpe sees a different function of the tree of Gernika, that of "our consolation" (tenth stanza), again emphasizing the importance of history and of the symbols of the Basque Country.

UNITY AND DIVISION

To Erramuzpe, the tree of Gernika is both a symbol of those freedoms and of the unity of the Basques, which he praises. In the second stanza, he says that the "oak of Gernika" is the "bond" among the seven peoples and emphasizes that "all Basques" love each other "in brotherhood."

Nevertheless, he recognizes that the Basque Country is divided between two states ("Though the mountains split us in two"; "Nahiz bi aldetarat gauzkaten mendiek"), however, the tree of Gernika is the bond among all. He cites the mountains as the reason for the division, but later (fifth stanza) mentions Spain and France: "In Spain under the tree of Gernika / In France on the Rock of Uztaritz" ("Españan Gernikako arbolaren pean / Frantzian Uztaritzen Haitzeko gainean").

In stanzas nine through eleven, Erramuzpe again identifies the tree of Gernika as a gathering place for the Basques, and states that the plants growing from the seven acorns taken from the tree ("Seven acorns were planted"; "Zazpi ezkur zituzten ezarri erainik") will go to the seven provinces. In the eleventh stanza, he says that one of those plants was sent to Lapurdi, where it brought great joy ("Then we rejoiced all around / With love in our hearts and a smile on our lips"; "Orduan bozkarioz oro gira jarri / Bihotzez amodio ezpainetan irri").

In the eighteenth stanza as well, he notes the ability of the tree of Gernika to unite the Basques: "The tree of Gernika is our bond / Ever binding our hearts together" ("Gernikako arbola dugula lokarri / Beti tink atxikiak bihotzez elgarri"). For Erramuzpe, the solidarity and unity of the Basques are of the utmost importance.

LOVE FOR THE PEOPLE

Erramuzpe expresses his pride in being Basque in several verses. First, he says that the Basques honor Gernika (first stanza). He calls the shoot taken from the tree "incomparable child" (twelfth stanza) and promises that the Basques will always love it (fourteenth). He also praises the Basque language, saying that

"There is nothing else like it on earth" ("Berdinikan ez baitu lurraren gainian"; nineteenth stanza). He speaks about the Basques' blood (by which we understand their strength and vigor) in two stanzas: "Blood strong in their veins and brave of heart" ("Odol asko zainetan bihotzez suharrak") (seventh) and "We ourselves have the blood in our veins" ("Odolikan duguna guhaurek zainetan") (seventeenth).

Erramuzpe wants to see the Basques survive. He refers in the third stanza to the belief that they were a people on the brink of death: "Everyone said it had fallen / We Basques were lost forever ("Orok erraiten zuten eroria zela / Eskualdunak betikotz galduak ginela"). That is, should the tree of Gernika fall, the Basques would also disappear. At the beginning of the twentieth century it was widely believed that the Basques would disappear. But Erramuzpe is happy because the shoots from the dead tree are strong. He believes that the Basque Country is still strong, as he wants it to be: "We ourselves have the blood in our veins / In the words and deeds that make us Basque" ("Odolikan duguno guhaurek zainetan / Eskualdun izan gaiten hitz eta obretan") (seventeenth stanza).

In closing, he expresses his desire for the Basque language to survive: "Safeguarding the Basque language on our tongues [. . .] May it hold its place in heaven for all eternity" ("Eskuarazko hizkuntza atxikiz mihian [. . .] Zeruan izaiteko eternitatean").

But the end of the seventh stanza deserves further examination: "Our enemies' fears never ceased" ("Inoiz ez du baratu etsaien beldurrak"). A few years later, in his verses about WWI, he describes the Germans as the enemy. Here, however, we understand the enemies to be Spain and France, who stole the Basques' "holy liberty" ("libertate saindua").

In short, the message of this set of verses is completely patriotic: Erramuzpe praises the unity of the Basques, bemoans the loss of their rights, wants the Basque language and people to live for all eternity, and names those against the Basques as enemies.

FROM GERNIKA TO VERDUN: WHAT CHANGED?

Although in his verses about the tree of Gernika, Erramuzpe says, "In Spain under the tree of Gernika" ("Españan Gernikako arbolaren pean") and "In France . . . [in] Uztaritz" ("Frantzian Uztaritzen") (fifth stanza), and "French Basques" ("Frantses euskaldunak") (thirteenth stanza), all the stanzas nevertheless fully uphold the Basque Country and focus on the Basque Country and its unity.

How then are we to interpret the French patriotism that appears in his verses about WWI? Could Erramuzpe's political views have changed? Did the patriotism that he showed in his 1908 set of verses fade? Or did his loyalty to France increase? Or was he loyal to both countries before and after the war?

The contrast between these two sets of verses supports the idea that WWI was a key event in the Frenchification of the Basques. And Erramuzpe himself fought in the war, as did his brothers.

Erramuzpe went to war on August 31, 1914, and remained in service until February 21, 1919.[39] There were nine children in his family, and seven brothers were eligible to go to war.

Jean (born November 20, 1881) went to war on June 18, 1917, first with the Twelfth Infantry Regiment, and then, beginning on August 30, 1917, with the 335th.[40]

Bertrand (July 20, 1883) was an objector and did not report for the draft. On August 7, 1920, he was removed from the list of objectors and reported to the army offices in Bayonnne. Bertrand lived in the United States, in Reno, Nevada, in 1906 and in Ogden, Utah, in 1910.[41]

Sauveur (April 5, 1885) went to war early, on August 4, 1914. He received two recognitions and a War Cross for his service as a "very good soldier."[42]

Jean (November 14, 1886) joined the army on August 2, 1914, but was not sent to war until October 22, 1916. He was a very good soldier and was awarded a War Cross. In 1916, he was wounded in the thigh. After the war, he lived in San Francisco and Seattle.[43]

Gaston (September 27, 1888) went to war with the American army on November 6, 1917. He was initially considered an objector because he had not reported for the draft. However, by then he was living in the United States, in Ogden, Utah, like his brother Bertrand. Even though he did ultimately fight in the war, in 1922 he was condemned to six months in jail for being an objector. He later lived in Geneva, Idaho and Rock Springs, Wyoming.[44]

Jean (October 28, 1890) did not go to war. In 1914, he was living in Rock Springs, where he remained until 1925, when he moved to Geneva, Idaho.[45]

RESULTS: A DEAD OFFSHOOT?

One conclusion that can be drawn from a comparison of these two sets of verses is that, after having fought in the war for four years for France, Erramuzpe's loyalty to France increased, as it did in others. But the patriotism that is so apparent in the verses about the tree of Gernika shows us that it is not entirely true that by the end of the nineteenth century, national loyalties lay with France. Although we cannot generalize, it is clear that Basque patriotism was present on the farms of the Northern Basque Country. A sprig of patriotism remained.

It was a young shoot, however, and fragile. France's efforts to civilize and Frenchify its citizens were far greater. And with WWI, the emerging sprigs of Basque patriotism were uprooted. These verses written by Erramuzpe before and after the war bear witness.

RESOURCES

Altzibar, Xabier. "Zazpiak bat gaia XIX. Mendean (The zazpiak bat topic in the XIXth century)." In Antoine d'Abbadie (1897–1997), Congrès International Eusko Ikaskuntza, Ez ohizko kongresua. Eskualtzaindia. XIV biltzarra, 663–68. Donostia: Eusko Ikaskuntza, 1998.

Arrizurieta, Irene. "1913ko uholdeak gogoan." Berria, June 1, 2013. https://www.berria.eus/paperekoa/1562/046/001/2013-06-01/1913ko-uholdeak-gogoan.htm. Accessed December 8, 2021.

"Bankako bertsulari ohien koblak." Banka: Euskal Kultur Erakundea eta Bankako Herria, 2013.

Barbier, Jean. Piarres I. Ramon Sanchez edition. Donostia: Euskal Editoreen Elkartea, 1992.

———. Piarres II. Ane Loidi edition. Donostia: Euskal Editoreen Elkartea, 1996.

Bidegain, Eneko. Gerla Handia, muga sakona. Donostia: Utriusque Vasconiae, 2009.

———. "Lehen Mundu Gerra." Eskualduna, 29. Iker. Bilbo: Euskaltzaindia, 2013.

———. Lehen Mundu Gerra eta Euskal Herria. Baiona: Elkar, 2014.

Bilbao, J. B., and Juan Bautista Bilbao Elgezabal. Hau mundu arrano hau 1914-1916. Zarautz: Susa, 1997.

Caron, Jean-Claude, and Michel Vernus. L'Europe au XIXe siècle: des nations aux nationalismes: 1815–1914. Paris: Colin, 1996.

Charriton, Piarres. Jean Etchepare mirikuaren idazlanak. III. Kazetaritza (A) (1903–1915). Donostia: Elkar, 1988.

———. Jean Etchepare mirikuaren idazlanak. IV. Kazetaritza (B) (1916–1935). Donostia: Elkar, 1992.

Dolosor, Franck. Matxin Irabola: senpereko bertsularia. Baiona: Elkar, 2010.

Elias, Norbert. La civilisation des mœurs. Translated by Pierre Kamnitzer. Paris: Agora, 1985.

Elissalde, Jean. LVII.a gerlan. Patri Urkizu edition. Irun: Alberdania, 1995.

Forcade, Olivier. La censure politique en France pendant la Grande Guerre. Thèse de doctorat, Université Paris-X Nanterre, 1999.

Gerbod, Paul. L'éthique héroïque en France (1870–1914)." Revue Historique, October 1982: 409–29.

Kaleko Urdangak. Morts Pour La Patrie. EP. Vis Vires. Iruñea: Tough Ain't Enough Records, 2019. https://open.spotify.com/track/10IWFMRGFdqWj4eKJrAOwp. Accessed December 9, 2021.

Kirsch, Fritz Peter. Ecrivains au carrefour des cultures: études de littérature occitane, française et francophone = Estudis de literatura occitana, francesa e francofona. Pessac: Presses Universitaires de Bordeaux, 2000.

Knörr, Gorka. Nik nahi dudana. LP. Artezi, 1975.

Lestocquoy, Jean. Histoire du patriotisme en France. Des origines à nos jours. Paris: Albin Michel, 1968.

Montoia, Xabier. Hezur gabeko hilak. Zarautz: Susa, 1999.

Peruarena Ansa, Mikel. Su zelaiak. Zarautz: Susa, 2014.

Saint-Pierre, Jean "Anxuberro." 14eko Gerla Handia. Piarres Xarriton edition. Klasikoak collection. Donostia: Euskal Editoreen Elkartea, 1998.

Sohier, Anne. "L'enfant et la guerre à l'école primaire: en Bretagne 1871–1914." In Mémoire et trauma de la Grande Guerre. Bretagne, Catalogne, Corse, Euskadi, Occitanie, by Gwendal Denis, 11–30. Rennes: Rennes 2 Université Haute Bretagne, 2010.

Soule, Beñat. Neurtizlari Bertsulari Iparraldez. Bilbo: Euskalzaleen Biltzarra, 2011.

Thiesse, Anne-Marie. Ils apprenaient la France: l'exaltation des régions dans le discours patriotique. Paris: Éditions de la Maison des Sciences de l'Homme, 1997.

Toledo Lezeta, Ana María. "Jean Barbier-en 'Piarres' XX. mendearen lehen erdiko euskal eleberrigintzan." Fontes linguae vasconum: Studia et documenta 50, No. 125 (2018): 221–50.

Urkizu, Patri. 1914–1918 lekukoak. Baiona: Maiatz, 2015.

Vigier, Philippe. "Régions et régionalisme en France au XIXe siècle." In Régions et régionalisme en France du XVIIIe siècle à nos jours, edited by Christian Gras and Georges Livet, 161–76. Paris: Presses Universitaires de France, 1977.

Weber, Eugen. La fin des terroirs, la modernisation de la France rurale, 1870–1914. Translated by Antoine Berman and Bernard Genies. Paris: Fayard, 1984.

NOTES

1   Beñat Soule, Neurtizlari Bertsulari Iparraldez (Bilbo: Euskalzaleen Biltzarra, 2011), 136.

2   "Bankako bertsulari ohien koblak" (Banka: Euskal Kultur Erakundea eta Bankako Herria, 2013), 4.

3   Irene Arrizurieta, "1913ko uholdeak gogoan," Berria, June 1, 2013 , https://www.berria. eus/paperekoa/1562/046/001/2013-06-01/1913ko-uholdeak-gogoan.htm.   Accessed December 8, 2021.

4   Eneko Bidegain, "Lehen Mundu Gerra 'Eskualduna' astekarian" 29, Iker (Bilbo: Euskaltzaindia, 2013).

5   Eneko Bidegain, Gerla Handia, muga sakona (Donostia: Utriusque Vasconiae, 2009).

6   Jean "Anxuberro" Saint-Pierre, 14eko Gerla Handia, Piarres Xarritonen edition, Klasikoak collection (Donostia: Euskal Editoreen Elkartea, 1998).

7   Piarres Charriton, Jean Etchepare mirikuaren idazlanak. IV. Kazetaritza (B) (1916–1935) (Donostia: Elkar, 1992); Piarres Charriton, Jean Etchepare mirikuaren idazlanak. III. Kazetaritza (A) (1903–1915) (Donostia: Elkar, 1988).

8   Jean Elissalde, LVII. a gerlan, Patri Urkizu edition (Irun: Alberdania, 1995).

9   Jean Barbier, Piarres I, Ramon Sanchez edition (Donostia: Euskal Editoreen Elkartea, 1992).

10   Jean Barbier, Piarres II, Ane Loidi edition (Donostia: Euskal Editoreen Elkartea, 1996).

11   Ana María Toledo Lezeta, "Jean Barbier-en 'Piarres' XX. mendearen lehen erdiko euskal eleberrigintzan." Fontes linguae vasconum: Studia et documenta 50, No. 125 (2018): 221–50.

12   Bidegain, "Lehen Mundu Gerra 'Eskualduna' astekarian."

13   Bidegain.

14   Toledo Lezeta, "Jean Barbier-en 'Piarres' XX. mendearen lehen erdiko euskal eleberrigintzan," 236.

15   J. B. Bilbao and Juan Bautista Bilbao Elgezabal, Hau mundu arrano hau 1914–1916 (Zarautz: Susa, 1997).

16   Franck Dolosor, Matxin Irabola: senpereko bertsularia (Baiona: Elkar, 2010).

17   Patri Urkizu, 1914–1918 lekukoak (Baiona: Maiatz, 2015).

18   Gorka Knörr, Nik nahi dudana, LP (Artezi, 1975).

19   Kaleko Urdangak, Morts Pour La Patrie, EP, Vis Vires (Iruñea: Tough Ain't Enough Records,   2019),   https://open.spotify.com/track/10IWFMRGFdqWj4eKJrAOwp. Accessed: December 9, 2021.

20   Mikel Peruarena Ansa, Su zelaiak (Hiria; Susa, 2014).

21   Xabier Montoia, Hezur gabeko hilak (Zarautz: Susa, 1999).

22   Anne Sohier, "L'enfant et la guerre à l'école primaire: en Bretagne 1871–1914," in Mémoire et trauma de la Grande Guerre. Bretagne, Catalogne, Corse, Euskadi, Occitanie, by Gwendal Denis (Rennes: Rennes 2 Université Haute Bretagne, 2010), 384.

23   Jean Lestocquoy, Histoire du patriotisme en France. Des origines à nos jours (Paris: Albin Michel, 1968), 136.

24   Paul Gerbod, "L'éthique héroïque en France (1870–1914)," *Revue Historique*, October 1982.

25   Eugen Weber, La fin des terroirs, la modernisation de la France rurale, 1870–1914, translated by Antoine Berman and Bernard Genies (Paris: Fayard, 1984), 20.

26   Philippe Vigier, "Régions et régionalisme en France au XIXe siècle," in Régions et régionalisme en France du XVIIIe siècle à nos jours, edited by Christian Gras and Georges Livet (Paris: Presses Universitaires de France, 1977), 167.

27   Jean-Claude Caron and Michel Vernus, L'Europe au XIXe siècle: des nations aux nationalismes: 1815–1914 (Paris: Colin, 1996), 434.

28   Weber, Eugen Weber, La fin des terroirs, la modernisation de la France rurale, 1870–1914, 23.

29   Norbert Elias, La civilisation des mœurs, translated by Pierre Kamnitzer (Paris: Agora, 1985).

30   Fritz Peter Kirsch, Ecrivains au carrefour des cultures: études de littérature occitane, française et francophone = Estudis de literatura occitana, francesa e francofona (Pessac: Presses Universitaires de Bordeaux, 2000).

31   Anne-Marie Thiesse, Ils appreniaient la France: l'exaltation des régions dans le discours patriotique (Paris: Éditions de la Maison des Sciences de l'Homme, 1997).

32   Xabier Altzibar, "Zazpiak bat gaia XIX. Mendean (The zazpiak bat topic in the XIXth century)," in Antoine d'Abbadie (1897–1997), Congrès International Eusko Ikaskuntza, Ez ohizko kongresua. Eskualtzaindia. XIV biltzarra (Donostia: Eusko Ikaskuntza, 1998), 663–68.

33   Caron et Vernus, L'Europe au XIXe siècle, 343.

34   "Bankako bertsulari ohien koblak," 18–19.

35   Eneko Bidegain, Lehen Mundu Gerra eta Euskal Herria (Baiona: Elkar, 2014), 142.

36   Olivier Forcade, La censure politique en France pendant la Grande Guerre (Thèse de doctorat, Université Paris-X Nanterre, 1999), 125.

37   Bidegain, "Lehen Mundu Gerra 'Eskualduna' astekarian."

38   "Bankako bertsulari ohien koblak," 15–17.

39   earchives.le64.fr/archives-en-ligne/ark:/81221/r67921zv147vmk/f1?context=militaire::95924. Accessed: December 6, 2021.

40   earchives.le64.fr/archives-en-ligne/ark:/81221/r72874zb2sbnjk/f1?context=militaire::100880. Accessed: December 6, 2021.

41   earchives.le64.fr/archives-en-ligne/ark:/81221/r81029zlkb8knk/f1?context=militaire::109035. Accessed: December 6, 2021.

42   earchives.le64.fr/archives-en-ligne/ark:/81221/r88330z8lqrkpk/f1?context=militaire::116360. Accessed: December 6, 2021

43   earchives.le64.fr/archives-en-ligne/ark:/81221/r93054zf6ph3xk/f1?context=militaire::121090. Accessed: December 6, 2021.

44   earchives.le64.fr/archives-en-ligne/ark:/81221/r101309zvqp8wk/f1?context=militaire::129352. Accessed: December 6, 2021.

45   earchives.le64.fr/archives-en-ligne/ark:/81221/r108227zb7xq2k/f1?context=militaire::136270. Accessed: December 6, 2021.

4

THE AMERICAN WESTS

HISTORY, FICTION, MYTH

Monika Madinabeitia

"The past is a foreign country: they do things differently there" is the first line of L. P. Hartley´s 1953 novel, *The Go-Between*.[1] Our history, our histories, are felt as distant, unreliable, and hence intangible and even lost. At best, they are half-remembered and half-reproduced; at worst, twisted and obscure. Our history/ies pose the challenge to reconfigure the past to chronicle individual and collective memory.[2]

As collective memory begins to fade and blur, and even later decades of the last century are becoming history, myth, or legend to more people, there are certain conflicts between temporality and memory. "Human memory may well be an anthropological given, but closely tied as it is to the ways a culture constructs and lives its temporality, the forms of memory will take are invariably contingent and subject to change."[3] Hence, memory and representation play a crucial role. All representation, "in language, narrative, image, or recorded sound—is based on memory. Re-presentation always comes after, even though some media will try to provide us with the delusion of pure presence."[4] The past is not simply in memory; it must be rephrased and articulated to become memory. Memory itself, particularly in its belatedness, is based on representation. There is an unavoidable split between experiencing and remembering an event. This fissure gives way to cultural and artistic creativity. This frail gap between past and present constitutes memory, making it powerfully alive and vibrant. The vessels through which memory is articulated may both illuminate certain episodes and characters and conceal and belittle others. As suggested in this chapter, these vessels may also be mechanisms that revisit and combat reductionist views and diminishing articulations.

Although the debate on the definition of literature is not the primary goal of this chapter, it should be stated that there are different scopes and approaches to it and that its definition has varied over time. Etymologically, the term derives from Latin *litaritura/litteratura*, which means "a body of written words"; however, this definition is misleading for it may also include spoken or sung texts. It has been traditionally "applied to those imaginative works of poetry and prose distinguished by the intentions of their authors and the perceived aesthetic excellence of their execution."[5] Nineteenth-century critic Walter Pater referred to "the matter of imaginative or artistic literature" as a "transcript, not of mere fact, but of fact in its infinitely varied forms."[6] Others regard " '... not only what is written but what is voiced, what is expressed, what is invented, in whatever form'—in which case maps, sermons, comic strips, cartoons, speeches, photographs, movies, war memorials, and music all huddle beneath the literary umbrella;"[7] or, as Arthur Krystal himself claims, it can be regarded as "a record of one human being's sojourn on earth, proffered in verse or prose that artfully weaves together knowledge of the past with a heightened awareness of the present in ever new verbal configurations."[8]

As for history, from Greek *historia*, it means "inquiry; knowledge acquired by investigation."[9] "History ... is the study of the past;"[10] it comprises past events, as well as their discovery, memory, collection, and interpretation. "History is the study of people, actions, decisions, interactions and behaviours. It is so compelling a subject because it encapsulates themes which expose the human condition in all of its guises and that resonate throughout time: power, weakness, corruption, tragedy, triumph ..."[11] Historians make use of oral accounts, written documents, and many other human and material resources to learn about these past events. The description and presentation of these events create narratives that organize and thus add order to societies. Certainly, "we seek to understand the past by determining and ordering 'facts'; and from these narratives we hope to explain the decisions and processes which shape our existence."[12]

History can be valid to approach problems of the present and the future. Similarly, it provides societies with a sense of identity, for it can help in understanding who we are and where we come from. In other words, history can supply a sense of context not only for our lives, but also for our existence. It may do so at an individual or collective level; even nationally. History has often been used as a weapon to shape people. Those who control the narrative are granted the power to dictate who and what is in or out; in other words, the main narratives can be used to discredit or legitimize people and events.

Until the nineteenth century, the study of history was, rather than a science, an art that blended fact and fiction, myth and reality. History usually covered major events, such as wars or revolutions, emphasized important rulers, and glorified founding legends to infuse patriotism and legitimize identity. Consequently, historians almost always skipped what they considered unimportant events and inconsequential people. History was considered a form of art; the ornaments of the medieval history books come as evidence. The nineteenth century brought a secular approach to the study of history, mainly through the works of the German philosopher and historian Friedrich Hegel. The nineteenth century reformulated the concept of history, which was divorced from the literary fiction—novels. In the twentieth century, historians became aware of the necessity for an interdisciplinary approach to broaden the picture, fill in voids, and understand the past better.[13]

Although historians arduously attempt to find the historical truth and do by striving for objectivity, trying to erase the interpretation factor and ideological burdens, the past remains subjected to new interpretations. The past continues to be contested, re-interpreted, and re-written. Gaps arise in the narrative of events. Because of these voids, historical narratives comprise an irreducible element of interpretation. Historians must interpret their data and exclude certain facts from their account because of the narrative purpose. In the endeavour to reconstruct what must have happened in a period of history, historians are forced to include plausible explanations. In other words, historians must fill in the gaps of their materials on inferential or speculative grounds, mixing adequately and inadequately events. The ultimate narration is an interpretation that passes for an explanation of the whole process.[14] Hence, and despite all the theories and efforts of historians to categorize history as science and not art, history remains a border discipline, which, since the beginning of time, vacillates between the concepts of fact and fiction. In fact, fiction has prevailed over fact in many cases.[15]

Fiction seems to be much more powerful than history, for it is easily popularized, and it reaches out to larger audiences. However, history and fiction share a common ground, for history needs narratives and representations to provide plausible explanations and scenarios. These representations are the outcome of a distorted view of reality, which is filtered by the hand of the person making inferences and speculations. Consequently, not much faith can be put into history and its stories, or rather what historians term as facts.[16] This blend between history and fiction, which has been presented as history and thus believed as true, has become a powerful tool to reach the mainstream and make it malleable. The relation between history and fiction is taken for granted and simply accepted as fact. Consequently, dominant representations color our world and affect the way we see ourselves and the world we live in. This perception of the world hence largely determines our behavior and identity.

The American West is a clear example of the interplay between history and literature.[17] The landmark essay of the American historian Frederick Jackson Turner,[18] "The Significance of the Frontier in American History," included in the annual report of the American Historical Association for 1893, became one of the major representations of the 1890 official closing of the frontier of the West. Turner revealed the exceptionalism of the American frontier as the process that evolved into the separation from Europe. Turner underscored the availability of unsettled land as the most important factor determining national development throughout much of the American history. The outcome was the grandeur of a unique America. Turner's thesis, also largely known as the frontier thesis, emphasized the frontier in shaping American character and influenced thousands of scholarly histories. For instance, by the time Turner died in 1932, 60 percent of the leading history departments in the US were teaching courses in frontier history along Turnerian lines.[19]

The widespread popularization of Turner's frontier thesis also influenced popular histories, motion pictures, and novels. In turn, all these artifacts glorified individualism, frontier violence, and rough justice as staples of the American West. Even Disneyland's Frontierland of the mid to late-twentieth century reflected and celebrated individualism as the American heritage.[20] Subsequent critics, politicians, and historians have followed Turner's trend and have applied his frontier thesis in, for example, technological or scientific innovation. John F. Kennedy explicitly called upon the ideas of the frontier at his acceptance speech for the Democratic presidential nomination on July 15, 1960. Kennedy called out to the American people, "I am asking each of you to be new pioneers on that New Frontier. My call is to the young in heart, regardless of age—to the stout in spirit, regardless of party."[21] Throughout his term in office, Kennedy cultivated the frontier ideology as a motto for progress, with an emphasis on technology and space exploration. The frontier or Turner thesis used by Kennedy hence kept its attachment to progress, as it had in the Old Frontier.

Turner admitted that "the conceptions of history have been almost as numerous as the men who have written history."[22] He also claimed that "each age tries to form its own conception of the past. Each age writes the history of the past anew with reference to the conditions uppermost in its own time . . . History is the biography of society in all its departments." He added that "there is objective history and subjective history. Objective history applies to the events themselves; subjective history is man´s conception of these events. As underscored, " 'the whole mode and manner of looking at things alters with every age,' but this does not mean that the real events of a given age change; it means that our comprehension of these facts changes."[23] From Turner´s perspective, "the aim of history . . . is to know the elements of the present by understanding what came into the present from the past. For the present is simply the developing past, the past the undeveloped present." Turner made a distinction between the historian and the antiquarian. The latter "strives to bring back the past for the sake of the past; the historian strives to show the present to itself by revealing its origin from the past. The goal of the antiquarian is the dead past; the goal of the historian is the living present."[24]

Turner's thesis evolved from his speech in 1893, three years after the official closing of the frontier in the West. The supposed end of the conquest of the West did not shed light on the reality, which comprehended unaccountable memories and dilemmas. The divide between past and present that resulted in 1890 posed an obstacle to understanding issues widely believed to be ended. The conquest contested the ideals of Americans and profoundly affected both the conqueror and the conquered. History is made by the ones in power; they are the ones who decide what is relevant and what needs to remain in history. That is to say, the ones in power choose who and what is to be remembered and celebrated. As a result, history is what historians make of it. As a result, to some, the conquest of the West did take place and did end in 1890. For others, this never happened as it is told.

In the imagination of present America, "the West has come to stand for independence, self-reliance, and individualism . . . modern westerners see themselves as part of a lineage that conquered a wilderness and transformed the land; they spring from a people who carved out their own destiny and remained beholden to no one."[25] Expansionists in the nineteenth century thought that the US "was an empire of liberty peacefully extending itself into an untamed wilderness and populating the empty land with settlers thankful for the empire's blessings."[26] For more than a century, the American West has been the most strongly imagined section of the US. It began being imagined even before the conquest of the area was fully complete. Shows, such as Buffalo Bill's Wild West show, nourished the imagination of thousands of people, more particularly outside the West itself. The etched vivid images that populated the fantasy and the imagination of people turned into stories about the West, which then evolved into a particular genre, the Western. Novels first, and films later, became a consolidating element of American popular culture, which has also affected the global imaginary of the West. The voracious consumption of fictions about the West clearly intruded and influenced the historical narrative of this area. For example, authors such as Louis L'Amour fed the way people believed the true West was. L'Amour´s novel *How The West Was Won* (1963) describes the author as "our foremost storyteller of the authentic West . . . by bringing to vivid life the brave men and women who settled the American frontier."[27] Part one of the novel starts claiming that "the shining land lay open—ready for conquest, . . . that led ever onward into the heart of the dangerous but unawakened land where riches waited for the bold and the strong."[28]

Such fiction has furnished and filled in the voids that historians could not reach. It has similarly accentuated selected and selective events in history. As previously stated, fiction is more powerful than history, for it reaches the mainstream more easily. The actual West, often nostalgically referred to as the Old West, is constantly in conversation with the imagined West, also known as the mythic West. The American West constitutes the invention of a myth.[29] As a construct of the imagination, the West has become an exceptional place. Historian Richard Slotkin talks about a national mythology that attempts to fabricate an "American epic."[30] This mystique has generally hindered coming to terms with the real past and the present of this large part of the United States.[31]

To start with, the Old West has been mistakenly labeled under the adjective old, since this side of the continent was chronologically the last to be conquered. The Old West usually has to do with the history related to the region beyond the Mississippi River and the second part of the history of the American West.[32] The term old evokes nostalgic sentiments because of the longing for a past regarded as better than the present.[33] This disproportionate relevance of the West is in great part the result of a phenomenon known as the myth of the West. Although critics often use the phrase "myth of the West," there is not "just one single myth about the West."[34] Likewise, there is not "a single imagined West"[35] either. The West has hence become an abstract term to define, a term of multiple definitions.[36] The myth temporally referred to the historical process that is regarded as the frontier or westward movement, considering the frontier as the meeting point between civilization and wilderness, which moved westward from the Puritan era to the 1890s. Spatially, the myth refers to a West which did not become geographically fixed till the end of the frontier era.[37]

Among the people doing the imagining, there are at least two main groups: on the one hand, residents of the West, who have constructed various local versions of a collective past; on the other, professional writers, who include journalists and filmmakers, often located outside the West.[38] The first group includes people such as Buffalo Bill Cody, who did not discover the Wild West, but was able to formulate a popular image of the frontier that dominated the interpretations of the West till much later. In fact, Buffalo Bill, more than any other figure, is responsible for . . . the myth of the American West."[39] Aside from James Fenimore Cooper, who did more than any other writer to popularize the frontier during the first half of the nineteenth century, before midcentury, artists, explorers, and historians introduced other elements about the West,[40] which in turn marked the history of the West and its perception.

Mythmakers usually draw from history, for they use actual people or events; they may add characters, change details, and generally rearrange events to make the meaning of the stories clearer. Historians, as do mythmakers, also draw from history and are selective. Historians select from numerous available facts to create a story about the past. Both historians and mythmakers attempt to order the past in a way that conveys meaning; they both tell stories. Nonetheless, historians are not allowed to reorder facts, or invent new ones; by the code of their craft, they must write stories with veracity. This constricts them as opposed to the liberty that mythmakers use. However, as people accept and assimilate myths, they act on the myths, and the myths become the basis for actions that shape history. If myth is a historical product, history is also a product of myth. In fact, "the mythic West imagined by Americans has shaped the West of history just as the West of history has shaped the West that Americans have imagined and created."[41] Edward Abbey's second published novel, *The Brave Cowboy* (1956), which later inspired the motion picture *Lonely Are the Brave*,[42] is a fictional example of how the mythic West molds actual westerners. This novel is the story of Jack Burns, a loner cowboy at odds with modern civilization. He follows a personal code of ethics and lives as cowboys did in the old times. He refuses modern society and rejects modern technology. His escape from prison on horseback and his end convey the twilight of the old times against the encroaching modern West. Claude Dallas is a real instance to also bear in mind. Dallas was released on February 7, 2005, after twenty-two years of prison, for killing two Idaho State fish and game wardens in the 1980s. He was pursued throughout the West for fifteen months and although finally captured and accused of manslaughter, Dallas was celebrated as one of the last free and independent men in the West among certain fringe factions. He is a well-known figure in the state of Idaho, where some see him as a murderer and others still view him as a nostalgic vestige of the Old West. To this time, Dallas is remembered by many in Idaho. Basque American writer Frank Bergon wrote a novel, *Wild Game* (1995),[43] based on the figure of Dallas. In addition, there are at least two other books that deal with the 1980s event related to Claude Dallas: Jack Olsen's *Give a Boy a Gun: A True Story of Law and Disorder in the American West* (1985)[44] and Jeff Long's *Outlaw: The True Story of Claude Dallas* (1985).[45] These two books are presented as narrations or accounts of what really happened in the Idaho-Nevada frontier in the 1980s.

Dallas became so popular that even a film was made from his story, *Manhunt for Claude Dallas,*[46]based on Long's book *Outlaw*, and a song, "Claude Dallas."[47] The lyrics of the song capture the lingering Old West ambience and how Dallas, born in the East, moved West fascinated by the etched vivid images that hunted into his imagination.

In a land the Spanish once had called the Northern Mystery
Where rivers run and disappear
Mustang still lives free
By the Devil's Wash and the Coyote Hole
In the wild, Owyhee Range
Somewhere in the sage tonight
The wind calls out his name
Aye Aye Aye
Come gather 'round me buckaroos
a story I will tell
Of the fugitive Claude Dallas
Who just broke out of jail
You may think this tale is history
From before the West was won
But the events that I'll describe took place in 1981
He was born out in Virginia
Left home when school was through
In the deserts of Nevada
He became a buckaroo
And he learned the ways of cattle
And he learned to sit a horse
And he always packed a pistol
And he practiced deadly force
Then Claude he became a trapper
And he dreamed of the bygone days,
And he studied bobcat logic
And their wild and silent ways
In the bloody runs near Paradise

In monitors down south
Trapping cats and coyotes
Living hand to mouth
Aye Aye Aye
And Claude took to living all alone
Out many miles from town
A friend Jim Stevens brought supplies
And he stayed to hang around
That day two wardens Pogue and Elms
Drove in to check Claude out
They were seeking violations
And to see what Claude's about
Now Claude had hung some venison
He had a bobcat pelt or two
Pogue claimed they were out of season
He said "Dallas, you're all through"
But Dallas would not leave his camp
He refused to go to town
As the wind howled through the bull camp
They stared each other down.
It's hard to say what happened next
Perhaps we'll never know
They were gonna take Claude into jail
And he vowed he'd never go
Jim Stevens heard the gunfire
And when he turned around
Bill Pogue was falling backwards
Conley Elms he fell face down
Aye Aye Aye
Jim Stevens walked on over
There was a gun near Bill Pogue's hand
It was hard to say who'd drawn his first
But Claude had made his stand
Claude said, "I am justified, Jim.
They were gonna cut me down . . .
And a man's got a right to hang some meat
When he's livin' this far from town."
It took eighteen men and fifteen months
To finally ran Claude down

In the sage outside of Paradise
They drove him to the ground
Convicted up in Idaho
Manslaughter by decree
Thirty years at maximum
But soon Claude would break free
There's two sides to the story
There may be no right or wrong
The lawman and the renegade
Have graced a thousand songs
The story is an old one
Conclusion's hard to draw
But Claude's out in the sage tonight
He may be the last outlaw
Aye Aye Aye
In a land the Spanish once had called the Northern Mystery
Where rivers run and disappear
The mustang still lives free
By the Devil's Wash and the Coyote Hole
In the wild Owyhee Range
Somewhere in the sage tonight
The wind calls out his name
Aye Aye Aye

Bergon's novel and the books about him also underscore Dallas's fascination with the West, the imagined West. Dallas was not born a cowboy, a buckaroo, but he wanted to eagerly become one. He did so by gluttonously consuming fiction about the West and imitating the morals and messages in it. Dallas illustrates the use to which an invented West could be put.

The song on Dallas also specifies the divided views and approaches toward his growing popularity: some lionized him and turned him into an anti-government folk hero—a reputation that was heightened by his 1986 jailbreak; to others, he was a ruthless criminal and a psychopath. One way or the other, Dallas was acquiring an iconic status in the western folklore with books, films, documentaries, news, poems, and songs being written about him. His figure, real and imaginary, was becoming a blurry mixture of fantasy and reality. Bergon was not pleased with the overromanticized attention that Dallas was receiving, and hence decided to take the debate to a novel. Without distorting its historical possibilities, Bergon decided to take the stance of a novelist and freely dramatize the story.

Bergon invented a character, Jack Irigaray, of Basque heritage, as a literary artifact to tell the story. As did the other two books, Bergon also used the court transcripts to write the novel. To put it another way, Bergon selected the materials and details, added characters and rearranged events to make the meaning of the story clearer. To represent the figure of Claude Dallas, Bergon created the counterpart Billy Crockett, which is the merging of two of the Wild West and frontier prototypes, Billy the Kid and Davy Crockett. The latter negated the accepted values of the East and existed beyond the boundaries of civilization.[48] Davy Crockett became "a legend on America's colonial frontier when violence and danger were everywhere. He was a scout and a soldier, an explorer and a homesteader. . . ." After his death, "he became a legend of mythic proportions. Today he symbolizes the spirit of those pioneers who settled the untamed lands of a young country and is recognized as a man who fought for the common people, defining for their time what it means to be an American."[49] Of all American personages, more fallacies, misrepresentations, legends, and myths have been presented than any other concerning alias Billy the Kid. His biography was so distorted with lies that there is little, if any, resemblance between what is told about him and his actual life. He was like Robin Hood to some, a cold-blooded murderer to others. Marshall Ashmun Upson wrote the book *The Authentic Life of Billy the Kid* and consequently gave birth to a legend. He had little regard for the facts and as a result, he embellished a lowly outlaw, a common murderer, into the western counterpart of Robin Hood or El Zorro. This frothy mixture created a blurry image of a young man who then captured the imagination of a nation.[50] The choice to merge both figures in the name Billy Crockett nails the debate that emerged around Claude Dallas.

Another literary artifice used by Bergon to reveal the cosmetic fabrication of heroes and the legacy of the myth of the frontier is to include two fictionalized books in the novel: *Desperado: The True Story of Billy Crockett* and *Quick Draw: A True Story of Violence in the American West*. These titles recall the two books so far available on Dallas, which Bergon used as research material. Another reference is that Irigaray was interviewed for both books, but that "neither writer got much right."[51] As Irigaray explains, the writer of Desperado did not listen to him because "he seemed to already know what he intended to write. In his book, what happened in Little High Rock Canyon came totally from Billy's false testimony . . . he'd understood that Billy was trying to live out an Old West fantasy, and everyone was buying it."[52] This reflection brings to mind the end of the Western *The Man Who Shot Liberty Valance*[53] and its popular film line: "This is the West, sir. When the legend becomes fact, print the legend" by the journalist Maxwell Scott to the senator, Ransom Stoddard.

The 1890s produced two traditions for interpreting the frontier and the American West: one was the tradition that emerged from the previously cited Frederick Jackson Turner, who distinguished the emergence of the West's history as an important field of scholarship. His thesis marked the writing of American history and western American history for generations after. Turner and the academics accepted the Turner or frontier interpretation, which celebrated the frontier experience as the most significant ingredient of American history. The other tradition was the one started by Buffalo Bill, who was influenced by the Cooper and dime-novel tradition. Buffalo Bill differed from Turner in the image of the West he was creating: Buffalo Bill's was a story of adventure, drama, and competition. These "shows were extravaganzas, emerging straight out of the imaginations of showmen eager to keep the spirit of the West at the forefront of the public's mind."[54] The shows would start with an announcement asserting the show's authenticity. According to Buffalo Bill, the shows were not performances, and the actors were not actors; "they simply appear just as they are ... nothing more, nothing less."[55] These two traditions may seem to clash at first sight, but in reality, they were both narrations that compensated each other. That is, the Wild West shows exacerbated the uniqueness and grandeur of the West; likewise, and quite paradoxically, Turner's emphasis on the frontier helped keep alive the more popular Wild West tradition.[56] The crossroad and the consequent liminal or in-between zone between these two trends have fabricated what we primarily know about the West today. Actual events merged with the imagined and invented, and stories have drawn and fed back into history.

The two main traditions established in the 1890s result from the construction of narratives. The intersection between them acts as a productive space for playing with the dynamics of fact and myth. Likewise, this crossroad opens the debate between voicing and silencing, oblivion and memory. History is made by the ones in power, the ones who decide what is important and what needs to remain in history. Since history starts from a text that is further turned into a narrative, just like fiction, then the so-called objectivity and respect for the historical truth is yet just another story, and history and fiction are closer to each other than previously believed.[57] The historian's distortion is not just technical, it is ideological. This distortion is released into a world of racing interests and any chosen emphasis—regardless of whether it is intended or not—supports some kind of interest, economic, political, racial, national, or sexual. The quiet acceptance of conquest and murder in the name of progress or the treatment given to heroes and victims are only part of a specific approach to history, in which the past is told from the perspective of conquerors, governments, diplomats, and leaders.[58]

The history of the West is continuously demystified in contemporary fiction, an action whose purpose is to argue that history is nothing but fiction. History is subject to constant reviewing, correcting, revision, and victim of falsification and misunderstanding. By proposing alternative histories, post-Western[59] or late Western[60] authors, such as Larry McMurtry, the already mentioned Frank Bergon, Sherman Alexie, Joan Didion, Rebecca Solnit, Claire Vaye Watkins, Jon Raymond, among many others, are trying to make people aware that nothing should be taken for granted. The history/ies they produce may be smaller, but their words still serve the purpose to give voice to the minorities, human and/or not human.

Fiction is not solely exclusive to written text, which means that cinema and film productions are to be taken into consideration as well: *The Three Burials of Melquiades Estrada*;[61] *Brokeback Mountain*;[62] *No Country for Old Men*;[63] *Cowboys & Aliens*;[64] *The Revenant*;[65] *The Homesman*;[66] *Hell or High Water*;[67] and *First Cow*,[68] for instance, are revisions, corrections, and in essence, alternative histories. Films also attempt to raise awareness and therefore debate on what has been presented as a fact through history. Indeed, as opposed to written literary fiction, films have the capacity to reach the mainstream more easily and hence contribute to drawing back curtains to reveal glaring realities that have been hidden or silenced. Films can shake the audience and arm it with new perspectives. Needless to say, media, particularly through new technologies and digitalization, are even more persuasive forces to shape behaviors and mindsets. It would be interesting to analyze the intersection of history and fiction at a time of encroaching digital gluttony. Another area to explore would be what is preserved and what is not, what is protected and promoted and what is not, when texts and different products are being digitalized.

Overall, the role of historians may be to look to the past to better understand and illuminate how our present came to exist. Nonetheless, the results are more than likely to be conditioned by the contending interests, perspectives, and the enduring power of the structures around these historians. Hence, these histories require reconstructing. Likewise, narratives that have been lost in dominant historical accounts need to be recovered. Fiction, in the form of written or oral texts, shows, or media can underscore the chief versions, as illustrated through the myth of the West and the frontier or Turner thesis. The intersections between history and fiction may thus create a selected and selective image of the West. Since historians are unable to reveal the complexity and plurality of the past, and they are limited in recording diverse ideas and experiences, they fail to expose different thoughts and relations to the world around them. Fiction, regardless of the format, can be of paramount importance in recovering and reconstructing what has been subsumed and forgotten. The authors and films mentioned in this article are examples of how these histories can be revisited and rewritten. Historians need to be acknowledged in their arduous job, but fiction, in whichever format, must be also validated as a means that opens spaces of critical debate and contests dominant standpoints, from which the audience may learn that the West is much more than a cosmetic fabrication. In consequence, the interplay or intersection of history and fiction should be considered an in-between zone where dominant histories may still be accented, but the histories of minorities, of the fringe, of the unselected, have a chance to come to the front and make a difference in the way we perceive ourselves and the world in which we live.

RESOURCES

Athearn, Robert G. *The Mythic West in Twentieth-Century America.* Lawrence: University Press of Kansas, 1986.

Bergon, Frank. *Wild Game.* Reno: University of Nevada Press, 1995.

Bergon, Frank, and Zeese Papanikolas. *Looking Far West: The Search for the American West in History, Myth, and Literature.* New York: New American Library, 1985.

Bogue, Allan G. "Frederick Jackson Turner Reconsidered." *The History Teacher* 27, no. 2 (1994): 195–221. https://doi.org/10.2307/494720.

Boia, Lucian. *Jocul Cu Trecutul: Istoria Între Adevăr Și Ficțiune.* București: Editura Fundației Humanitas, 2002.

Brokeback Mountain. Directed by Ang Lee. Starring Heath Ledger and Jake Gyllenhaal. Focus Features, 2005. Film.

Chirobocea-Tudor, Olivia. "Perspectives on the Relation between History and Fiction." *Philologica Jassyensia,* 2017, 191–202.

"Claude Dallas." Written by Ian Tyson and Tom Russell. In *Cowboyography,* by Ian Tyson, 1986. In *Cowboy Real,* by Tom Russell, 1992. Song.

Cline, Donald. *Alias Billy the Kid: The Man behind the Legend.* Santa Fe, NM: Sunstone Press, 1988.

Cowboys & Aliens. Directed by Jon Favreau. Starring Olivia Wilde, Daniel Craig, and Harrison Ford. Universal Pictures, Paramount Pictures, 2011. Film.

Etulain, Richard W. *Telling Western Stories: From Buffalo Bill to Larry McMurtry.* Albuquerque: University of New Mexico, 1999.

Faragher, John Mack (Commentary). *Rereading Frederick Jackson Turner: "The Significance of the Frontier in American History" and Other Essays.* New Haven: Yale University Press, 1998.

First Cow. Directed by Kelly Reichardt. Starring John Magaro and Orion Lee. FilmScience, IAC Films, 2019. Film.

Hartley, L. P. *The Go Between.* Harlow, England: Pearson Education, 2008.

Hell or High Water. Directed by David Mackenzie. Starring Jeff Bridges, Chris Pine, Ben Foster, and Gil Birmingham. Lionsgate, CBS Films, 2016. Film

Hoare, Natasha. "The Past Is a Foreign Country." *The White Review,* October 11, 2017. https://www.thewhitereview.org/feature/the-past-is-a-foreign-country/.

Huyssen, Andreas. *Twilight Memories: Marking Time in a Culture of Amnesia.* Taylor and Francis, 2012.

Janda, Richard D., and Brian D. Joseph. "Introduction: On Language, Change, and Language Change—Or, Of History, Linguistics, and Historical Linguistics." Introduction. In *The Handbook of Historical Linguistics,* edited by Brian Joseph D. and Richard D. Janda, 3–180. Oxford: Blackwell, 2005.

Krystal, Arthur. *This Thing We Call Literature.* New York: Oxford University Press, 2016. E-book.

L'Amour, Louis. *How the West Was Won: A Novel.* New York: Bantam Books, 1963.

Lonely Are the Brave. Directed by David Miller. Starring Kirk Douglas and Walter Matthau. Universal Pictures, 1962. Film.

Long, Jeff. *Outlaw: The True Story of Claude Dallas.* New York: McGraw-Hill, 1986.

Macauley, Justine. "How the West Was Played: The Influence of Wild West Shows on American Identity and Perceptions of Gender, 1870 to 1920." *Historical Perspectives: Santa Clara University Undergraduate Journal of History,* II, 15, no. 7 (May 2010): 24–43.

Malone, Michael P., and Richard W. Etulain. *The American West: A Twentieth-Century History.* Lincoln: University of Nebraska Press, 1989.

Manhunt for Claude Dallas. Directed by Jerry London. Starring Matt Salinger, Claude Akins, and Beau Starr. 1986. Film.

Meldrum, Barbara Howard. *Under the Sun: Myth and Realism in Western American Literature.* Troy, NY: Whitston Publishing Company, 1985.

Morrow, Bradford. *World Outside the Window: The Selected Essays of Kenneth Rexroth.* New York: New Directions Publishing Corporation, 1987.

Murdoch, David Hamilton. *The American West: The Invention of a Myth.* Cardiff: Welsh Academic Press, 2001.

No Country for Old Men. Directed by Joel Coen and Ethan Coen. Starring Tommy Lee Jones, Javier Bardem, and Josh Brolin. Miramax Films, Paramount Vantage, 2007. Film.

Olsen, Jack. *Give a Boy a Gun: A True Story of Law and Disorder in the American West.* New York: Dell Pub., 1986.

Reddin, Paul. *Wild West Shows.* Urbana: University of Illinois Press, 1999.

Slatta, Richard W. "Taking Our Myths Seriously." *Journal of the West* 40, no. 3 (2001): 3–5.

Slotkin, Richard. *Regeneration through Violence: The Mythology of the American Frontier, 1600–1860.* Middletown: Wesleylan University Press, 1974.

Sorensen, Theodore C. *Let the Word Go Forth: The Speeches, Statements, and Writings of John F. Kennedy 1947 to 1963.* New York: Delcorte Press, 1991.

Stanley, George E. *Davy Crockett: Frontier Legend.* New York: Sterling, 2008.

"Story." Cambridge Dictionary. Accessed December 21, 2021. https://dictionary.cambridge.org/dictionary/english/story.

"Story Definition & Meaning." Merriam-Webster. Merriam-Webster. Accessed December 21, 2021. https://www.merriam-webster.com/dictionary/story.

The Homesman. Directed by Tommy Lee Jones. Starring Tommy Lee Jones, Hilary Swank, and Meryl Streep. Roadside Attractions, EuropaCorp Distribution, 2014. Film.

The Man Who Shot Liberty Valance. Directed by John Ford. Starring John Wayne, James Stewart, Lee Marvin, and Vera Miles. Paramount Pictures, 1962. Film.

The Three Burials of Melquiades Estrada. Directed by Tommy Lee Jones. Starring Tommy Lee

Jones, Barry Pepper, Julio Cedillo, Dwight Yoakam, and January Jones. Sony Pictures Classics, 2005. Film.

The Revenant. Directed by Alejandro Gonzalez Iñarritu. Starring Leonardo DiCaprio and Tom Hardy. Twentieth Century Studios, 2016. Film.

Turner, Frederick Jackson. *The Significance of the Frontier in American History.* Mansfield Centre, CT: Martino Publishing, 2014.

"What Is History?" History Today, August 2020. https://www.historytoday.com/archive/head-head/what-history.

White, Hayden. "Interpretation in History." *New Literary History* 4, no. 2 (1973): 281–314. https://doi.org/10.2307/468478.

White, Richard. *"It's Your Misfortune and None of My Own": A New History of the American West.* Norman: University of Oklahoma Press, 1993.

Zinn, Howard. *A People's History of the United States: 1492–2001.* New York: HarperCollins, 2003.

NOTES

1　L. P. Hartley, *The Go Between* (Harlow, England: Pearson Education, 2008).

2　Natasha Hoare, "The Past Is a Foreign Country," *The White Review*, October 11, 2017, https://www.thewhitereview.org/feature/the-past-is-a-foreign-country/.

3　Andreas Huyssen, *Twilight Memories: Marking Time in a Culture of Amnesia* (Taylor and Francis, 2012), 2.

4　Huyssen, *Twilight Memories*, 2.

5　Bradford Morrow, *World Outside the Window: The Selected Essays of Kenneth Rexroth* (New York: New Directions Pub. Corp., 1987), 275.

6　Morrow, *World Outside the Window*, 275.

7　Arthur Krystal, *This Thing We Call Literature* (New York: Oxford University Press, 2016), e-book.

8　Krystal, *This Thing.*

9　Richard Janda and Brian Joseph, "The Handbook of Historical Linguistics," in *The Handbook of Historical Linguistics*, ed. Brian Joseph and Richard Janda (Oxford: Blackwell, 2005), 3–180, 163.

10　Peter N. Stearns, "Why Study History?" (1998) | AHA, accessed December 21, 2021, https://www.historians.org/about-aha-and-membership/aha-history-and-archives/historical-archives/why-study-history-(1998).

11　"What Is History?" *History Today*, August 2020, https://www.historytoday.com/archive/head-head/what-history.

12　"What Is History?"

13　Olivia Chirobocea-Tudor, "Perspectives on the Relation between History and Fiction," *Philologica Jassyensia*, 2017, 191–202, 191–192.

14　Hayden White, "Interpretation in History," *New Literary History* 4, no. 2 (1973): 281–314, https://doi.org/10.2307/468478, 281.

15　Chirobocea-Tudor, "Perspectives," 127.

16　Lucian Boia, *Jocul Cu Trecutul: Istoria între Adevăr Și Ficțiune* (București: Editura Fundației Humanitas, 2002), 8.

17　As of this point, literature will be primarily limited to fiction in this chapter.

18 Frederick Jackson Turner, *The Significance of the Frontier in American History* (Mansfield Centre, CT: Martino Publishing, 2014).

19 Allan G. Bogue, "Frederick Jackson Turner Reconsidered," *The History Teacher* 27, no. 2 (1994): 195–221, https://doi.org/10.2307/494720, 195.

20 Richard W. Slatta, "Taking Our Myths Seriously," *Journal of the West* 40, no. 3 (2001): 3–5.

21 Theodore C. Sorensen, *Let the Word Go Forth: The Speeches, Statements, and Writings of John F. Kennedy 1947 to 1963* (New York: Delcorte Press, 1991), 101.

22 John Mack (Commentary) Faragher, *Rereading Frederick Jackson Turner: "The Significance of the Frontier in American History" and Other Essays* (New Haven: Yale University Press, 1998), 11.

23 Faragher, *Rereading Frederick*, 18.

24 Faragher, *Rereading Frederick*, 19.

25 Richard White, *"It's Your Misfortune and None of My Own": A New History of the American West* (Norman: University of Oklahoma Press, 1993), 57.

26 Richard White, *"It's Your Misfortune,"* 85.

27 Louis L'Amour, *How the West Was Won: A Novel* (New York: Bantam Books, 1963), back cover.

28 L'Amour, *How the West Was Won*, 1.

29 David Hamilton Murdoch, *The American West: The Invention of a Myth* (Cardiff: Welsh Academic Press, 2001).

30 Richard Slotkin, *Regeneration through Violence: The Mythology of the American Frontier, 1600–1860* (Middletown, CT: Wesleylan University Press, 1974), 3.

31 Michael P. Malone and Richard W. Etulain, *The American West: A Twentieth-Century History* (Lincoln: University of Nebraska Press, 1989), 11.

32 Richard White, *"It's Your Misfortune,"* 4.

33 Robert G. Athearn, *The Mythic West in Twentieth-Century America* (Lawrence: University Press of Kansas, 1986), 20.

34 Barbara Howard Meldrum, *Under the Sun: Myth and Realism in Western American Literature* (Troy, NY: Whitston Pub. Co., 1985), 2.

35 White, *"It's Your Misfortune,"* 617.

36 Frank Bergon and Zeese Papanikolas, *Looking Far West: The Search for the American West in History, Myth, and Literature* (New York: New American Library, 1985), 2.

37 Meldrum, *Under the Sun*, 2.

38 White, *"It's Your Misfortune,"* 614–615.

39 Richard W. Etulain, *Telling Western Stories: From Buffalo Bill to Larry McMurtry* (Albuquerque, NM: University of New Mexico, 1999), 2.

40 Etulain, *Telling Western Stories*, 2–3.

41 White, *"It's Your Misfortune,"* 616–617.

42 Directed by David Miller, starring Kirk Douglas and Walter Matthau, Universal Pictures, 1962, film.

43 Frank Bergon, *Wild Game* (Reno: University of Nevada Press, 1995).

44 Jack Olsen, *Give a Boy a Gun: A True Story of Law and Disorder in the American West* (New York: Dell Pub., 1986).

45 Jeff Long, *Outlaw: The True Story of Claude Dallas* (New York: McGraw-Hill, 1986).

46 Directed by Jerry London, starring Matt Salinger, Claude Akins, and Beau Starr, 1986, film.

47   Written by Ian Tyson and Tom Russell. First released by Ian Tyson, in *Cowboyography*, in 1986, and by Tom Russell, in *Cowboy Real*, in 1992.

48   White, *"It's Your Misfortune,"* 620.

49   George E. Stanley, *Davy Crockett: Frontier Legend* (New York: Sterling, 2008), back cover.

50   Donald Cline, *Alias Billy the Kid: The Man behind the Legend* (Santa Fe, NM: Sunstone Press, 1988), 7.

51   Bergon, *Wild Game*, 248.

52   Ibid.

53   Directed by John Ford, starring John Wayne, James Stewart, Lee Marvin, and Vera Miles, Paramount Pictures, 1962, film.

54   Justine Macauley, "How the West Was Played: The Influence of Wild West Shows on American Identity and Perceptions of Gender, 1870 to 1920," *Historical Perspectives: Santa Clara University Undergraduate Journal of History* 15, no. 7 (May 2010): 24–43, 28.

55   Paul Reddin, *Wild West Shows* (Urbana: University of Illinois Press, 1999), 61.

56   Etulain, *Telling Western Stories*, 29–30.

57   Chirobocea-Tudor, "Perspectives," 200.

58   Howard Zinn, *A People's History of the United States: 1492–2001* (New York: HarperCollins, 2003), 8–9.

59   See, for example, Neil Campbell´s *Post-Westerns: Cinema, Region, West* (2013) or Susan Kollin´s *Postwestern Cultures: Literature, Theory, Space* (2007).

60   See Lee Clark Mitchell´s *Late Westerns: The Persistence of a Genre* (2018).

61   Directed by Tommy Lee Jones, starring Jones, Barry Pepper, Julio Cedillo, Dwight Yoakam, and January Jones, Sony Pictures Classics, 2005, film.

62   Directed by Ang Lee, starring Heath Ledger and Jake Gyllenhaal, Focus Features, 2005, film.

63   Directed by Joel Coen and Ethan Coen, starring Tommy Lee Jones, Javier Bardem, and Josh Brolin, Miramax Films, Paramount Vantage, 2007, film.

64   Directed by Jon Favreau, starring Olivia Wilde, Daniel Craig, and Harrison Ford, Universal Pictures, Paramount Pictures, 2011, film.

65   Directed by Alejandro Gonzalez Iñarritu, starring by Leonardo DiCaprio and Tom Hardy. 20th Century Studios, 2016, film.

66   Directed by Tommy Lee Jones, starring Jones, Hilary Swank, and Meryl Streep, Roadside Attractions, Europacorp Distribution, 2014, film.

67   Directed by David Mackenzie, starring Jeff Bridges, Chris Pine, Ben Foster, and Gil Birmingham, Lionsgate, CBS Films, 2016, film.

68   Directed by Kelly Reichardt, starring John Magaro and Orion Lee, FilmScience, IAC Films, 2019, film.

5

CONSTRUCTING THE AGRARIAN MARTYR IN MAURICIO MAGDALENO'S *EMILIANO ZAPATA*

A SHARED READING BETWEEN HISTORY AND LITERATURE

Andrea Perales-Fernández-de-Gamboa[1]

On September 12, 1909, Emiliano Zapata was elected president of the municipal council of his hometown, Anenecuilco (Morelos). His reputation as a horseman and horse han7dler made him famous both in his state and around Mexico City. But it was at that specific moment in 1909 that Zapata's fate changed to become a military and political leader in the Mexican revolution.[2] His leadership encompassed more than a military campaign; his manifestos, letters, and decrees state a political and ideological project which transcended a Mexico immersed in a process of unequal modernity, where the Indigenous communities were relegated to exclusion and extreme poverty. His project encapsulated centuries of local indigenous resistance for land and community rights toward the policies enacted, first by the colony and later by the liberal governments and Porfirio Díaz's dictatorship.[3] For the community, land was not merely a space or property, rather ". . . it was history, rights and tradition—it was place. *Reivindicación* and restitution signified the return of lands but also validated a community's historical and 'sacred' rights as a pueblo and *municipio libre*."[4] The nature of Zapata's project was of an intercommunity, where the rural peasantry was expected to take over the lands that rightfully were theirs, as their ancient legal documents proved. Furthermore, it was a national political project that aimed at establishing a plurinational democracy where the ancestral customs and laws of the original communities of Mexico would be enacted.[5] This ambitious process, however, was blurred in Mexico's historical narrative as the hero that became Emiliano Zapata was consecrated in the national imaginary.

Nine years after the revolution erupted, on April 10, 1919, Zapata was assassinated in Chinameca (Morelos) after the *carrancista* colonel Jesús Guajardo framed him. The pictures of his dead body soon appeared in national newspapers, so "in that way, 'those who desired to or might doubt' could see that 'it was actual fact that the famous jefe of the southern region had died.'"[6] Although several newspapers claimed that Zapata's body was taken to the capital, he was buried in Cuautla, under strict surveillance, to avoid any popular insurrection. All the headlines in the national newspapers in the next days after the assassination represented Zapata either as a ruthless warmonger or an ideal knight who sacrificed himself for the sake of his suffering community;[7] moreover, many headers asserted how *zapatismo* was dead. In that sense, for his fellow country people, Zapata's death meant losing any hope to restitute their land rights. This despair led to the circulation of many rumors and legends that ended up becoming part of national representation of Zapata, as well as to the emergence of a regional cult which aimed at keeping *zapatismo* as a movement. The remaining zapatista leaders disseminated manifestos in which they represented Zapata as "the fiery apostle of the *agrarismo*," a "redeemer of the indigenous race[8] representations that later were transferred to the city by curious visitors and writers who were in search of the exoticism related to Zapata's revolution. In this sense, and even though the Mexican revolutionary state became a macro structure which controlled the Revolution's narrative, Thomas Benjamin contends that "in Mexico memory, myth and history were elaborated not by the state but by diverse individuals sympathetic to the promises of revolutionary transformation."[9] There was an implicit need to justify why the civil war turned out the way it did, but mostly a desire to construct a homogenous narrative in which all the agents involved were fighting for a common cause: the nation. Thus, a national project emerged, where some of those who had fought and died vicariously became martyrs of the Revolution.[10]

In Zapata's case, an oral tradition was in the making in Morelos with the legends, *corridos* (folk songs), and tales of Zapata's heroic and romantic deeds. In the aftermath of the revolution, and during Álvaro Obregón's government (1920–1924), many avant-garde artists from the capital visited Morelos in search of Zapata's real and human self. They observed the impact of the southern hero in the lives of these indigenous communities and soon realized, alongside with the political institutions, that Zapata was a key figure in the construction of the Mexican national identity. Zapata became a symbol to unify the nation. The *morelense's* image, however, needed to be rehabilitated, as Brunk asserts, and from being the Attila of the South (as some newspapers called him), he was gradually transformed into the Agrarian martyr:[11] "Zapata, tragic hero as the Greek Dionysius, stopped being dangerous for the city when he was added to the mysteries, to the official rite."[12] Hence, his insurgent and anti-centralist project was blurred as his image was resignified to serve the state project.

The projected image of national Zapata in the narrative of the Revolution was expanded to all artistic expressions, including literature. Mauricio Magdaleno's 1932 play *Emiliano Zapata* is no exception to this treatment of the historical figure; furthermore, it falls under the myths created around the general. Despite the author's attempts to present a humane portrait of the revolutionary hero, the play constitutes another instance of the coloniality of power, the epistemic hegemony which established the narrative of modernity and condemned non-Eurocentric communities to silence and ostracism.[13] Thus, this chapter is constructed upon a shared reading of the play and some pieces from the manifestos enacted by Zapata and his *Ejército Libertador del Sur,* along with the works of some Zapata scholars. Magdaleno's work brings to light the tensions inherent in a process of unequal modernity in which majorities become silenced in the creation of the modern nation-state, the rehabilitation and reconstruction of Emiliano Zapata's image being an example.

DANGEROUS LIAISONS: THE RELATIONSHIP BETWEEN CULTURE AND STATE IN POST-REVOLUTIONARY MEXICO AND THE CONSTRUCTION OF NATIONAL ZAPATA

The importance of the intellectual elite in Mexico's post-revolutionary state does not exclusively trace back to that époque; from the *científicos* (scientists) who consolidated Porfirio Díaz's regime, to those previous scholars and writers who began forging the nation, the relationship between the state and the intelligentsia has been a constant. Despite the tensions that in some cases emerged between both structures, both were aware of how they needed each other to survive. Ángel Rama[14] comments upon these dangerous liaisons over time, claiming that "two forces were combined: the desire of the intellectuals to join the literate city that surrounded the central power, . . . and the desire of the latter to attract them to their service, obtain their cooperation and even subsidize them, forging a relationship which lasted during the twentieth century."[15] Amid these scholars, the *Ateneo de la Juventud* stands out as the most relevant civil society of the time; figures such as Alfonso Reyes, Pedro Henríquez Ureña, and José Vasconcelos were members of that society. Furthermore, Vasconcelos became the secretary of public education and became the "cultural *caudillo*" of the Mexican Revolution.

Vasconcelos as the secretary of public education (SEP) initiated an array of projects between 1921 and 1924 which aimed not only at educating the illiterate communities, but also at defining the Mexican character, which mostly encompassed the notion of *mestizaje*. Murals were painted across the country in federal buildings, and the great muralists Diego Rivera, José Clemente Orozco, and David Alfaro Siqueiros became the pictorial narrators of Mexico's glorious past, creating art that would educate the people on their identity.[16] These murals evoked the notion *mestizaje* and indigenism as central to the country's identity, following Vasconcelos' central thesis in his book *La raza cósmica*.[17] However, the *indigenista* project was not considering the communities living at the time, as they wanted them to assimilate into that emergent modern Mexico through education and civil assimilation.[18] The original communities were the others that needed to disappear and be nostalgically remembered as Mexico's glorious past, those whose world was denied in their current existence and was placed as a heirloom in the museums, murals, and textbooks. This negation of the existence of the other does not fit in the narrative established by the Eurocentric hegemony has been conceptualized as the coloniality of Being, derived from the notions of the coloniality of power and knowledge. As Maldonado-Torres puts it, the concept "responded to the need to thematize the question of the effects of coloniality in lived experience and not only in the mind."[19] Paradoxically, these communities' current realities were negated, yet their ancestors were regarded as the founding fathers of the nation.

In this sense, Zapata's presence in these murals was not casual; since the Mexican *científicos* were trying to assimilate the indigenous peoples into the national plan to modernize the country, they needed an example of what a modern *mestizo* could be. Zapata embodied the traits of this modern *mestizaje*: he belonged to a humble but well-situated family, he was literate and did not dress like a peasant, and, most importantly, he was a mass hero with followers all over the country. Moreover, it was not only Zapata, but his movement as well, as "*indigenista* reformers like Gamio (and even Vasconcelos), ...chose to see Zapatismo, in retrospect, as the awakening of the Indian people of Morelos."[20]

As an example, Rivera painted Zapata in a mural created in Cortés' Palace in Cuernavaca (Morelos). He was portrayed wearing a white shirt and trousers and a straw hat, like some of his fellow zapatistas did. Conversely, the best-known pictures of the revolution reveal that Zapata used to dress as a *charro* (horseman), given that it was his job. Consequently, the nostalgic and idyllic vision of the conflict, where Zapata's image is reduced to that of a bucolic indigenous farmer, demonstrates to which extent the national project appropriated, for their own purposes, the image of Zapata. On that note, Rueda Smithers comments on that when he asserts that Zapata:

> His monstrous, uncontrollable figure was changed, from the real rebel, to the harmonic, identifiable, of the plastic hero. His painful essence of a man of flesh and blood also changed. Within the ritual, he transformed into a man of a gentle nature, albeit with a fearsome hint of restrained strength. The uncompromising man was forgotten in favor of the locatable, "paintable" martyr, a work of art that rides a horse that flies without moving from its place. And Zapata was the Attila while he threatened the city, and he became a hero when the city again subdued the countryside, when he won the war.[21]

Rehabilitated Zapata was not only a constant in the murals and narratives of the Mexican state, but also became a common figure in the literary and folkloric works of the time, along with other recovered historical figures such as Cuauhtémoc. The turbulent post-revolutionary times, which included the *Cristero* Wars, coexisted with the proclamation of the new constitution of 1917 and flourishing *avant-garde* movements that either tried to evade the reality in which they lived or aimed to portray the turbulence and velocity of Mexico's everyday nature. In that sense, the novel of the Mexican Revolution followed the narrative initiated in muralism, whereas the *Contemporáneos* aligned with a cosmopolitan vision of the existence, and a demand to transgress folklore and nationalist arts. The *Estridentistas* aligned with the latter's need to renovate art, but they also agreed that art needed to have a social function and it could be used as a pedagogical tool.[22] Some of the members of this group shared a fascination with Zapata: such was the case with Germán and Armando List Arzubide who, in addition to fighting in the civil war, also contributed to the mystification of the hero. The former wrote *Emiliano Zapata: Exaltación* (1927, in which he "presents Zapata as an agrarian prophet . . ., died a martyr's death, and became a symbol of the continuing struggle for the agrarian reform."[23] The latter took on a popular genre as the *corrido* and wrote, "On the Death of Emiliano

Zapata," included in many of the *corrido* anthologies from the revolution and which reinforced some of the myths around the hero's life.[24]

Despite all the attempts to forge a homogenous cultural expression that narrated Mexican history, some agents besides the *Contemporáneos* tried to provide a critical stance toward the official narrative. Mauricio Magdaleno and Juan Bustillo Oro founded *El Teatro de Ahora*, an outcasted theatrical movement where the play *Emiliano Zapata* is located. Even if the authors' position was of radical opposition to the official narrative of the Revolution, this play falls under a similar folklorization of the general's life. Magdaleno's attempt to provide a more humane Zapata ends up becoming another simulacre of the revolutionary hero, where his complexities, discordances, and political and social impact are erased to promote the image of a larger-than-life martyr and hero.

MAURICIO MAGDALENO'S EMILIANO ZAPATA:
FORGING THE FATHERLAND WITH THE REVOLUTIONARY HEROES

El Teatro de Ahora was a short-lived theatrical movement (1932–1934), yet it was one of the most assertive movements in the search for *mexicanidad*.[25] Fellow playwrights attempted to create a national theater whose main theme would be linked to the social reality of the country.[26] Magdaleno's and Juan Bustillo Oro's *El Teatro de Ahora* constituted an example of the artistic trend, since Magdaleno's main goal was to put into light the unjust political system and society that was in the making.[27] Magdaleno himself described *El Teatro de Ahora* as:

> nationally inspired theater. Realistic theater, perhaps harsh, lacking in literary polish, but, without a doubt, live theater, full of suggestion, dramatic, strong, which brought to the scene the language and personality of the people, their problems, their demands for justice and freedom, their breath of thirsty earth, orphan of understanding.[28]

The intention of providing a space for catharsis and criticism toward the government was not well received by the audience because they were used to epic drama which would rather exalt the virtues of the Mexican past. Moreover, their epistemic disputes with the *Contemporáneos* also contributed to the short life of the movement. Consequently, *El Teatro de Ahora's* plays were only performed in the 1932 season, with *Emiliano Zapata* the first to be showcased. Since patronage was something necessary to succeed in the theatrical sphere, Magdaleno and Bustillo Oro were soon displaced when Vasconcelos was no longer secretary of education. Given the situation, both authors traveled to Madrid and published their plays even though they were, once again, censored when they returned to Mexico. Conrado J. Arranz considers that "literary creation, political responsibility, censorship, and silence intersected in the cultural relationships of the time,"[29] and the juncture of these four elements constituted the emergent Mexican national culture. Whichever cultural artifact that did not adhere to the state ideology was blacklisted. Still, it is curious to note how *Emiliano Zapata,* despite its mythical portrait of the hero, was not absorbed as part of that narrative. Nevertheless, it could be argued that despite Magdaleno's attempt to portray a real Zapata, his play belonged to the avant-garde and, furthermore, that it collaborated in the mystification process of Zapata as a national hero.

ZAPATA'S LAST YEARS OF LIFE:
THE LIGHT AND SHADOWS OF A LARGER-THAN-LIFE HERO

Emiliano Zapata offers a panoramic overview of Zapata's last years of life; their focus on such a historical moment wanted to demonstrate how the civil war had not really served at changing their reality.[30] The play can be placed between 1917 and 1919, since it begins with Otilio Montaño's[31] execution in 1917 and culminates with Zapata's assassination in 1919. The author intersperses Zapata's life and events of the revolution with fictional elements that tried to give a melodramatic twist to his work. Many of the scenes are conversations between Zapata and his fictional love interest, Remedios. This focus on the romance, however, damages any social protest that the author attempted to make.[32] Marcela del Río asserts that Magdaleno's play explores Zapata's real implication in some of his cruelest actions, like Montaño's assassination, and states that it is a historical theater with the necessity of self-reflection on the implications and consequences of the revolution itself.[33] Similarly, Arranz Mínguez mentions that Magdaleno converses with history, but he is also interested in the human side of the southern general, and tries to move away from the barbaric image that the inhabitants of the urban area had of Zapata.[34] Arranz Minguez's vision, however, seems problematic: the play premiered twenty-one years after the conflict ended and, in addition, Zapata's name had already been inscribed in golden letters in the walls of Congress, becoming officially a national hero. There was no real need to rehabilitate again the southern leader, as he already was the agrarian martyr of the revolution. Nonetheless, representing Zapata's humanity in the play seems a priority, since from the very beginning there is a sense of tiredness from the civil war and a need to stop the conflict. Furthermore, and as it will be demonstrated later, this fictional Zapata seems to surrender to that tragic end to offer himself for his community, thus following the contemporary depictions of Zapata, the apostle of agrarianism.

The piece is divided in three acts that focus on his interpersonal relationships: the whole play is structured around his romantic partnership with

Remedios, his confidant who serves not only to provide the melodramatic vibe but also to stage Zapata's fears and longing. In contrast, the first act focuses on the last conversations that Zapata and Montaño had before the the latter's execution, while the second and third acts focus on the protagonist's and Jesús Guajardo's relationship. The cruelty of the assassination somehow aided in the rehabilitation of the southern hero. It seems as if Guajardo's treason was what shed light around the corrupted national image of Zapata and transformed the Attila of the South into a Catholic martyr, something that the play signifies with a gradual brightening of theatrical lights as the story advances "from the darkness of the armed struggle to the enlightening of the caudillo, a glorification that passes through suffering and death."[35] Still, in this play, another treason takes place at the beginning, but in this case is undertaken by the agrarian apostle, which demonstrates the inherent tensions between light and darkness present in Zapata's fictional body.

LOYALTY OR LEAD: THE EXECUTION OF OTILIO MONTAÑO

The play opens with two choral characters on scene, an old lady, an indigenous old man called "El Pinto," and a man with malaria. The three of them show the ravages of the revolution; their physical aspect represents the poverty present in rural areas, while their conversations reflect how the common people felt toward the conflict. According to them, the revolution changed nothing, and they express their desire to go home.[36] Silence and darkness characterize this setting, and Magdaleno uses these choral characters to express the general feeling of despair, with some hints of hope. The old woman, specifically, seems to represent the community, as she expresses: "And so, as they took our lands, many years ago, so they will return them to us: with our pistols in hand."[37]

This old lady makes the first reference to Zapata, showing her total trust toward him.[38] The audience gets some grasps about the hero through Remedios and the old lady. Montaño appears onstage and searches for the leader to claim for forgiveness. Soon after, Zapata makes his entrance, and both become protagonists. Zapata's appearance offers some indications from the playwright, stating that his glance is " ... suspicious, meek, sad."[39] Zapata's eyes have been explored, both in literature and historical research,[40] and it is no coincidence that Magdaleno mentions his gaze as a way to delve into his humanity. The conversation fluctuates between a defense of Montaño, when the general defends his former comrade, claiming he "was the oldest revolutionary ... "[41] Research shows, however, that by 1919, Zapata and Montaño had already had some major disagreements that had set them apart for a long time.[42]

Zapata's appearance provokes Montaño's call for justice, arguing that he cannot continue in the cause if Zapata's fellows "persist in making the revolution an instrument of banditry and crime."[43] Expecting no banditry to exist at this point in the revolution was quite naïve for Montaño; however, it is interesting to share Zapata's take on the subject. For example, in a notice sent on April 16, 1916, the general encampment gave permission to the brigade commanders to discipline whoever seemed to be over the law, an issue that is explored in different documents.[44] It is clear that Zapata and his army were trying to control the banditry, which was inevitably occurring, and they were providing their subalterns with the instrument needed to avoid insurrections. A conversation around banditry in the play, however, seems a good excuse to show Zapata's human side and contradictions, by means of his attitudes toward Montaño: he mostly ignores and scorns the rural teacher, and he also accuses him of treason; briefly, however, we notice some instances of camaraderie from the general toward Montaño.[45]

Given the importance of these two characters' relationship in the play, it seems important to see the experts' take on this matter. Scholars did show in their works how long their comradeship lasted; while Womack claims that Zapata never really liked Montaño since he was more of an intellectual than an action man and had betrayed the southern revolution a few times.[46] In addition, Brunk comments on Montaño's importance in the creation of the Ayala Plan and asserts that it was Montaño's involvement in a rebellion that actually caused his execution—not the liberation of some prisoners.[47] Thus, it seems as if both revolutionaries had long drifted apart, but the playwright seems to hang on the dramatism present on this breakup. Magdaleno takes a poetic license when fictional Zapata accuses Montaño of having betrayed him three times. The biblical parallel drawn by the playwright directs the audience to that representation of Zapata as the Agrarian Martyr and tragic hero, an ideal vision of Zapata enacted by the state.[48] Similarly, the hero was considered a man of the people, something that Magdaleno underlines in different instances, such as when Zapata claims that he was aware of Montaño's betrayal, or when the teacher himself pleads for mercy "because you cannot get your hands dirty with an innocent man's blood!."[49] Nonetheless, Zapata's sense of justice operates in this scene and sends Montaño to die. Therefore, we observe how consecrated to the cause and social justice the protagonist is, as he lets the teacher die, demonstrating that Zapata, human as he was, also had light and shades.

Magdaleno fluctuates on his representation of Zapata, as he moves between the state's representation of Zapata and his attempt to humanize him, but he also seems to simplify Zapata's political and social impact. On the one hand, the playwright puts in the protagonist's mouth what his revolution was about: ". . . we do not fight more than the right thing: our lands. When our ideals are realized and the Indian has a piece of land where he can recline to die, all this that now scares you will be justified."[50] This sentence clearly states how the national project of whitewashing Zapata had been successful, as he was only remembered as the martyr who wanted to return the land to the indigenous people. Conversely, his mission, present in his manifestos,[51] went further beyond their recovery of their lands; as stated at the beginning, it was a project which attempted at reconstituting the customs, traditions, and communitarian laws of the peoples of Mexico, a plan to constitute a plurinational Mexico. These communities had guarded through centuries their knowledges otherwise, that is their own theory and praxis of their own existence, in their oral traditions.[52] In the revolution, they incorporated the social practices and modern discourses with written manifestos, as a way of transcending that unequal process of modernity and, consequently, reverting what Walter Mignolo defined as the colonial difference.[53]

Amid these manifestos and legal documents, the "general law on municipal liberties" from 1916 gave the communities and town councils the opportunity to legislate themselves according to their own customs and traditions: "Each municipality will enjoy absolute freedom to provide for local needs and to issue the regulations, parties and provisions that it deems necessary for its internal regime."[54] These documents are proof that Zapata and the *Ejército Libertador del Sur* envisioned something that went beyond the mere redistribution of lands; it departed from that necessity, but it expected that the communities would regain their own sovereignty. This first act, then, sets in motion the ideological apparatus of Magdaleno, who far from showing Zapata's humanity, constantly falls under the national rhetoric which constructed Zapata as a tragic hero.

RIDING TOWARD HIS SUNSET: ZAPATA'S AND GUAJARDO'S MEETING

The second act begins with a "light and sunny afternoon" in a rural setting, with Emiliano dressed as a charro onstage giving orders on how to proceed with an ex-zapatista commander.[55] The surrender letter from Colonel Jesús Guajardo arrives at the same time, something which does not seem to surprise Zapata because he asks one of his aides to address his people to "tell them that the promises I made to them are being kept. That the triumph of the Ayala Plan is a matter of months . . . that everyone will have their piece of land, and can keep the rifle to wield the plow."[56] These statements, as mentioned earlier, oversimplify Zapata's mission, and are proof of the success of the narrative of the Revolution. Additionally, and as research shows, Guajardo was just a part in the plot to kill Zapata, as it was really General Pablo González who orchestrated everything.[57] The official revolutionary narrative, however, chose who to blame for this act. Similarly, in 1918, the zapatista movement was in a critical situation: the *carrancistas* were gaining territory because the alliance between Pancho Villa's North Division and the Southern revolution was deteriorating because of several losses and González's devastation of Morelos, which caused the abandonment of some of Zapata's men; the general's original men, though, remained loyal to the cause.

Remedios appears onstage, and shares with Zapata her happiness over the end of the conflict, mostly in relation to what it meant for women.[58] At this moment, she becomes a choral character, too, expressing the concerns and expectations of women in Morelos. The idea of ending the revolution brings to his mind the people who died along the way, such as his brother, Eufemio: "They mutilated me the day they laid him dying."[59] This sentence is embedded with emotions, and it is no coincidence that it is placed in a conversation with Remedios. She brings out Zapata's humanity, and their fictional love story allows the playwright to represent Zapata as humane and not just as a larger-than-life-hero.[60] His humanity is also represented by means of his blind trust on Jesús Guajardo. Zapata's squad also believe in Guajardo because of his bravery. Furthermore, Zapata exalts the colonel's strategic and military abilities, and since he is an underdog, he believes he must be well intentioned.[61] It is interesting to see how Magdaleno constructs a bond between both figures, taking their humble origins into account. Guajardo himself makes a full emotional act, hugging Zapata as well as showing his fear of not being trusted by the southern general,[62] while Zapata fully exposes himself through his feelings, and allows Guajardo to see to which extent he can develop his plan. The latter's treason and Zapata's representation as a "fool" respond is a license taken by the author in which he represents the protagonist and the antagonist as diametrically opposites, as a reference to Shakespearian tragedies.[63] The audience already knows of the betrayal, thus this representation permits the author to praise, once again, Zapata as this semi-messianic figure.

In some stances, however, Guajardo reveals his true self: for him, any action in the revolution seems an opportunity to enrich himself, while Zapata understands that "they are just armed peasants."[64] Even though this should alarm the southern leader, he still trusts him blindly. There are more instances where this trust is at the verge of breaking, such as when the two Sierra Indian leaders talk to Zapata and call for justice, implying that some *carrancista* leaders have to be executed. Guajardo refuses to obey Zapata's orders, yet he ends up fulfilling them, saying: "I am a man of convictions, Emiliano, and I know how to keep my word, even if I die!"[65] This act ends with the execution of the fifty-nine soldiers and the promise of Guajardo's loyalty. The audience knows to whom Guajardo is being loyal, yet, onstage, Zapata keeps being a trustworthy human who is walking toward his own assassination.

ON HIS WAY TO CHINAMECA: ZAPATA'S ELEVATION TO MARTYRDOM

This act begins on April 9, 1919, one day before the ambush. It is interesting to note how the lighting onstage has dramatically changed from the darkness and sunset of the previous act to a sunny noon. As it was mentioned earlier, it seems as if Magdaleno wanted to metaphorically display the hero's trans-formation over the years; from being a bandit and the Attila of the South to becoming the Agrarian martyr. In a scene analogous to the first act, some of the characters appear onstage and comment on the upcoming peace and the triumph of the zapatista revolution, attributing it to some extent to Jesús Guajardo's collaboration.[66] *El Pinto*, one of the choral characters, soon refutes that claim, stating that it had been Zapata and his people the ones who won the revolution. Zapata is regarded as the ideological leader, the cult hero, whereas Guajardo is represented as the military man who brought strategy to the southern rebels.

The setting is festive, and Zapata's men are organizing a party while Zapata is onstage preparing to depart to Chinameca. Zapata himself is in a festive and hopeful mood as he tells his secretary Palacios: "Nobody tells me, but I know what is going on with them. They are hopeful that they are finally going back to their ranches."[67] His empathy underlines his humanity, and it is in this conversation where we see, once again, the triumph of the official narrative of the Revolution. They mention the collective notion of zapatismo, the accom-plishment of the Ayala Plan and their mission, which according to fictional Zapata was ". . . land and freedom for the Indian people."[68] This motto has been wrongly attributed to Zapata as a way of simplifying his political and social efforts. It was the anarchist leader Ricardo Flores Magón (1873–1922) who signed his manifestos with this slogan. Conversely, Zapata signed all the doc-uments with "Reform, freedom, justice and law," for example, the "Manifesto to the nation" signed on June 1, 1913.[69] Furthermore, the term "Indian people" is not found amid his documents because they would always talk about com-munities, respecting the ethnic diversity of Mexico. Moreover, fictional Zapata envisions post-revolutionary Morelos as a bucolic Arcadian land, where "the little ranches would peacefully work in the shared terrains . . . all of us planting corn . . . women making *tortillas*, the men, happy."[70] The playwright lacks this historical approach to Zapata's life, work. and philosophy, thus falling under the narrative of rehabilitated Zapata, and constructing him through the colonial gaze of the good savage figure.

Despite this hope toward the end of the revolution, Zapata's only wish is to disappear, as if he was sensing his tragic ending. The audience gets a glimpse of this during his conversation with Remedios, who is scared and urges him to leave.[71] Magdaleno, with Remedios' clairvoyance and fear toward Zapata's assassination, takes on some of the folk tales which emerged after April 10, 1919. One of them, in particular, said that a woman tried to prevent him from going to Chinameca, aware as she was of his destiny.[72] Zapata ignores Remedios's plead and, with the entrance of Guajardo and his men, he plans the Chinameca meeting, and lets the *carrancistas* leave as means of securing his own protection.[73] Soon after, Zapata reflects on his own decisions, and Magdaleno's stage direction shows that he does not seem to leave for Chinameca.[74] He talks to his comrades, and he shows his apathy toward the meeting and the revolution itself. He talks about his own suffering, how not many men have suffered as much as him, and how his real wish is to ride his horse far away and work anywhere.[75] The longing for anonymity shows, again, the human Zapata that Magdaleno wants to display. Finally, Zapata and his men ride toward Chinameca while Remedios again envisions her love's tragic destiny. His last words in the campsite for his people are clear: "As long as I live, the lands will be theirs and, when I die, they should only trust their own strength, and they should defend their lands with their arms in their hands."[76] Little could Magdaleno imagine that many decades later, rebellions around Mexico would erupt in search of their sovereignty, such as the 1994 rise of the *Ejército Zapatista de Liberación Nacional*.

The audience knew how the play would conclude, yet as it occurs with the other executions, they only hear about it; Guajardo, ironically repeats that "Jesús Guajardo knows how to keep his word, even if he dies!"[77] thus revealing the trope of treason which was the backbone of the play: that he would only remain loyal to *carrancismo*. Zapata seems to ride toward his death, ready to sacrifice himself if that meant the end of the conflict. Thus, his characterization falls upon his representation as a martyr, rather than the human being with contradictions that Magdaleno wanted to represent.

As it was earlier mentioned, Zapata was inscribed in the Pantheon of heroes in 1931, along with Venustiano Carranza himself, the leader who had ordered his death. Zapata's plurinational mission is blurred on this play and follows the official narrative which constructs the southern general as a larger-than-life hero. The cultural and social politics in the post-revolutionary period marked the multiple representations of Zapata. His assassination brought an array of reactions, but, overall, it was the popular moan what showed the potential of appropriating his figure. The intellectuals of the time, despite some divergences, became the spokespersons who disseminated an edulcorated version of the conflict. Since the implicit violence was impossible to erase, they opted for removing any trace of conflict between the revolutionary factions, and they carefully chose whom to elevate as heroes. Magdaleno's play, despite his conscious attempt at confronting this official narrative, falls also upon a mythical rather than human representation of Zapata. His piece, even if it showed the contradictions inherent to any human being, consciously underlines Zapata's martyr condition, and further reinforces the national discourse where indigenous communities were depicted as peacefully living in their terrains, planting corn, and making *tortillas*.

The triumph of the lettered city is inevitable in this depiction of Zapata. Fortunately, a shared reading with some of the written manifestos of the *Ejército Libertador del Sur*, along with the impeccable research of some of Zapata's scholars allows us to shed light on the incongruences of this play. Pretending to humanize a simulation of Zapata is rather difficult, especially if the sources are folk tales, legends, and rumors from Morelos. Still, this play enables us to observe the multiple mechanisms in which the colonial scaffolding is structured: Zapata is depicted as a semiliterate martyr whose only goal is to disappear and peacefully work in his land, while his peoples are all depictions of the good savage, ignoring their realities, knowledges otherwise, and ancestral traditions present in the manifestos. Magdaleno constructed Zapata's universe and last years of life through a Eurocentric vision where there is no possibility for indigenous communities to construct alternative ways of existing and thinking. Zapata's legacy, present in the *Ejército Zapatista de Liberación Nacional* and in an anthology of manifestos, correspondence, and written pieces, illustrate a foundational ethos based on ancestral knowledge, while Magdaleno's play, contrarily, exemplifies how nation-states appropriate and resignify their symbols, territories, and folklore.

RESOURCES

Arranz Mínguez, Conrado J. *El universo literario de Mauricio Magdaleno (1906–1986)*. Doctoral dissertation, National University of Distance Education, 2014.

Anreus, Alejandro, Robin Adele Greely, and Leonard Folgarait. *Mexican Muralism: A Critical History*. Berkeley: University of California Press, 2012.

Benjamin, Thomas. *La Revolución: Mexico's Great Revolution as Memory, Myth, and History*. Austin: University of Texas Press, 2000.

Brunk, Samuel. *¡Emiliano Zapata! Revolution and Betrayal in Mexico*. Albuquerque: University of New Mexico Press, 1995.

_____. "The Eyes of Emiliano Zapata." *Heroes and Hero Cults in Latin America*, eds. Samuel

Brunk and Ben Fallaw, 109–127. Austin: University of Texas Press, 2006.

_____. *The Posthumous Career of Emiliano Zapata: Myth, Memory, and Mexico's Twentieth Century.* Austin: University of Texas Press, 2008.

Craib, Raymond B. *Cartographic Mexico: A History of State Fixations and Fugitive Landscapes.* Durham, NC, and London: Duke University Press, 2004.

Cisneros, Sandra. "Zapata's Eyes." *Women Hollering Creek and Other Stories,* 85–113. New York: Vintage Books Random House, 1992.

Corona, Ignacio. "Emiliano Zapata y el fluctuante archivo de la imagen: del héroe trágico a la nostalgia neoliberal." *La luz y la guerra: El cine de la Revolución mexicana,* eds. Fernando Fabio Sánchez and Gerardo García Muñoz, 595–648. Mexico City: CONACULTA, 2010.

Escobar, Arturo. "Worlds and Knowledges Otherwise. The Latin American modernity/coloniality research program." *Cultural Studies* 21.2-3 (2007), 179–210.

Espejel, Laura, Alicia Olivera and Salvador Rueda Smithers. *Emiliano Zapata: Antología* Mexico City: Instituto Nacional de Estudios Históricos de la Revolución Mexicana, 1988.

Gilbert, Dennis. "Emiliano Zapata: Textbook Hero." *Mexican Studies/Estudios mexicanos* 19 (2003), 127–159.

Joseph, Gilbert M. and Jürgen Buchenau. *Mexico's Once and Future Revolution. Social Upheaval and the Challenge of Rule since the Late Nineteenth Century.* Durham, NC, and London: Duke University Press, 2013.

Knight, Alan. "Race, Revolution, and Indigenismo" in *Race and Nation in Modern Latin America,* eds. Nancy Appelbaum, Anne S. Macpherson and Karin A. Rosenblatt, 71–113. Chapel Hill: University of North Carolina Press, 2003.

Katz, Friedrich. *The Life & Times of Pancho Villa.* Stanford: University of California Press, 1998.

Magdaleno, Mauricio. "Emiliano Zapata," *Teatro revolucionario mexicano,* 93–164. Madrid: Cenit, 1933.

Maldonado-Torres, Nelson. "On the coloniality of Being" *Cultural Studies 21,* no. 2-3 (March–May 2007), 240–270.

Martinot, Steve. "The Coloniality of Power: Notes Toward De-Colonization." Open Computer Facility Berkeley. November 30 2021. https://www.ocf.berkeley.edu/~marto/coloniality.htm.

Mason Hart, John. *Revolutionary Mexico. The Coming and Process of the Mexican Revolution* (Berkeley: University of California Press, 1997.

Mignolo, Walter and Catherine E. Walsh. *On decoloniality. Concepts, Analytics, Praxis.* Durham, NC: Duke University Press, 2018.

Niemeyer, Katharina. "Arte-vida: ¿Ida y vuelta? El caso del estridentismo" in *Naciendo el hombre nuevo. Fundir literatura, artes y vida como práctica de las vanguardias en el Mundo Ibérico,* ed. Harald Wenttzlaff-Eggebert, 187–212. Madrid: Iberoamericana, 1999.

O'Malley, Ilene V. *The Myth of the Revolution: Hero Cults and the Institutionalization of the Mexican State, 1920–1940.* Westport, CT: Greenwood Press, 1986.

Ortiz Bullé Goyri, Alejandro. "Cultura y políica en el drama mexicano posrevolucionario (1920–1940)." *Cuadernos de América sin nombre,* 20, 2007.

Perales-Fernández-de-Gamboa, Andrea. *Desaprendiendo las múltiples significaciones de Emiliano Zapata: Hacia una lectura decolonial.* Doctoral dissertation. Knoxville: University of Tennessee, 2017.

Quijano, Anibal and Michael Ennis "Coloniality of Power, Eurocentrism, and Latin America." *Nepantla* 1.3 (2000), 533–580. https://muse.jhu.edu/article/23906/pdf.

Rama, Ángel. *La ciudad letrada.* Montevideo: Arca, 1998.

del Río Reyes, Marcela. *Perfil y muestra del Teatro de la Revolución mexicana*. Mexico City: Fondo de Cultura Económica, 1997.

Rueda Smithers, Salvador. "Emiliano Zapata: Entre la historia y el mito" in *El héroe entre el mito y la historia*, edited by Federico Navarrete Linares and Guilhem Olivier, 251–264. Mexico City: UNAM, 2000.

_____. *El paraiso de la caña: historia de una construcción imaginaria*. Mexico City: Instituto Nacional de Antropología e Historia, 1998.

Sánchez, Fernando Fabio. "Contemporáneos y Estridentistas ante la identidad y el arte nacionales en el México post-revolucionario de 1921 a 1934." *Revista de Crítica Literaria Latinoamericana* 33, no. 6 (second semester 2007), 207–223.

Schmidhuber de la Mora, Guillermo. *El advenimiento del teatro mexicano*. México: Instituto de Cultura de San Luis Potosí-Editorial Ponciano Arriaga, 1999.

Sotelo Inclán, Jesús. *Raíz y razón de Zapata*. Mexico City: Cien de México, 2011.

Stern, Alexandra M. "From Mestizophilia to Biotipology: Racialization and Science in Mexico, 1920–1960" in *Race and Nation in Modern Latin America*, eds. Nancy Applebaum, Anne S. Macpherson and Anne S. Rossemblat, 186–209. Chapel Hill: University of North Carolina Press, 2003.

Vevia Romero, Fernando Carlos. *Teatro y Revolución mexicana*. Guadalajara: U. de Guadalajara, 1991.

Womack Jr., John. *Zapata and the Mexican Revolution*. New York: Vintage Books, 1970.

NOTES

1   All translations from sources in Spanish are made by the author.

2   This chapter makes a conscious use of the lower and upper case in the word "revolution." Given that the nature of this chapter is to offer a shared reading of Zapata's myth and memory, we agree with Joseph and Buchenau's take on this matter. For these scholars, revolution is the term which defines the historical period of insurgency in modern Mexico between 1910 and 1920. In contrast, Revolution refers to the macronarrative and national building process initiated by the Mexican state in 1920 (2013, 2). See Joseph, Gilbert M. and Jürgen Buchenau. *Mexico's Once and Future Revolution. Social Upheaval and the Challenge of Rule since the Late Nineteenth Century* (Durham, NC, and London: Duke University Press), 2013.

3   John Mason Hart. *Revolutionary Mexico. The Coming and Process of the Mexican Revolution* (Berkeley: University of California Press, 1997); Salvador Rueda Smithers. *El paraiso de la caña: historia de una construcción imaginaria* (Mexico City: Instituto Nacional de Antropología e Historia, 1998); Jesús Sotelo Inclán. *Raíz y razón de Zapata* (Mexico City: Cien de México, 2011).

4   Raymond B. Craib. *Cartographic Mexico: A History of State Fixations and Fugitive Landscapes* (Durham and London: Duke University Press), 243.

5   For a more thorough take on this, see the compilation of Zapata's manifestos: Laura Espejel, Alicia Olivera, and Salvador Rueda. *Emiliano Zapata: Antología* (Mexico City: Instituto Nacional de Estudios Históricos de la Revolución Mexicana, 1988).

6   Samuel Brunk. *The Posthumous Career of Emiliano Zapata: Myth, Memory and Mexico's Twentieth Century* (Austin: University of Texas Press, 2008), 42.

7   Ilene V O'Malley. *The Myth of the Revolution: Hero Cults and the Institutionalization of the Mexican State, 1920–1940* (Westport,CN: Greenwood Press, 1986), 43.

8   Brunk, *The Posthumous Career*, 48.

9   Thomas Benjamin. *La Revolución: Mexico's Great Revolution as Memory, Myth, and History* (Austin: University of Texas Press, 2000), 32.

10   It is interesting to note that even though Zapata was immediately elevated to the Pantheon of heroes (O'Malley, *The Myth of the Revolution*, 23), Pancho Villa remained an outcast for a long time. See Friedrich Katz. *The Life & Times of Pancho Villa* (Stanford: University of California Press, 1998).

11   Brunk, *The Posthumous Career*, 69.

12   "Zapata, héroe trágico como el Dionisos griego, dejó de ser peligroso a la ciudad cuando se le incorporó a los misterios, al rito official." Salvador Rueda Smithers. "Emiliano Zapata: Entre la historia y el mito" in *El héroe entre el mito y la historia*, eds. Federico Navarrete Linares and Guilhem Olivier (Mexico City: UNAM, 2000), 259.

13   "The coloniality of power constitutes a matrix that operates through control or hegemony over authority, labor, sexuality, and subjectivity—that is, the practical domains of political administration, production and exploitation, personal life and reproduction, and world-view and interpretive perspective. The forms these have taken are the nation-state, capitalism, the nuclear family, and eurocentrism. Eurocentrism functions as the ideological valorization of Euro American society as superior, progressive, and universal, though it really represents white supremacy, capitalist profitability, and EuroAmerican self-universalization." Steve Martinot. "The Coloniality of Power: Notes Toward De-Colonization," OCF Berkeley, November 30, 2021. Check Quijano's and Mignolo and Walsh's works in the bibliography to obtain a more thorough explanation on the axis of coloniality.

14   Rama's study of the Lettered City provides an overview of the power of the written discourse in the formation of Latin American nations, mostly focusing on the role that cities had in utilizing and disseminating that power. His analysis includes the challenges faced by the *letrados* since their roles in these emerging new societies widened as the nineteenth and twentieth centuries arrived. It underlines the complexity of the relationships between the emerging nations and its intellectuals, as well as the roles that the latter played in the creation of the national narratives.

15   "Two forces were combined: the desire of the scholars to join the literate city that surrounded the central power, . . . and the desire of the latter to attract them to their service, obtain their cooperation and even subsidize them." Ángel Rama. *La ciudad letrada* (Montevideo: Arca, 1998), 93.

16   Fernando Fabio Sánchez. "Contemporáneos y Estridentistas ante la identidad y el arte nacionales en el México post-revolucionario de 1921 a 1934." *Revista de Crítica Literaria Latinoamericana* 33, no. 6 (second semester 2007), 209.

17   *The cosmic race* (1925), written by José Vasconcelos established that the future of Mexico relied on *mestizaje* as the only means in which the country would progress.

18   Alexandra M. Stern. "From Mestizophilia to Biotipology: Racialization and Science in Mexico, 1920–1960" in *Race and Nation in Modern Latin America*, eds. Nancy Appelbaum, Anne S. Macpherson, and Karin A. Rossemblatt. (Chapel Hill: University of North Carolina Press, 2003), 189.

19   Nelson Maldonado-Torres. "On the Coloniality of Being," *Cultural Studies* 21, no. 2-3 (March–May 2007), 242.

20   Alan Knight. "Race, Revolution, and Indigenismo" in *Race and Nation in Modern Latin America*, eds. Nancy Appelbaum, Anne S. Macpherson, and Karin A. Rossemblatt. (Chapel Hill: University of North Carolina Press, 2003), 77.

21 Cambió su figura monstruosa, incontrolable, del rebelde real, por la armónica, identificable, del héroe plástico. Cambió también su esencia dolorosa de hombre de carne y hueso. Se transformó dentro del ritual en hombre de naturaleza apacible, aunque con un dejo temible de fuerza contenida. Se olvidó al hombre intransigente en favor del mártir ubicable, "pintable", obra de arte que cabalga en un caballo que vuela sin moverse de su lugar. Y Zapata fue el Atila mientras amenazó a la ciudad, y se hizo héroe cuando la ciudad sometió nuevamente al campo, cuando le ganó la guerra. Rueda Smithers. "Emiliano Zapata: Entre la historia y el mito," 259.

22 Katharina Niemeyer. "Arte-vida: ¿Ida y vuelta? El caso del estridentismo" in *Naciendo el hombre nevo. Fundir literatura, artes y vida como práctica de las vanguardias en el Mundo Ibérico*, ed. Harald Wentzlaff-Eggebert (Madrid: Iberoamericana, 1999). 188–189.

23 Dennis Gilbert. "Emiliano Zapata: Textbook Hero." *Mexican Studies/ Estudios mexicanos* 19 (2003), 136.

24 Brunk, *The Posthumous Career,* 75.

25 Guillermo Schmidhuber de la Mora. *El advenimiento del teatro mexicano.* (México: Instituto de Cultura de San Luis Potosí-Editorial Ponciano Arriaga, 1999), 35.

26 Alejandro Ortiz Bullé Goyri. "Cultura y política en el drama mexicano posrevolucionario (1920–1940)". *Cuadernos de América sin nombre*, 20 (2007), 75.

27 Conrado J. Arranz Mínguez. *El universo literario de Mauricio Magdaleno (1906–1986).* Doctoral dissertation (National University of Distance Education, 2014), 66.

28 "Teatro de inspiración nacional. Teatro realista, quizá bronco, escaso de pulimento literario, pero, sin duda, teatro vivo, pleno de sugestión, dramático, fuerte, que llevó a la escena el lenguaje y la personalidad del pueblo, sus problemas, sus reclamos de justicia y libertad, su aliento de tierra sedienta, huérfana de comprensión." Cited in Arranz, *El universo literario,* 70.

29 "Creación literaria, responsabilidad política, censura y silencio se entrecruzan a lo largo de las relaciones culturales del momento." Arranz, *El universo literario,* 72.

30 Fernando Carlos Vevia Romero. *Teatro y Revolución mexicana* (Guadalajara: U. de Guadalajara, 1991), 14.

31 Otilio Montaño Sánchez (1877–1917), rural teacher and revolutionary leader who was the intellectual author of the "Plan de Ayala" (1911), a document by which the southern insurrection officially took up arms. As the revolution moved along, Zapata and Montaño grew apart because of ideological differences but mostly to the influence of other revolutionary leaders on Zapata.

32 Schmidhuber de la Mora. *El advenimiento del teatro mexicano,* 40.

33 Marcela del Río Reyes. *Perfil y muestra del Teatro de la Revolución mexicana* (Mexico City: Fondo de Cultura Económica, 1997), 146.

34 Arranz, *El universo literario,* 107.

35 Vevia Romero. *Teatro y Revolución mexicana,* 51.

36 Mauricio Magdaleno. "Emiliano Zapata," *Teatro revolucionario mexicano* (Madrid: Cenit, 1933), 94.

37 Magdaleno, *Emiliano Zapata,* 95–96.

38 Magdaleno, *Emiliano Zapata,* 95.

39 Magdaleno, *Emiliano Zapata,* 106.

40 Sandra Cisneros, "Zapata's Eyes." *Women Hollering Creek and Other Stories* (New York: Vintage Books Random House, 1992), 85–113; Samuel Brunk, "The Eyes of Emiliano Zapata." *Heroes and Hero Cults in Latin America,* eds. Samuel Brunk and Ben Fallaw (Austin: University of Texas Press), 109–127.

41 Magdaleno, *Emiliano Zapata*, 101.

42 Samuel Brunk. ¡Emiliano Zapata! Revolution and Betrayal in Mexico (Albuquerque: University of New Mexico Press, 1995), 87.

43 Magdaleno, *Emiliano Zapata*, 107.

44 Laura Espejel, Alicia Olivera and Salvador Rueda. *Emiliano Zapata. Antología* (Mexico City: INAH, 1988), 337.

45 Magdaleno, *Emiliano Zapata*, 108–109.

46 John Womack Jr. *Zapata and the Mexican Revolution* (New York: Vintage Books, 1970), 284–285.

47 Brunk. *¡Emiliano Zapata!*, 205.

48 Ignacio Corona. "Emiliano Zapata y el fluctuante archivo de la imagen: del héroe trágico a la nostalgia neoliberal," *La luz y la guerra: El cine de la Revolución mexicana,* eds. Fernando Fabio Sánchez and Gerardo García Muñoz (Mexico City: CONACULTA, 2010), 595–648.

49 Magdaleno, *Emiliano Zapata*, 113.

50 Magdaleno, *Emiliano Zapata*, 101.

51 Espejel, Olivera and Rueda, *Emiliano Zapata. Antología.*

52 Arturo Escobar. "Worlds and Knowledges Otherwise. The Latin American modernity/ coloniality research program." *Cultural Studies* 21.2–3 (2007), 179.

53 Andrea Perales-Fernández-de-Gamboa, *Desaprendiendo las múltiples significaciones de Emiliano Zapata: Hacia una lectura decolonial*, Doctoral dissertation (Knoxville: University of Tennessee, 2017), 16.

54 Espejel, Olivera and Rueda, *Emiliano Zapata. Antología*, 352–356.

55 Magdaleno, *Emiliano Zapata*, 121.

56 Magdaleno, *Emiliano Zapata*, 122.

57 Brunk. *¡Emiliano Zapata!*, 190; Womack, *Zapata and the Mexican Revolution*, 268.

58 Magdaleno, *Emiliano Zapata*, 123–125.

59 Magdaleno, *Emiliano Zapata*, 125.

60 Arranz, *El universo literario*, 74.

61 Magdaleno, *Emiliano Zapata*, 130.

62 Magdaleno, *Emiliano Zapata*, 132.

63 Schmidhuber de la Mora. *El advenimiento del teatro mexicano*, 40.

64 Magdaleno, *Emiliano Zapata*, 136.

65 Magdaleno, *Emiliano Zapata*, 141.

66 Magdaleno, *Emiliano Zapata*, 147.

67 Magdaleno, *Emiliano Zapata*, 150.

68 Magdaleno, *Emiliano Zapata*, 150.

69 Espejel, Olivera and Rueda, *Emiliano Zapata. Antología*, 134–136.

70 Magdaleno, *Emiliano Zapata*, 151.

71 Magdaleno, *Emiliano Zapata*, 155–156.

72 Brunk, *The Posthumous Career*, 43.

73 Magdaleno, *Emiliano Zapata*, 158–159.

74 Magdaleno, *Emiliano Zapata*, 159.

75 Magdaleno, *Emiliano Zapata*, 160.

76 Magdaleno, *Emiliano Zapata*, 162.

77 Magdaleno, *Emiliano Zapata*, 162–164.

INDEX

Note: End note information is indicated by n and note number following the page number.

ABOUT THE AUTHORS

LARRAITZ ARIZNABARRETA

Ariznabarreta graduated and obtained her doctorate at the University of Deusto, Bilbao. Her fields of research deal with the analysis of various expressions of Basque culture and their relation with power structures. Ariznabarreta is the author of the books *Martin Ugalde: Cartografías de un discurso* (Ekin. Buenos Aires, 2015), *Notes on Basque Culture: The aftermath of epics* (CLAEH, Montevideo, 2019), *Memory and Emotion: (Basque) Women's Stories. Constructing Meaning from Memory* (co-edited with Nere Lete) (CBS Press, 2022), and *Bertso Eskolak. Basque Improvisational Poetry Schools* (co-edited with Inaki Arrieta-Baro and Xabier Irujo) (CBS Press, 2023).

XABIER IRUJO

Born in exile in Caracas, Venezuela, in 1967, Xabier Irujo is the director of the Center for Basque Studies at the University of Nevada, Reno, where he is professor of genocide studies. Holding master's degrees in philology, history, and philosophy, he also possesses two doctorates in history and philosophy. Irujo was the inaugural guest research scholar of the Manuel Irujo Chair at the University of Liverpool, a William Douglass visiting lecturer at the University of Massachusetts Amherst, and an Eloise Garmendia Chair at Boise State University. He has presented lectures across nearly a hundred American and European institutions, including universities, governments, parliaments, museums, and libraries. His research primarily delves into Basque history, politics, and genocide studies, particularly focusing on physical and cultural extermination. He contributes to the scientific committees of six academic and university presses spanning Europe and the Americas and is the author of over fifteen books and numerous articles in specialized journals. Among his recent publications are *Gernika: Genealogy of a Lie* (Sussex Academic Press, 2018), *Gernika 1937: The Market Day Massacre* (University of Nevada Press, 2015), and *Charlemagne's Defeat in the Pyrenees: The Battle of Rencesvals* (Amsterdam University Press, 2021).

IDOIA ARRIETA ELIZALDE

Born in Donostia in 1962, she studied Contemporary History at the Autonomous University of Madrid, then earned her PhD in history after completing her doctoral thesis at the University of the Basque Country on the impact of the Basques on the colonization of Upper California. She is a member of the History Department of the Udaco Basque University and is a secondary school history and art history teacher in Zumaia, Spain. She has been working on the Ikastola project on the history of the Basque people. The Martin Ttipia Cultural Association named her Navarrese of the Year for her research. She is the author of *Ilustración y Utopía: Los frailes vascos y la RSBAP en California* (1769-1834), Donostia; *Real Sociedad Bascongada de Amigos del País,* 2004; and *Angel de Gorostidi y Guelbenzuren: Getariako albisteak,* Getaria, Getaria City Council, 2005 as well as several articles.

ENEKO BIDEGAIN

Bidegain has a PhD in Basque Studies, is lecturer in the Audiovisual Communication Degree, and is a Basque Culture Master at Mondragon University and a member of its Biziguneak research group. Previously he has worked for many years as a journalist in the newspapers *Euskaldunon Egunkaria* and *Berria*. His research focuses on Basque Media, Culture, and Identity. He is also the author of several books (novels and essays).

MONIKA MADINABEITIA

Madinabeitia is an associate professor at the Faculty of Humanities and Education (HUHEZI), at Mondragon University since 2005. In March 2023, Etxepare Euskal Institutua appointed her as Director for the Promotion and Dissemination of the Basque Language. She holds a degree in English Philology (1994) and a PhD in Western American Literature from the University of the Basque Country (2006). Madinabeitia focuses her research work on Basque identities, culture, migration, and diaspora. In 2018 she published the illustrated book *Petra, My Basque Grandmother,* in collaboration with the Center for Basque Studies at the University of Nevada, Reno.

ANDREA PERALES-FERNÁNDEZ-DE-GAMBOA

As an assistant professor at the Department of Didactics of Language and Literature at the University of the Basque Country, she holds a Bachelor of Arts in English Studies from the University of the Basque Country and a PhD in Modern Foreign Languages and Literatures (Latin American Studies) from the University of Tennessee. She is a member of the research team *País Vasco, Europa y América: Vínculos y Relaciones Atlánticas* (University of the Basque Country). She has been a recipient of several grants and awards from USAC, the University of Tennessee, or the town council of Vitoria-Gasteiz, among others, which have allowed her to focus on her research. Her research lines are varied, including Latin American cultural studies, Intercultural Education, and Multilingual Education, as her publications show.

Made in the USA
Middletown, DE
04 November 2023

41709530R00104